Decks & Patios

Decks & Patios

Plus Other Outdoor Projects

KENT KEEGAN
PAMELA KEEGAN
DENNIS GETTO
ERIC BRUBAKER

CREATIVE HOMEOWNER PRESS®.

A DIVISION OF FEDERAL MARKETING CORPORATION,
24 PARK WAY, UPPER SADDLE RIVER, NEW JERSEY 07458

Manufactured in United States of America

Current Printing (last digit)
16 15 14 13 12 11

Editor: Shirley M. Horowitz
Art Director: Léone Lewensohn
Proofreader: Marilyn M. Auer
Technical Assistance: Tarun Naik, Asst. Profes-
sor, School of Engineering, University of
Wisconsin-Milwaukee; Frank Randall, Portland
Cement Assn.; Gerard Rewolinski

Jacket design and cover photo: Jerry Demoney

Library of Congress Cataloging in Publication
Data

Decks & Patios.

   Includes index.
   1. Decks (Architecture, Domestic)
2. Patios. 3. Garden structures. I.
Keegan, Kent.
TH4970.D42   690'.184   80-12177
ISBN 0-932944-16-7 (pbk.)
ISBN 0-932944-15-9

CREATIVE HOMEOWNER PRESS*
BOOK SERIES

A DIVISION OF FEDERAL
MARKETING CORPORATION
24 PARK WAY,
UPPER SADDLE RIVER, NJ 07458

Acknowledgments

We wish to take this opportunity to extend our appreciation for the many artistic and technical contributions that made this book possible. Specific photographic and line illustration identifications and credits are given here. The addresses for the organizations and individuals listed below will be found in Appendix 2.

Michael Bliss 10 upper right, 11 upper center, 12 upper left, 13 upper right, 14 upper left, 15 right, 19, 20 upper, 22 upper left, 23, 28 right and lower left, 31, 32, 101, 103, 108 left, 109, 111 lower right, 112 right center

Bowmanite Corporation 24 lower

Brick Institute of America 30 top and bottom, 39 left, 40 lower left, upper right and lower right, 41 upper left, 86, 105 lower left, 106 left, 107 lower left, 108 center, 111 lower left, and 112 lower left and center

Eric Brubaker 40 upper, 64 upper left

California Redwood Association 18 upper, 21, 33, 34 bottom, 35 bottom, 69 center and lower right, 71 right, 73 upper right, 74 right, 75 lower, 76 lower right, 77 left and center right, 78 center and right, 79, 80 upper, 82, 85, 89, 94 left, 95 lower right, 98, 99, 100, 101, 117, 118 upper left, 122 lower left, 131 upper and center, 134 upper left, 137 left, right center and lower right

Rick Clark 40 lower right, 49 lower right and left, 54 lower left, 64 lower left, 65, 121 upper, 123, 125 lower, 136, 140, 141, 142, 143, 144, 145

Ego Productions 22 right, 8, 10 left, 12 lower left, 14 center, 18 left, 27 right, 28 upper left

Erecto-Pat/Oakwood Manufacturing, Inc. 20 left

Georgia-Pacific 94 right

Dennis Getto 27 left, 39 upper, 43 center, 60 left

Herb Hughes 35 upper, 36 right, 40 upper left, 45, 46, 47, 120

General Electric/Lamp Division 146, 147, 148

Philip Graham 9, 13 lower right, 14 upper right, 112 upper right

Johnson's Nursery, Inc. 36 left, 104 lower right

Kent Keegan 50, 67, 87, 104

Koppers Co., Inc. 68 lower left and right, 70 center right, 73 left, 76 left center, 77 center and upper right, 78 left, 80 lower right, 83 lower right, 93, 141 lower right

Leviton Manufacturing Co., Inc. 151

Lied's Green Valley Gardens 10 lower right, 11 left and right, 14 lower right, 15 lower left, 16, 17, 22 center left and lower left, 24 center, 25 right, 26 upper right and lower, 44, 110 upper right

Midwest Plan Service 119, 130

National Concrete Masonry Association 25 left, 41 right, 42, 112 left center, 113 left and upper right, 137 upper

National Swimming Pool Institute 92

Richard V. Nunn 57 left, 60 right, 61 left, 125 upper

Portland Cement Association 38 center right, 51, 53, 54 right, 55, 56 lower right, 57 center, 58, 113 lower right (3), 114, 115, 116

Reichhold Chemical/Reinforced Plastics Div. 100 center

Wausau Tile 43 upper left

Western Wood Products Association 11 left center, 25 upper left, 29, 30 left, 34 upper, 37, 72, 77 lower right, 84, 88, 101, 107 upper right, 118 upper right, 127 center, 128 right, 131 lower, 132, 134 left, 135, 138, 139

Wonderbrix 24 upper, 38 lower right

Contents

Decks and patios can be an extension of the indoor living space — an "outdoor room". Before beginning deck or patio construction, undertake a thorough investigation of the elements that influence the shape and fit of a deck or patio. Probably the most important questions to be asked are:

(1) What do you want from your deck or patio?
(2) How is it to be used?
(3) Will its purpose be to extend an already overused interior room?

A well-designed outdoor space, large or small, should be almost entirely determined before any physical construction is begun.

FUNCTIONAL CONSIDERATIONS

By answering the question, "What do I want from an "outdoor room?" you initiate the ideas that will lead to a successful design solution. Consider whether you want a very formal outdoor area primarily for entertaining larger groups of people, or an outdoor area for family use only, or space for informally entertaining small groups of people. Will you use the area for sunbathing or as the location of a swimming pool? Will you need space accessible for the handicapped or the very elderly? Is it to be completely secure from the outside, and is privacy a priority item on your checklist? If so, it might mean that the outdoor area must be fenced in or enclosed with trees, evergreens or shrubs in arrangements that will prevent invasion of the patio or deck.

After answering these questions, as well as the ones listed below, and carefully evaluating your lifestyle, you can choose what type of outdoor space you will want and how it will best suit your needs.

Functional Checklist

How are your present living spaces used? In answering this question, keep in mind that a patio or deck is most often

A completely screened-in cement patio overlooks the pool area, with access from the living room and an upstairs bedroom. Circling the pool is a broad ribbon of broom-finished cement — a non-skid surface that ensures safe footing for bathers.

located near a kitchen area or family room. Another popular location is near or adjacent to the dining room. The location should be near the largest traffic flow in the house, as well as being an area that can be easily modified without drastically changing the everyday operations of the household. Proximity to a kitchen often assures an easy flow of food and beverages without excessive footwear. Less frequently, one sees a small private deck or patio off a bedroom or bathroom.

How large a deck or patio do I need? To give a blanket size does not take into account individual needs. Recommended dimensions provide for 20 square feet per person — a space that is comfortable without being excessive. This converts to an area of 4 ft. by 5 ft., and includes a chair and area in which to circulate. If you contemplate entertaining a group of 15 to 25 people, the corresponding size in area would be: 500 sq. ft., or an equivalent size of 20 ft. by 25 ft. Keep in mind that there are limits to what a reasonably sized deck or patio can hold. If the immediate

area around the contemplated deck or patio is accessible for larger groups, you might find that a smaller deck will function far more efficiently than a more grandiose one. Be realistic about your space needs. Often a clever arrangement of furniture or plants will give the impression of a much larger space and yet still keep the charm of a more intimate area. Where much larger groups than 15 to 25 are contemplated, the deck or patio must be situated so as to take advantage of your site. This will handle overflow without overcrowding.

Which should I choose — a deck or a patio? A deck is a wooden platform that is raised above the gound while a patio is a platform that is formed on, and near level with, the ground.

Your specific needs might be limited by your site configurations (see site considerations), or the position of the entry or exit area in relation to the ground. A deck situated at a second floor level is often the only alternative available on a sloping site. A patio at ground level provides a

Mature trees on a sharply sloping site create an opportunity for a deck with a tree-house atmosphere. The corner tree dictates the size and shape of the structure. Foliage from nearby trees assures almost total privacy.

Because the deck connects to an outreaching second story, support columns were provided under the ledger strip attached to the house. Additional support is given by a column located at the triangular end of the deck.

larger surface, which might be required for your particular needs and by your site. It also offers a wider choice of construction materials. In some areas, a combination of patio and deck have been used very effectively to integrate the outdoors with the interior rooms.

How will I use the deck or patio? Decide first whether you need a formal or informal area. A deck or patio subjected to considerable wear and tear from children or pets must be sturdy as well as be suitable for adult requirements. An informal arrangement often requires less attention to specific detail and gives more options as to the various ways the deck or patio can be arranged.

Walls of cement block or cinderblock can take a coating of plaster to create a stucco texture. Different surface textures can be achieved by adjusting the application technique.

Built-in furniture reduces the need to purchase outdoor furniture to meet seating requirements; the built-in units stay fixed and are not as susceptible to damage. In a formal deck or patio, more fragile materials might be used — along with delicate flower borders, trellises, slate, or cobblestones.

Is privacy a concern? The openness of a deck or patio is most often determined by the degree of privacy desired. While there are other determinants (refer to cli-

Serious gardeners find that a formal patio often displays their efforts to best advantage. A concrete and brick base of symmetrical design forms the central portion. A clipped box hedge borders the front.

Open spaces were left in this concrete block patio for formal planter beds and borders. The wrought-iron fence emphasizes the elegant design.

Lath is attached in a dense louvered pattern to provide shade and to define a small patio area. Screen of bamboo or reed can be substituted for the lath.

An overhead structure can carry more than one type of infill. As shown, some of the eggcrate pattern is permanently filled in with wood insets. Other sections take plastic screens that may be either permanent or removable; the remainder of the pattern is left open for full sunlight.

mate and site) that will affect the decision of openness, the need for privacy often dictates the final design solution. Keep in mind that there are three types of privacy:

(1) visual privacy;
(2) acoustical privacy;
(3) physical privacy.

Identification of the three types is important because you may be concerned with one, two, or all three. Each type requires a specific architectural treatment. Special considerations for each type are as follows:

Visual Privacy. Ask yourself: is protection from being seen, or from seeing others necessary? You may discover that the most desirable exposure for the deck or patio may face an unsightly yard, street, or railroad tracks — not to mention the houses or apartments nearby that can easily peer onto your outdoor space. To correct this and gain visual privacy, here are several recommendations. A simple wood fence (see materials for wood types) high enough to screen out the undesirable view, or low brick or decorative concrete block walls in conjunction with vertical shrubs, often create an effective screen. Rows of shrubs of varying height will also limit the view into and out of the space. A lattice covered with ivy or similar material is also an effective screen technique. For those sites where enclosure is desired above the contemplated deck or patio, a trellis roof structure in combination with ivy or other similar material should be considered, although it may reduce the overall light level. Another option is to build a wood roof structure and insert translucent plastic or fiberglass panels. This guarantees a high level of privacy from any overhead viewing.

Acoustical Privacy. Do you need protection from unwanted or bothersome noises? While no method is perfect, acoustical isolation — using readily available materials and landscaping — in most instances can offer protection from distracting noise. The best method uses layers of shrubs or evergreens. For example, evergreens placed in rows perpendicular to the noise source will break up the noise so it will merge with other background noises. An urban or suburban lot will require more privacy than an isolated country site. A fence, in combination with vertical evergreens or shrubs, will give additional isolation from noise sources that are exceptionally severe. Since it is impossible to stop all noise from penetrating your outdoor area, keep in mind that an outdoor deck is by its nature open. The greater the closure of the area, the more likely that it will lose its flexibility and desirability. A balance must be kept between all your needs.

Physical Privacy. This includes protection from intrusion of uninvited guests, or pets, and can also be called "security." While fences with controlled access or lockable gates can prevent strangers from wandering in off the street, low walls with evergreens or shrubs may provide all the physical privacy you need. To evaluate your specific needs, determine: (1) whether a controlled access to the outdoor area is needed; (2) what kind of security is required — this will partially depend on whether or not the deck is enclosed in any manner; (3) whether you need a method of keeping youngsters out of (or inside) the area.

If you have a swimming pool with your deck or patio, your "attractive nuisance" should be inside a secure fence. Low walls with dense shrubs also furnish a very serviceable wall without a high fence.

Brick patio is bordered by a low retaining wall of Lannon stone. The tall trees contribute visual and acoustical privacy, so that a higher wall is unnecessary.

This two-tiered deck was constructed around existing trees and shrubs. The wooden wall offers visual and physical privacy. It also becomes the backing for, and gives additional strength to, built-in benches that are supported by the deck posts.

The feeling of an old country bridge has been created with a long narrow deck that extends over the edge of a ravine. Placement takes advantage of the shade and screening of nearby trees. A gravelled patio area leads to the deck.

SITE CONSIDERATIONS

Now that you have identified what you want from an outdoor room, the next step in evaluating your needs is to understand the physical and environmental limitations of your site. These restrictions have as much influence over the physical design as your functional requirements. It is essential to the success of your deck or patio that you evaluate the following considerations.

Site Checklist

Terrain. The location of the deck or patio, or the choice of which you will build, may be dictated by the terrain. A flat area of ground just off the kitchen or family room is obviously suitable for either a deck or a patio. If the terrain is excessively pitched either to the house or away from the house, your only alternative may be a deck — unless price is no object. In that case, almost anything can be built.

The effect of the slope of terrain in relation to the level of your house is very important. The most economical solution will most often be one that uses the least amount of material to support a deck — or in the case of a patio, the minimum amount of retaining wall to stabilize the soil in order to maintain a level outdoor platform. Generally a 5 or 6% slope is quite acceptable for the construction of a patio. If the ground slopes into the house rather than away from it, you will have to raise the patio surface higher than you would for ground that slopes away, no matter what material you choose. If there is a portion of the site that is quite steep, while the majority of it is flat or gently sloping, a retaining wall may be needed. If the retaining wall is a steep (three feet or higher) vertical embankment, it will usually prove beyond the abilities of the do-it-yourselfer, since a few harsh winters will cause the materials to give way. Shorter or stepped-back walls of boulders or railroad ties are sufficient for slope control at heights of three feet or less.

Plants and Trees. In planning an outdoor space, inventory the existing plants and trees in the areas under consideration. Evaluate the relative condition and the survival ability of each plant or tree to be moved to an alternate location. To move a mature tree that is located where you want the deck or patio is impractical, and cutting the tree down is not a good solution.

Rather than cut a mature tree down, a deck or patio can be constructed to include the tree in the design. This is most often done by leaving an opening around the trunk. Keep in mind that a minimum of transplanting and cutting is the most satisfactory course; this reduces your total replacement costs. Once a location has been chosen, check off those plants or trees that can be kept and those that must be moved. Your local nursery or grower should be consulted if you are unsure of a particular plant's hardihood.

Utilities. Prior to building a deck or patio, it is very important to determine the location of all underground utilities. Water, gas, sewage and telephone lines can influence the position of outdoor construction either by requiring special construction or by relocation of the lines or the deck. Many accidents have occurred as a result of not knowing where the lines were located, and at what depth in the ground.

To locate these utility lines, check with your local utility companies through their customer-service section. They will help you determine the specific location of their service. They will also suggest ways of building over or around the problem. If your house was built recently, your local building inspector will normally have a copy of your utility, gas, water and sewage hookup location. This information should be kept in your files for future reference. You may discover that no connections or underground lines exist under the proposed patio or deck. However, if there is a conflict, consult with the service in question or your local building inspector in order to explore your options. Most often, the utilities are located in a zone from 2½ ft. to 8 ft. in depth. Normally, the major concern is that location of deep footings or retaining walls will conflict with the utility service.

Codes. Building codes were established to protect the public health and safety. They were originally developed to insure that all safety requirements and loadings were within reasonable and realistic limits. The building codes in use today are much more specific. Although local requirements vary, most building codes stipulate that all exterior decks that are not in direct contact with the ground must be able to support a minimum of 60 lbs. per sq. ft. of area. While this figure might appear to be excessive, it takes into

It is easier to build a brick patio that will incorporate existing trees and shrubs than it is to build a concrete patio or a deck around them. The tree is left in position and the brick pattern is set to leave enough space for the tree to grow. Room can also be left for plantings or night lighting.

An on-grade wood deck is extended on two sides by a wide band of red brick. A portion of the area is shaded by a trellis canopy that protects the deck from strong sunlight.

The soft grey of weathered wood has been chosen to blend into this natural setting. The walkway up to the deck crosses a manmade stream and an oriental-style boulder garden.

consideration the effect of snow loads in northern climates as well as the effect of a large group of people standing on the deck. All design recommendations and sizes found in this book have been designed to meet that loading requirement. Building codes also stipulate that second-story railings, when exposed to the exterior, are either 36 in. or 42 in. high to keep the area safely contained.

Prior to any construction, a building permit must be obtained. To obtain one, contact your local building inspectors office. This office may require a set of plans (refer to Chapter 4 for how to draw a plan). In their review of your plan, they will make sure that your proposal meets all applicable codes. Once the permit is awarded, you may begin construction.

Zoning. Zoning codes were created to control land usage and the density of building in any one area. Zoning regulations indicate the setback requirements. These requirements determine how closely you may build to your property lines, how high fences or trellises may be, and in some cases, what materials may be used. Your local building inspector will be able to furnish you with the necessary information.

Determine if any easements are located on your property. These rights of way might limit the building of your deck or patio. Your property deed should indicate if any easements are in force.

Soil Conditions. While soil conditions around your house are most often stable, it is important to keep in mind that minor excavation should be filled in as soon as possible to reduce settlement of the slab or supports. Generally, soils with a large clay content tend to swell during the spring; this can cause movement of the patio or deck. The movement is easily controlled by introducing construction joints in the patio, and allowing the piers

Open and screened-in areas are both elements in this redwood deck design. The roofed portion will withstand wet weather as well as screen out bugs.

to float independently in a deck. Most other types of soil are considered quite stable for the support of a deck or patio.

Pools. If you are planning to have ornamental or reflecting pools as part of your design, locating the closest water supply source is important. Try to minimize the length of run of pipe required to service the pool. In northern climates, insure that the pipe can be pitched from a high to low level so it can be drained.

Electrical needs. Electrical service for power outlets and/or lighting must also be determined well in advance of the construction. Underground service from your power panel, or through-the-wall service, should be considered in your location of the patio or deck. It is important to minimize the degree of difficulty for the electrical service connection.

CLIMATIC CONSIDERATIONS

This section covers environmental and physical factors that will affect the amount and type of light, the volume and direction of wind, and the control of rain or snowfall on your patio or deck design. An exterior space that is oriented solely for a view might become unusable if the elements are not taken into account. The following list will assist you in understanding basics of environmental design.

The deck surrounding this pool slopes gently away to allow for drainage. This is particularly important in areas where there are heavy rains that could cause the pool to overflow.

Climate Checklist

Orientation. This involves deciding what direction your planned outdoor living area will face, which will affect the amount of sun and shade received.

A north-facing space in the northern hemisphere will primarily be in shade most of the day. This is the most desirable exposure in a southern climate, but could be cold and uncomfortable in northern climates. In a southern climate, the next-best orientation is an easterly exposure, so that the morning sun falls on the outdoor area. In colder or more severe climates, to make outdoor spaces usable as long as possible, a southwest exposure provides full afternoon and late afternoon sun. This results in a warmer outdoor area on many cooler spring and fall days.

The activities you are planning for the deck or patio can influence its orientation. Sunlight may or may not be a desirable factor, whatever the climate. It is up to you to evaluate your own specific needs regarding the quality of light needed. Northern light tends to be far more dif-

This aluminum awning shields the concrete patio and the living room. The wrought-iron supports were installed before concrete was poured.

fused than sunlight. Understanding that difference can increase your plans for the overall level of sunlight.

The position of the sun in the sky, and the angle of the sun, are also worth concern. During the summer months, the angle of the sun is higher than in the winter. This means that during the winter months a southern-oriented deck will receive less direct sunlight than during the summer months. If you should be considering a fence or other obstacles toward the south, there is the possibility that very little sun will penetrate during the winter months. However, sunlight will fall across most of the surface of the outdoor area during the summer. Particularily in the southern regions, overhead trellises or lanais are used as sunscreens to permit a controlled amount of light. They are used less often in northern climates because they may offer too much shade.

Wind. If excessive, wind can create a very uncomfortable and unusable deck or patio even if all the other conditions are just right. Planning so you accommodate the wind's movements means that you must observe the wind pattern around your house. Try to recall where leaves collect in the fall; this might indicate a zone that has little air movement. If the site experiences a constant breeze over the entire day, some form of windbreak is in order, if only to keep the napkins on the table.

In a southern climate, air movement is considered a definite advantage. Air moving under a screening or a shading device will feel cooler than when exposed to di-

This backyard has been organized into three recreational areas. The patio closest to the house is set off with overhead cover and seating. Trees and the slope of the ravine shade most of the other areas in the yard, while the pool receives nearly full sunlight.

A gate to the backyard area serves as a screen for the deck as well. If the currently screened-in area had been left open, a wind tunnel would have been formed.

This all-redwood gazebo features a potting area in the lower level, with trellisses on three sides. A beamed stairway leads to an upper level that allows a view of the ocean and has a high rail for safety.

Stepping stones laid on pea gravel, a cedar post fence, and oriental garden accessories, lend a flavor of the Far East. This is an inexpensive but effective, consistent landscape design.

rect sunlight. The temperature is about the same, but the moving air gives a cooling sensaton. A sunshade can in fact aid in the cooling of the interior of the house, even though situated outside. Depending on the location of the sunshade, preferably on the windward side of the house, this cooling effect can be achieved. Evaluate the position of the deck or patio in terms of the day breeze and the night air movement. If you are fortunate enough to have a consistent wind pattern during the day, position the area to take advantage of it. Breezes are easily directed and controlled. In zones where the air movement is minimal, locate the deck in a position where the air will be funneled through the deck and amplified.

Rain. Rain falling on a deck or patio can have interesting consequences. If the deck or patio has not been pitched to shed the water, ponding or puddling is produced. The result, in some cases, is minor flooding — especially if the deck or patio is on the same level as the house. This is why it is often wise to lower the deck or patio several inches. On the other hand, rain falling on a deck can create patterns and movements that can be aesthetically pleasing to the ear, although detrimental to your house if the roof is pitched toward the deck or patio. Keep in mind that all horizontal surfaces should be pitched away from the house no less than an ⅛ in. per ft. A ¼ in. per ft. slope is best for most outdoor areas, as it provides positive drainage even in the heaviest of rain. If the proposed deck or patio is 10 ft. wide, it should drop from the house side to the outside edge by about 2½ in., in order to minimize any flooding or ponding. Be sure that the adjacent area is capable of handling the concentrated rain accumulated by the deck or patio, or you may wash out in areas you had not anticipated.

Snow. The effects of snow are similar to the effects of rain in their weathering of the deck or patio. All materials will tend to deteriorate under the influence of weathering. Your outdoor area and the materials will naturally change over the years. Each material has its own patina of weathering. A well-selected grouping of materials may appear visually incompatible during construction, but after several years of exposure to the elements will blend together in a most pleasing manner. Find examples that you like of weathered material. Select based on what it will look like two years from now rather than tomorrow, when it is first built.

Freezing and Thawing. Northern cli-mates, where freezing and thawing occur, have the potential for the greatest damage to building materials. Concrete slabs will crack and heave if not properly constructed and reinforced. Wooden decks can separate from their supports if not properly anchored. Roof structures will separate at the joints if improperly detailed. Brick walls will crack or break up if not properly flashed. All these problems are caused by the freezing of tiny particles of water which expand when frozen. It is imperative that you select materials appropriate to your climate. You must control the method of construction enough to minimize the risk of disaster due to freezing and thawing. The introduction of expansion joints, as well as proper weather protection of susceptible materials, will reduce overall decay due to weathering.

CREATING THE DESIGN
The functional, site, and climatic considerations discussed above take into account physical realities that influence your plans. The design ideas and methods offer a means of converting your needs and desires into physical design solutions. The opportunity still exists, in this process, to modify or reevaluate your

course of action by simply altering your original criteria and their requirements.

Determining the design, once you have your mental shopping list, can be a very rewarding experience. Now you can turn all those ideas into reality. There are several ways in which you can proceed. You can look through photographs of existing decks, patios, walls, outdoor furniture, trellises, screens, as well as patterns and colors that have been gathered from magazines or other sources. Another method is to find a specific design, commercially available or other, that can be modified to suit your specific needs. You might also try — and in many ways this is the most effective solution — to list all your requirements and the sizes that you require. From this list, search for pictures and materials that best meet your needs. All of these methods should lead you to the same set of conclusions, and hopefully produce a clear visualization of your project. The following checklist is intended to assist you in the designing process.

Design Checklist

Shape. What forms and shapes are compatible with the outdoor space? Select a familiar shape such as a square, rectangle, triangle, hexagon or circle. From the physical features of your existing outdoor space you should be able to determine which of those geometric forms would best fit. Use the dominant geometry as the base, then integrate other shapes around the main form. For example, if your outdoor space is predominately rectangular, use a rectangle as the basic form. Then break up the rectangle by using smaller shapes such as squares, triangles or smaller rectangles. Keep in mind that you are designing a space in which people will walk. Try to be as simple as possible while offering enough space for various activities.

This red brick — called medium iron spot — combines with the Lannon wall for a rustic look. The brick patio meets a fence that supports a table-height surface for potting.

Shown is the bed before brick or 3x3 aggregate steppers have been laid down. The form is of railroad ties that also serve as permanent construction joints.

A series of rectangles — first in the low redwood deck and then in the patio that extends out to also serve as a walk — ties together the several types of materials used.

On-grade near the house, with the edge extending beyond a drop in grade, is this all-redwood patio designed to wrap around a new family room. Sturdy railings and a built-in bench are placed to provide protection as the land slopes away from the deck floor.

A steel column supports this second-story deck, that can capture evening breezes that never touch the ground. Trees incorporated into the design provide shade and serve as a noise barrier.

Material Compatibility. What materials will suit the style of your house? Choose a main building material that is in keeping with the style of your house or the architecture of the area. While there are many ideas and possibilities available, the choice of material will strongly influence your design options.

Many times, the material selected will dictate the style of deck or patio. A strong geometric material such as brick, for example, is not very easily integrated into a circular motif.

Try to keep your selection limited to no more than two materials. Use of a wide variety of materials can lead to overly complex and poorly executed constructions. By restricting the materials to no more than two types, you will discover that you will have greater flexibility in the actual construction of the deck or patio and in the final outfitting of the area. Even a single material will give you a very effective overall look if combined with outdoor furniture and flowers, and offers greater flexibility if you desire to change the look on a seasonal basis.

Patio Height. There are three likely choices for the height of your patio surface: (1) the top of the patio area is flush with the ground level; (2) a 4-in. concrete slab on ground level; (3) a raised patio with a wearing surface designed to be level with the interior house floor or 6 in. below it. The choice will depend on whether the patio is free-standing or attached and the access from the house to any adjoining slab.

Deck Level. There are several deck types that are available to you.

Deck on grade. Where the site you have selected is quite level, with a minimum amount of obstacles, a wood deck built just above grade is recommended. It is the least expensive, since it often requires little in the way of posts or footings. It is often built to, or just below, the interior floor level.

A deck on grade can be attached to the main house or it can be free-standing. Deciding which is best often depends on the type of house construction and its material. Free-standing decks can be placed almost anywhere within the site, and thus reduce or eliminate any need for connection to the house.

Two-story deck with site sloping away. Where the site or location you have selected has a terrain that slopes away

The lower deck tier acts as a wide, shallow step down to ground level. Built-in perimeter seating doubles as a railing, and permits a sweeping, hilltop view.

Concrete offers exceptional shape flexibility, and can easily be dressed up with permanent wood strips that serve first as forms and then as expansion joints. The patio, combined with a low wood deck, offers access from both the living room and the bedroom.

Low steps and railings combine with a partial shade trellis to add drama to a simple arrangement of squares and rectangles.

from the house, you will have to build the deck above the sloping site. To do this requires posts and cross-bracing to stabilize the deck. Access to the site is most often accomplished by exterior stairs. Building codes often dictate that a raised deck have two means of entrance or exit. The deck on a sloping away site can, if you desire, step down in a series of platforms. The complexity of construction, however, might deter you from creating a multi-level deck. Keep in mind that a stepped deck is simply a combination of smaller decks that are connected together.

Two-story deck with site sloping up. Where the site or terrain drops down to the house or building, using the slope of the site will allow you to terrace down to the desired level. Part of the deck could be on grade, while the rest of it would be elevated in order to achieve the proper level. Where the site is sloping up, it is recommended that your deck be accessed directly from the house rather than through steps down to the deck. Decking stairs are awkward if directly out of the house to the deck, and can be difficult when carrying cooking supplies, etc.

Deck as a cantilever. There are some situations where you will be unable to extend and support a deck on the site. The most obvious solution to this problem is a cantilevered deck. The requirements are much more complex than those required for a site connection. In this case all the pieces of the deck must be attached to the house for support. As a result, the house or support must be capable of withstanding the additional loads. Consult with an architect, engineer, or contractor to work out the technical details necessary.

Access. From your site analysis, you have already decided whether to build a deck or a patio. Other considerations should be made regarding access from the house, as well as from various points on the site. Will fencing or walls be required? If so, where and how much will be needed?

Adjacent, Attached, or Free-standing? A more formal space arrangement is usually enhanced by a free-standing platform, whereas a patio — built flush to the side of the house — suggests an informal arrangement. Plan your space to enable differing furniture layouts rather than just one.

Roofing. Is a roof structure or awning desired? Do you need just partial coverage? Will overhead coverage have the same shape as the deck or patio? (See also Chapter 2.)

In most cases you will want to locate the overhead cover above the deck or patio. You may either have support posts positioned within the interior of the deck or patio — which involves preplanning and structural considerations noted in Chapters 5, 6, and 7 — or you may position the support columns around the perimeter of the deck or patio. In the latter case, size limitations may prevent your providing cover for the entire deck or patio area. The dimension in one direction may be too long to be spanned by support columns placed outside the deck or patio.

The most important point in planning the roofing structure for your deck or patio is to try to build the overhead framing first, before beginning construction of the deck or patio. This will prevent conflict of the necessary roofing support structure with already constructed deck or patio construction.

Landscaping. How much landscaping will be required? Building a deck or patio

When extending an eave for shade needs, plan carefully so that there is no obvious break between the original roof line and the extension. This is easiest with a flat, or nearly flat, roof.

Compacted earth braced with railroad ties forms this house-hugging garden that leads along a path to a backyard deck. This type of garden, bordering a patio, helps achieve proper drainage away from the house.

will necessitate additional landscaping. On the plan of your deck or patio, locate the relative position and types of flowers, plants and shrubs. Indicate which ones are new material. If your patio is flush with the house, do you plan to locate any landscaping material next to the wall? Patios are often built at some distance away from the home's foundation in order to have a line of shrubs, flowers or plants conceal an unsightly foundation — as well as to soften the overall effect of the house on the planned area.

Decorative Elements. You may want to incorporate flower boxes, ornamental and reflecting pools, outdoor fireplaces, built-in seating, railings, stairs and tree tubs or openings. You will need visual samples or technical information for each one desired. Try to integrate them into the geometry of the outdoor area, keeping it as simple as possible.

Patterns. Choose the types of paving or deck patterns that are most appropriate to your needs. Not only will different patterns require specific methods of material assembly, but a pattern that fits into the overall geometric scheme will make construction easier.

Building a bench into the railing area of this second story deck reinforces the guard rails and cuts down on outdoor furniture costs.

A prefabricated wrought-iron railing bolts onto the deck for a fast answer to safety and decor needs.

2 How Materials Influence Your Design

Whatever material you select will strongly influence the design of your deck or patio. There are many possible combinations of materials for patio and deck designs. Some materials are more suitable for northern climates, and others for southern climates. Plan to select materials that are durable, pleasing to the eye, easy to obtain, maintenance-free, easy to work with, and within your budget.

CHOOSING A PATIO MATERIAL

A patio, because it is usually built on or into the ground, allows for a great range of material choices. Patios are built into a prepared ground level (refer to Chapter 5). Choosing a patio material means finding a surface material that fits the colors and the architectural design of your house, as well as the overall feeling of the outdoor area. It calls for use of locally available materials and, whenever possible, materials that require minimum maintenance.

Brick

Brick fits in almost anywhere. It evokes feelings of solidity, warmth, permanence and economic well-being. Brick is available in almost all locations and is competitively priced with other patio building materials. The coloration of brick is extensive, from yellow ochres to deep earth browns and blacks. The textural qualities vary from smooth to rough or grainy. Brick is a relatively easy material to handle, yet it provides a decorative effect that appears complex. New, used or salvaged brick can be pleasing in a variety of patio designs. Brick with a ceramic coating on one face can be used as a highlight element or in high traffic areas. The ceramic coating comes in a large range of colors to complement the regular brick pattern.

There are many different sizes of brick. A trip to a local brick yard or building materials dealer will provide you with actual samples and give you an idea of the range of patterns and textures available.

Brick set in a basketweave pattern results in a colorful and nonslippery surface for a pool surround. Southwestern landscaping makes frequent use of the brick-stucco combination.

Concrete

Concrete has become a universal material. It can be used in a variety of ways and in many types of construction. It has few design limitations and can be self-supporting if necessary. Concrete does not fit into all designs well, due to its visual hardness. It often best suits a contemporary scheme.

There are many kinds of concrete finishes available. It can be finished in a very flat, smooth style, or a very rough surface with an uneven texture depending on the desired effect and usage. Most concrete patios are constructed on a well-prepared and tamped gravel base. The concrete is then poured over the gravel base to the desired thickness. It is at this time that additional materials may be inserted or a surface pattern inlaid. Aggregate may be exposed or recessed. Sand may be strewn over the curing surface to provide a grit finish. Edging or pattern materials such as railroad ties, brick, or wood boards can be used as formwork and left in the slab to produce a very pleasing and decorative element. Since concrete starts out as a thick paste, introducing coloring agents into the mix

before it cures will produce very subtle color blends.

Concrete has the advantage of flexibility; it can be cast in a variety of shapes and forms. Other positive aspects of concrete are that it is readily available in a pre-mixed or dry form, is moderately inexpensive and easy to form, and provides a workable surface in less than a week. However, it does have disadvantages. Due to its porosity, concrete stains easily and the stains are almost impossible to remove. Due to its compressive strength, concrete is a very hard material underfoot and produces a hard, nonresilient surface. Concrete absorbs heat during the summer and cold during the winter, which could cause discomfort to the user. In regions of the country where frost penetrates the ground even a few inches, concrete slabs are subject to pitching and heaving. If a heavy rain follows a severe winter, the concrete patio can send water alongside your foundation and into your basement. If frost heaving or settling in soft soils is especially severe, a concrete patio will crack, and become more damaged each season. Concrete cracks when improperly constructed or reinforced. These cracks

A do-it-yourself dress-up for concrete comes from Wonderbrix. Patterns of tape are covered with a material that hardens to look like brick — or flagstone, or some other stone or block surface. The tape is then removed to reveal a pattern that looks better than concrete, but is easier to achieve than a patio of brick or stone.

Even in winter, this concrete patio is striking. Each square of concrete has a broom-finished center that contrasts with the smooth texture of the outer rim. The design is enhanced by the band of gravel surrounding the patio.

are impossible to repair properly or to remove without replacing the entire section. Contacting your local concrete supplier will give you an idea of the type of material available, special-order information, and the minimum order for on-site delivery.

Concrete Patio Blocks
Patio blocks are becoming more popular because they come in a variety of shapes and sizes and are an inexpensive surfacing material. An individual unit of concrete block is easily replaced if stained or broken. Concrete block is adaptable for use with a range of edging materials. It is an effective patio or walk choice in combination with railroad ties, brick, cobblestones, or wood board. The block is also

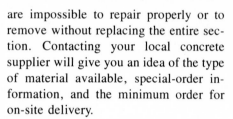

Bowmanite can dress up your new patio, or can revive an old, drab patio. It must be applied by a licensed contractor. The pattern above left simulates a brick running bond. What appears to be brick with a concrete border is really concrete with a Bowmanite surface. Shown at right is a simulation of concrete block with mortar.

Concrete block patios can be set in many patterns, and may be placed on either a sand or a concrete setting bed.

available in several colors — grey, green, and red.

Patio block is available at most building supply stores, lumber yards or concrete suppliers. Construction is similar to that for brick. The blocks tend to be heavier and larger than brick.

In warmer climates patio blocks are laid into a sandsetting bed. In northern climates, where freezing and thawing are severe, a concrete setting bed will minimize frost heave.

Flagstone

Flagstone, being a natural material, looks good in nearly any setting. It is particularly suited to a garden patio with a rustic atmosphere. Its highly irregular shape and color are an advantage where visual texture is desired. Flagstone does not mix well with other materials because of this irregular shape. When combined with more geometric materials, its distinctive irregular quality is reduced.

One disadvantage of flagstone is that it fractures quite easily if improperly laid. The problem can be solved by placing the stone in a mortar setting bed, and by purchasing flagstone with the highest degree of hardness. Always ask for the hardest grade of flagstone. The harder the flagstone, the longer and more permanent the wearing surface will be. Once the flagstone is properly installed, it will provide you with a lasting beautiful surface.

Flagstone is a relatively expensive building material. It is not always available or available in sufficient quantities to complete a job. Be sure to check on color and quantity to ensure that your patio will not look spotty.

In a warm climate flagstone may be laid in a simple sand bed. In a northern climate, place the stone in a mortar setting bed.

Gravel

Gravel is one of the least expensive patio-building materials. It is available in a variety of sizes and colors. There are two types: peastone gravel, which is a natural rounded gravel, and a manmade gravel such as crushed stone or rock. Of the two types, peastone gravel is the most expensive and is not always available.

Gravel combines well with wood, concrete and metal edging strips. It can be placed and shaped into a variety of forms and textures that are visually interesting and natural. A gravel patio area is often considered best when used for informal needs; it is difficult to walk on gravel in high heels. Gravel may also be used on the perimeter of a patio to integrate walkways into the area. Gravel is effectively used under shrubs, evergreens, and flower beds to give a finished look and to help discourage weed growth.

When used as a patio, gravel needs raking almost daily. Gravel is a loose material; it scatters easily and tends to wash away in heavy rainfall zones. Gravel may also settle into the ground and require occasional replenishment. Contact your local gravel yard for specific information regarding the type of gravel available.

Grass

Grass is often taken for granted as just a ground cover, but it can also make a very attractive patio material. Its life span, durability, and health are dependent on specific climatic conditions and maintenance. Grass in combination with other edging or pattern materials can create a very interesting patio space. Using grass as an in-fill material in your patio results in a very subtle extension of your lawn.

Grass is an inexpensive material and its maintenance is familiar to almost everyone. There are many different varieties of grass; it is important that you select a type that will be able to withstand constant use. Sod farms in your area are excellent sources of healthy plant material. Sod can easily be replaced.

This Oriental setting took minimum of materials and cost. The awning used Construction Grade wood, with cedar shingles as the undersurface. Cedar posts were used for the awning supports and the fence. Pea gravel was spread as ground cover. The awning extends over an exposed aggregate walk that is wide enough to double as a small patio. The cedar used throughout the yard — in the fence, awning supports, and set in the ground at the entrance to the backyard — helps tie together the disparate elements and areas.

Patios may be built of wood if the ground is level enough and if the loads will be light. These modular units come pretreated. They enable greater design flexibility and opportunity for decorative shrubs and plantings.

Wood

Wood is used as a patio material when it is laid onto or into the ground surface. If properly treated with preservatives, it has a long life span, but is not as durable as concrete, brick or stone. Wood provides versatility as an edging or walk material. Railroad ties, sliced tree trunks, planks or used telephone poles cut down to size offer the potential for a variety of patterns, textures and colors. Weathered wood, such as barn boards, exterior siding, or ship planks, give a desirable visual patina. Although wood is almost always thought of as a deck material, a patio with wood accents or edging strips also gives an excellent use. You must ensure that wood selected has been properly treated for rot, insect and weather resistance.

The rough texture of cut stone offers a nonslippery surface to lake bathers. The rustic appearance of the stone patio and walkway are accentuated by brick, lannon stone, and railroad ties.

Preservatives are available from paint stores or lumber yards, but pretreated wood is usually strongest.

Other Patio Materials

There are additional patio materials, found in nature and available through most building material suppliers or gravel and concrete suppliers.

Stone. Crushed granite, metro pavers, cobblestones, slate, field stone and marble are some of the usable stone materials. Each one has a very specific quality and use. When marble is available, it is used primarily as a decorative material. It is a fragile material and rather expensive. Cobblestones are visually interesting, but are hard to find and often difficult to walk

Metro pavers (used paving stones left by the city after new road construction) were set into the ground to create this patio. Moss and sedum grow between the stones for a resilient ground cover. The edging and planter are formed of aluminum downspouts set an equal distance above and below the ground level. Cast or precast concrete blocks can be substituted for metro pavers.

Interlocking pavers come in several shapes. In the Finetta design shown, sand has been swept between the interlocking joints, resulting in a continuous, smooth surface.

on. Some equivalents in size and appearance are "metro pavers"; these are stones left over from city construction projects; they are usually free.

Concrete Paver Blocks. Interlocking paver blocks provide texture and pattern, and are easy to handle. They can interlock to form a solid surface.

Wood Materials. Bark chips, pine cone chips, and compacted earth materials are best used as ground cover under evergreens and shrubs. Because they are loose and tend to deteriorate quite rapidly, they are not commonly used for patios.

Metal. Metal edgings are often used in patio construction, and as accent strips in concrete slabs. Metal should either be galvanized or be a material such as brass that will not rust in weathering. Metal grating of the type found in factories and fire escapes has been used as a patio surface or inset into a concrete slab to increase the durability of the wearing surface. A visit to a local wrecking yard will reveal a variety of materials that could, if used correctly, become patio materials.

CHOOSING A DECK MATERIAL

A deck, because it normally sits on or is built above the ground, is limited to those materials that are lightweight and capable of spanning small distances without excessive flexing. A deck usually extends out from a house or is free-standing away from the house. It requires a foundation in order to support it in the ground, and therefore requires two types of materials — one for the superstructure and one for the foundation. As when selecting patio materials, keep your specific house architecture and setting in mind while choosing deck materials. This will result in a natural transition between the interior of your house and the exterior. The house exterior will flow and become an integral part of your deck.

These are the considerations in the selection of a deck material: choice of a spanning material in keeping with the sur-

Concrete block patios are very durable: this patio has survived 40 northern winters. Pattern options are similar to those of brick.

rounding architecture; local availability; reduced maintenance; pleasing colors and textures; economic guidelines; versatility and adaptability. The most popular deck material is wood.

Wood

Wood is the primary deck material. The visual qualities of wood — grain, texture, and color — make it a very exciting material to use.

Since all the wood will be used in a exterior application, good weathering ability and freedom from rotting and insect infestation are essential. Cypress, spruce and redwood exhibit excellent weathering durability and, if left unpainted, will gradually turn a soft, attractive grey. Wood preservatives, and wood

sold as treated exterior grade wood, are available to improve the overall durability.

There are an infinite number of design possibilities with wood — different patterns, spacings, edgings, and railings. Wood patterns may appear visually complex but are relatively simple to build by the homeowner. Wood structural components are available in a variety of sizes, shapes and textures. Your local lumber yard will have on display a range of materials to assist you in your selection. Be sure to select a material that will weather to the desired patina and color. Newly installed wood has very little of its later, weathered qualities. Make sure you see samples of material that have weathered in an exposure similar to the one you are

Pretreated wood comes in a variety of shades. This new deck has received an application of clear sealer to maintain the light wood color.

The hillside slope was graded and then held back by wood retaining walls aided by large boulders. A bonsai work center, with slats above, displays the plants and provides an excellent mixture of sunlight and shade.

using. If you do not, you could be very disappointed in two years. Wood can also be painted to keep the deck in the color scheme of the house. In this case, a lower grade of material can be used since the paint will cover most blemishes. Wood can be fastened with a variety of connectors; nails, bolts, split rings and gusset plates are available at most lumber yards.

An outdoor fireplace/oven styled on the old-fashioned kiln has been built into a raised brick patio. Its corner location channels the smoke away from seating and eating areas.

Other Deck Materials

Most other deck building materials fall outside the building ability capacity of the homeowner. Metal decking or steel supports and grating are sometimes used in a more "high tech" approach. In this case, a contractor would normally have to be retained. Precast concrete floor panels have also been used in exterior decks. They require heavy machinery to install and, as in the steel or metal deck, the cost is quite high.

CHOOSING FENCE, SCREEN, OR WALL MATERIAL

Screens are used in conjunction with a patio or deck to give privacy, spatial separation, and shade; they also protect against unusual wind movement or act as an accent. Fences are usually of wood, metal or plastic panels. Walls are of brick or concrete block. Fences and walls offer increased visual privacy and noise dispersal.

To become an effective sound isolator, a fence must have certain properties. It should be completely closed to prevent sound from moving through the material, high enough to deflect sound reflecting off the wall of your house into your space, and buffered with plants, shrubs, evergreens or trees. A wall provides many of the acoustical and physical privacy benefits that a fence does not. It is often solid, thick and sturdily built. Privacy is maintained by having the wall at a sufficient

Screen frames are set square to sloping terrain; infill is trimmed to adjust for the ground slope.

An unusual screen uses contrasting woods for the framing and the infill. The shrubs and potted plants are enhanced by the background of horizontal boards.

height to achieve security. Wall materials should be selected according to color, texture, pattern and durability. In the selection of a wall or fence material, keep in mind the following: (1) a fence is often far less expensive than the same sized wall; (2) walls are often more labor-intensive and require more materials than a fence; (3) a fence properly placed and built will last about the same length of time as a wall.

Select a material that is locally available and easy to install. Find a wall or fence style that is compatible with the architecture and color of your house. The wall or fence material should weather in the same manner as the material used for the deck or patio. Here are some of the most frequently used materials for fences and walls.

Wood Fencing

Wood is most popular for fencing, and is readily available in most parts of the country. It is supplied by a building materials dealer in pre-assembled modules ready to be put together. Fence designs commonly seen are: lattice, louvered, board and batten, grapestake, basket-weave, board, alternating widths, post and rail, stockade, picket, grille, diagonal lattice and board. Texture and color vary due to the different wood species. Wood most often used in fences include redwood, spruce, white cedar, fir, pine, cypress and hemlock. In selecting a particular wood species and fence design, keep in mind these criteria:

(1) How does that particular fence design fit into the overall outdoor scheme?

(2) Does the fence match the deck construction?

(3) What type of ground support does the fence require?

The selection of a fence style will often determine how it can be connected to the ground. Some zoning codes regulate fence heights and require that the good side of the fence be turned outward and not toward the deck or patio. If so, a split wood fence might not be acceptable, but a slat or board type with a good face on each side would be better. A louvered fence might be selected if sun control is important, whereas a slat fence provides more effective wind control. In the selection of the fence design, try to minimize the feeling of a closed-in space. You may want to include a gate-type opening to the outside if the area is fully enclosed. A gate should swing outwards to allow quick passage in case of an emergency.

Metal Fencing

Often referred to as chain-link or "cyclone" fencing, metal is competitively priced with wood fencing, available in a variety of sizes and types, and easy to erect and maintain. A chain-link fence, however, is visually open; if not used with shrubs or evergreens it will offer little acoustical privacy. It is regarded as the least aesthetically pleasing of all the fencing materials. Chain-link fencing is available through a fencing dealer or building materials supplier.

Plastic Panel Fencing

Panels of translucent fiberglass or corrugated plastic inserted into a wooden frame give visual privacy without excluding

Wood fences can take plastic panel insets for an easy-to-build, but different, effect.

natural light. The panels can be flat or corrugated, and come in a variety of colors. The cost is low and they are almost maintenance-free. They do, however, rely on a wooden frame for their stability. If damaged, the panels are easily replaced.

Brick Masonry Walls

Brick walls create an atmosphere of privacy not offered by many other forms of enclosure. Brick walls are solid when used in an exterior setting. If your house is built of brick, a brick wall in a traditional pattern bond is an elegant solution to providing enclosure.

The advantages of a brick wall are: security, attractive appearance, and a wide range of colors and patterns to choose from. The main disadvantage in colder climates of brick is the potential for heaving, and breaking up of the brick surface, due to freezing and thawing.

The two basic units of a masonry wall are, *stretchers* and *headers*. The stretcher is a brick that lies flat with its longest dimension lengthwise along the face of the wall; the header lies perpendicular to the face of the wall. Headers are often used to connect the two wythes in a wall and give it greater structural strength. Above, four courses of running bond alternate with a course of headers in a double-wythe (vertical series) wall.

Bricks require a substantial foundation to prevent them from cracking or tipping over. Brick walls can be used in most climates, although reinforcement is recommended in vertical and horizontal joints. Other notes: An improperly mixed mortar can result in the overall failure of the wall; brick walls are expensive and time-consuming to build.

Most brick used in wall construction is cored brick. This reduces the overall weight of the material and provides additional surface area for the bonding of the mortar and brick. For walls and screens,

The uneven wall surface is created by headers set to protrude from the wall. A strong texture and three-dimensionality result.

use cored brick. It is not designed to permit wearing on its flat surface, but rather on its edge or end. When using cored brick, you must substitute a solid brick where openings occur in exterior brick walls. This will ensure effective water control. For example, there are variations on brick walls where every other brick is left out to create a screen effect, while still maintaining the integrity of a wall. Another variation of the brick masonry garden wall is the serpentine wall or the zig-zag wall, where the panels are offset to let in the light.

Concrete Masonry Screen Walls

The preference for concrete masonry screen walls cuts across most climates and geographic locations. Created originally as a functional building element, the screen wall combines privacy with some openness, interior light with shade, and solar heat reduction and airy comfort with wind control. Screen walls are required to support little more than their own weight. They exhibit stability and safety. Due to the high percentage of openness on the face of the block, however, attention to reinforcement is required. Reinforcement of the vertical and horizontal joints is most common. The open area is created by using concrete masonry screen units with decorative openings in their face.

The number of shapes and sizes of concrete masonry screen units is unlimited; check with your concrete block supplier on the specific shapes and sizes available. Most screen units are available in a greyish tone. Special orders in other colors are possible. Most screen designs will be compatible with contemporary exteriors. Since the units are primarily rectangular or square, the repetition of the forms will result in a very strong geometric pattern. The homeowner is capable of building concrete masonry screen walls, with some preliminary experimentation, using available mortars.

Glass Block Walls

Glass block may be used as a screen material. The blocks are set in mortar, reinforced, and built in a manner similar to masonry units. They let in quite a bit of light. The main disadvantage is high cost, low availability and poor resistance to damage.

CHOOSING A ROOFING MATERIAL

A roof structure allows you to further define the outdoor living area. A roof can extend the area of a deck or patio; it can vary the height in relation to the house, or extend the structure beyond the deck to capture additional space.

Gazebo

The gazebo is a totally free-standing structure. It offers a special and separate space outdoors while still remaining part of the outdoor deck or patio. The traditional gazebo gives you an enclosed feeling while letting the light filter through onto your deck. Precut gazebos are available in most areas.

Trellis

A trellis is an open latticework sun roof over a deck or patio supported by vertical posts. A trellis can be free-standing or attached to the house. A trellis provides excellent shading qualities as well as vertical privacy. The free-standing trellis is supported by vertical posts. The attached trellis rests against the existing house and uses it as a support, extending outward to the edge of the deck or patio. A trellis is normally built from narrow pine or fir stock applied to a wooden frame. It is an excellent surface for climbing plants for added shade and visual privacy. A roof structure can integrate climbing plants as a sun screen, and at the same time control air movement. The overhead also provides a high degree of protection from external noise sources. It is important that a free-standing overhead structure — or an attached one — blend into the architecture of your house and the mood of the overall environment.

Wood Roof Structures

Wood is the most commonly used patio or deck roofing material. Wood is relatively lightweight, cost-competitive, and easy to fabricate and assemble. Its warmth, texture, color and pattern combined with a solid, stable structure account for its frequent use.

Most wood roof structures are limited in the length of their span. As a result, a wood roof structure has a small planning or design unit. You may, however, increase the number of units (modules) used in the design. Some of the most-used wood species for roof structures are: redwood, cypress, spruce, hemlock, pine and fir. As in deck construction, it is advisable to purchase wood already treated for exterior use, or purchase the chemical preservatives to treat it yourself.

Lath. Usually sized in very narrow rectangular form, the pieces are set into a crosspiece or nailed directly to the sup-porting members. This can be in a criss-cross or diagonal pattern.

Louvers. Horizontal wood slats similar to a wood blind or shutter. These are normally available in prefabricated units. They are unfinished and suitable for exterior use.

Reed or Bamboo. Often difficult to obtain, the visual effect of bamboo or reed is quite elegant. Cut into equal lengths and tied to the superstructure with rope, it produces a very natural or primitive effect. This material deteriorates rapidly and should be replaced frequently. The quality of filtered light that both reed and bamboo contribute is exceptional.

Other Inset Materials

Canvas. Canvas panels tied into a frame have a light and summery feeling. They give shade from the sun and protection from the wind and rain. Canvas is moderately priced and readily available. It does not, however, last as long as wood and must be replaced on a regular basis. Other advantages are that it comes in many different weights and colors, is easily cut and bound, and can add vivid touches of color. Canvas, stretched on a wood frame, can be suspended from the roof structure to create an effective temporary screen.

Plastic Panels. Corrugated or flat plastic panels are available in a variety of thicknesses and colors. The standard size is based on a two-foot unit. Panels can be cut using simple home tools. Other advantages worth noting are that plastic panels can easily be inset into a wood frame or roof structure, and will provide a diffused light. They withstand effects of most weathering other than extreme cold, are easy to maintain, and are relatively inexpensive.

Metal. There are many lightweight metal panels available for use as an inset roof material or as spanning elements. Corrugated aluminum or steel panels come in a variety of lengths, gauges and colors. They are strong, will stand up to long spans, and are easily cut and installed. They are maintenance-free and inexpensive, and give complete shading control and protection from rain. The major problem with metal panels is that they tend to expand and contract excessively in hot weather, making a variety of noises and causing separation of the panel connections.

A prefabricated wrought-iron railing is attached to a round deck that has roofing of spanish tile.

3 Structural Characteristics of Materials

There are many influences on the actual design and construction of a deck or patio. The Design Checklist in Chapter 1, and Chapter 2 on choosing the right materials for your design, point out many considerations that are crucial to the effectiveness of your design. This chapter will cover suitability of the materials for particular uses — longevity, size, stability, texture or strength — all of which are critical to the successful completion of any deck or patio.

WOOD

Wood is prized for its durability and structural capabilities. It has high resistance to impact and strength relative to its weight in compression. It can be worked easily into a variety of shapes without seriously altering its behavioral tendencies. Because wood has natural defects such as knots, splits, and checks, it may suffer shrinkage, decay and warpage.

Wood is available throughout the United States, but the species are varied and access to a particular type depends on geographic location. Wood is an economically stable material, although its cost increases based on demand. Wood used in deck, patio, fence or roof structure is referred to as "lumber". Lumber is the product of the saw and planing mill. It is produced in standardized sizes and exhibits characteristics that can be guaranteed by the manufacturer. This uniformity of strength and stability assures you that your material will behave in a very predictable manner.

Selection of Wood

Species. Wood is divided into two major groups. Softwoods are those materials that are taken primarily from coniferous trees such as fir, hemlock, red and white cedar, spruce, redwood or pine. The softwoods represent more than half the available lumber used for decks and patios. The softwoods are found in most geographic regions, although the availability of a particular species varies widely. Lumber used for most woodframe house construction is softwood.

Hardwoods are taken primarily from deciduous trees. These trees shed leaves and include maple, oak, elm, birch, ash, cherry, walnut, poplar and hickory. Hardwoods are normally used for interior paneling or funiture, as they are expensive and difficult to find. Hardwoods are denser than softwoods and thus better suited to the requirements of furniture. They are known for the visual appeal of their grain, color and texture. Hardwoods are also more susceptible to variations in dimension due to the influence of moisture.

Decay and Expansion. Wood is composed almost entirely of cells that are interconnected with a natural glue that gives it its strength. The cells make wood vulnerable to decay. Most lumber that is available today is heartwood, which is less subject to decay than sapwood. The porosity of wood, due to its cell structure, is also the cause of expansion as wood absorbs moisture, and contraction when it dries out. The expansion of lumber used in an exterior deck might be a concern in areas with a high moisture content in the air. Moisture in wood reduces the strength of lumber, and affects its size and ability to be painted or stained.

Grading. Wood has certain visual characteristics that determine its grading. All lumber is graded. The grading is a measure of the overall quality of the wood. Some of the visual defects that influence grading are:

(1) knots where branches once were in the trunk — lesser grades are permitted to have a far greater number of knots than the better select grades;

(2) shakes, a separation along the long grain — pitch pockets reflect a sep-

Infill for this fence consists of vertical, rough-textured split-rail lumber. The antique iron grill set into the fence was a lucky find that accents the oriental garden within.

aration of the grain in the short end grain of the material.

Curvature. Almost all material that is used as lumber today is plain sawn. This is true of all lumber available for framing and decking. Quarter sawing, a process of cutting the log in a diagonal fashion so that the wood will be uniform in its shrinkage, is used only for hardwoods. As a result, most lumber you will buy will have an end grain that will cause the piece to curve. Make sure that the decking will always curve downwards; the boards should be bark side up. This will prevent cupping. Look at the end of the board to determine which side is the right side.

Strength. The strength of wood is determined by cell wall thickness and adhesion between cells in the length of the material. Wood is not as strong perpendicular to the grain because that is the weakest area of the cell. Therefore, there are two strength considerations when using lumber: the strength parallel to the grain, which is the strongest, and the strength perpendicular to the grain.

Lumber Sizes. All lumber is delivered to your site based on a predetermined set of sizes. These sizes are often referred to as "nominal" sizes — as opposed to the "actual" wood sizes delivered. The standard lumber sizes are indicated in the accompanying chart.

LUMBER SIZES

Nominal Size	Actual Size
1x2	¾x1½
1x3	¾x2½
1x4	¾x3½
1x6	¾x5½
1x8	¾x7¼
1x10	¾x9¼
1x12	¾x11¼
2x2	1½x1½
2x3	1½x2½
2x4	1½x3½
2x6	1½x5½
2x8	1½x7¼
2x10	1½x9¼
2x12	1½x11¼
4x4	3½x3½
6x6	5½x5½

These sizes are based on the current industry standard. As you can see, a 2x4 is not really 2 in. by 4 in. The lumber sizes listed above represent all the sizes you will be working with and that are neces-

This deck comes in modular sections, enabling adjustment for trees, corners, or sloping ground.

sary to the construction of a wood deck, fence or roof structure. There are many more sizes, but they are not generally used for this scale of enterprise.

Each size listed is capable of supporting a certain amount of weight. The amount varies with the spacing, span distance, species used, and the method of connection employed. However, most building codes stipulate a specific load that the deck must be able to carry. Based on these requirements, a conservative beam and joist selection chart is provided.

BEAM SPAN TABLE

Beam size	Max. span allowed when laid on edge
4x4 or two 2x4s	4 ft.
4x6 or two 2x6s	6 ft.
4x8 or two 2x8s	8 ft.
4x10 or two 2x10s	10 ft.
4x12 or two 6x10s	12 ft.
6x10 or three 2x10s	12 ft.
6x12 or three 2x12s	14 ft.

For spans over fourteen feet, consult with your lumber dealer or a structural engineer. All of the above size and span recommendations take into account normal loadings on your deck. In the case where you would plan to have unusually heavy objects or pools located on the deck, the above sizes are not applicable.

The distance that the beams have to span is determined by the distance between the supporting posts or piers. Obviously, the longer the span the heavier will be the beam required. Spanning from beam to beam are joists or smaller beams spaced closer together. The joist size and spacing is determined by the distance between the beams. The following chart is based on flexing (deflection) limitations. This is desirable, since you do not want your deck to bounce or feel like a diving board every time you walk across it.

JOIST SPAN TABLE

Joist	Max. span allowed when laid on edge
2x6 (minimum)	@ 12 in. o.c. 8 ft.
	@ 16 in. o.c. 7 ft.
	@ 24 in. o.c. 5 ft.
2x8	@ 12 in. o.c. 10 ft.
	@ 16 in. o.c. 9 ft.
	@ 24 in. o.c. 7 ft.
2x10	@ 12 in. o.c. 13 ft.
	@ 16 in. o.c. 12 ft.
	@ 24 in. o.c. 10 ft.
2x12	@ 12 in. o.c. 16 ft.
	@ 16 in. o.c. 15 ft.
	@ 24 in. o.c. 14 ft.

O.C. stands for on center (of Joist)

The posts that are to support the beams, which in turn support the joists which then support the actual decking, are normally sized as: 4x4 timber post up to 6 ft. above finished grade and no further than 6 ft. o.c., 6x6 timber post for heights between 6 ft. and 12 ft. and no further than 10 ft. o.c. This produces a very safe load transfer from the post into the foundation to which it must be connected, and is necessary for posts that will also be supporting overhead cover.

Decking. Wood decking comes in various sizes and species. It is strongly recommended that you do not use decking any wider than 6 in. This is to minimize cupping and the potential for splitting along the length of the board. Normally, all 2x6 or 2x4 wood decking will span 4 ft. if laid on its side (flat) and continued over more than two spans. Most 1x4 or 1x6 wood decking is usually capable of spanning a maximum of 2 ft. if laid on its side (flat) and continued over more than two spans. Keep in mind that the shorter the span, the stiffer the deck. If you plan to have very heavy furniture or unusual loadings on the decking, the above recommendations are not applicable, and professional assistance is strongly recommended.

Lumber Grades. While there are many lumber grades and species, most of the lumber recommended for the construction of a deck, railings, stairs, fences, walls and overhead structures need not be any better than a No. 2 common. The Western Wood Products Association (WWPA) has standardized the grading of all lumber in the following order.

Select Structural: the best and strongest but most expensive
No. 1 Appearance: recommended for deck construction
No. 2 Appearance: recommended for deck construction
No. 3 Appearance: not recommended for deck construction
Construction: minimum recommended for deck construction
Standard: not recommended
Utility: not for use as supporting members; lowest grade and cheapest — not recommended
Stud: not applicable for decks, roof structures; not recommended.

In addition to the above grades, terms such as common and select are used to differentiate between wood used for framing and other general construction and

This easy-to-build divider screen anchors to a concrete footing that is raised above a planter bed. Anchor installation is simplest if positioned soon after concrete placement.

Alternating 4x4s and 1x6s are of construction grade redwood, a rough-textured, knot-containing garden grade. One 1x6 has been left out to leave space for a hanging plant. Top and bottom rails are 4x6s; stringers are 2x6s.

that used for wood trim. While a better quality of material such as a No. 2 or a Construction grade might appear to be more expensive than other grades, but your investment will guarantee you a sturdier and more permanent deck.

Wood Preservation. The best assurance of purchasing lumber free of decay is to purchase lumber in grades that exclude decay. Because wood is a natural material, it can be susceptible to various insects, fungi, molds or stains. To ensure that these forms of deterioration do not occur, it is important to purchase material with a moisture content of less than 20%. Most lumber that you will purchase is sold at 16% moisture content. Another method for minimizing the potential of rot is to separate the wood from known moisture sources. This will also help minimize the tendency for insects to bore into the material. Almost all wood used today requires some form of preservative or protective coating. Lumber used in exterior applications particularly calls for protection against insects and decay. The best lumber preservative is that injected into the wood by pressure. Pressure-treated wood for exterior use is available in most lumber yards, and when not available may be ordered without financial penalty. It is marketed under several trade names specifically for use in exterior decks or exposed wood structures and fences. Its primary benefits are that you do not have to treat the material by spraying, soaking or brushing. If available, it is recommended that you purchase pressure-treated exterior use material over that material that you would have to treat yourself. The chemicals used to treat the material are waterborne preservatives that contain some form of chromated copper arsenate or ammoniacal copper arsenate. These are odorless and will not stain or discolor. Wood preservatives are necessary for the satisfactory performance of your exterior wood deck. They are well worth the small additional investment. For your information, Chapter 9 indicates some simpler home-treatment methods.

Deck Patterns

Diagonal patterns are laid at an angle of 45 degrees to the joists. Diagonals can provide visual direction to the deck, or aesthetic aid for very regular deck shapes. Herringbone, zig zag, or radial patterns,

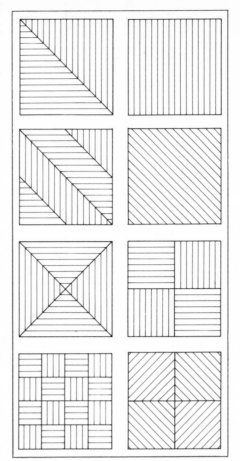

Here are some of the more popular wood deck patterns. They can, of course, be adapted to other deck shapes.

can at times cause undue repetition and as a result look too busy. When decking is set on a diagonal, the joist spacing will have to be reduced to compensate for the longer span. Illustrated here are some of the various pattern possibilities available to you.

In the case where you desire a more free-form arrangement, keep in mind that so long as you maintain the decking and joist arrangement previously discussed, you can achieve almost any form or surface pattern. Where a change in the direction of the decking occurs, additional reinforcement of a double joist must be laid parallel to the line of the cut. In the case of a herringbone pattern on a 48-inch grid, or a diamond pattern on a smaller or equal-sized grid, additional blocking must be added to each change in direction. It is suggested that changes in direction be made over joists or beams, and that additional blocking be added only to the changes occurring perpendicular to the joists or beams.

Framing Around A Tree. Where you are to frame around a tree, try to keep the deck as simple as possible. If you have a pattern that requires unusual footing requirements, digging into the roots of the tree is to be avoided at all costs. Plan the

Free-form deck patterns are feasible, but require careful planning of posts, beams, and joists to insure adequate support. Ends of joists are tied off into box around tree to carry load where joists have been cut off.

When the homeowners wanted a tree in the middle of their deck, they moved a large tree from one area of their lot to the deck site. The tree roots were wrapped, and the tree hauled to a hole that had been dug near the house. Trees must be in place before beginning construction of a deck or patio.

framing so that there is ample clearance for the tree. The tree will move and grow. The higher the deck is off the ground, the more the tree will sway. Allow enough room so the two can co-exist comfortably.

CONCRETE

Concrete is used in almost every type and size of architectural and engineering structure. In residential work, its major use is in the substructure of the building for foundation walls and footings. It is used extensively for flat concrete work such as floor, patio, garage, stairs, terraces, sidewalks, driveways and curbs. This section will concentrate on the use of concrete as applied to slabs on grade and to small-scale footings necessary to support posts of a deck or roof structure.

Use of concrete dates from a Roman discovery in 450 AD, when it was found that if a form of volcanic ash was mixed with water and combined with small amounts of sand and left to dry, the paste would turn into a hard and impervious block. The process has not changed much today. The concrete you will purchase is now made of manmade cement: a finely pulverized mixture of lime, silica, alumina, and iron fired together in an oven to produce a hard "clinker." The clinker is then pulverized and a small amount of gypsum is added. This very fine material is what we know as cement, a principal ingredient in concrete. To complete the list of ingredients for cement, you will need water and aggregate. The three combine to form a mixture that can be poured and set into an infinite variety of shapes.

Once poured, a curing process called "hydration" takes place. The hydration is the process by which the moisture in the mix evaporates, causing the mixture to harden. The usual length of time it takes for most concrete to achieve its full strength is 28 days from the intitial pour. If concrete is properly mixed and poured, the concrete will exhibit qualities of water tightness, strength, durability and longevity.

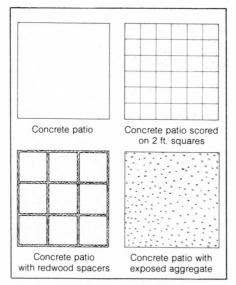

Concrete patio	Concrete patio scored on 2 ft. squares
Concrete patio with redwood spacers	Concrete patio with exposed aggregate

Shown are several of the treatments that can dress up a concrete patio. These methods can also be used in combination.

Concrete Ingredients

The materials that are normally used for exterior patios, sidewalks, slabs or terraces are available either ready-mixed or premixed in bags. Either way, concrete is composed of the following materials.

Cement. Cement is the catalyst that allows unlike materials to be formed into a single unit. The term portland cement is used in a "generic manner".

Portland Cement Type I and IA. This is a general purpose cement suitable for practically all exterior applications in residental use. The type IA refers to an air-entrained cement (see Concrete Admixtures).

Portland Cement Type II and IIA. This type generates less heat during the hydration process than does Type I, and has better resistance to sulfate attack. (Over time, sulfer can cause concrete to disintegrate.)

Portland Cement Type III and IIIA. This type is used when high early strength is required; for example, when forms must be removed as soon as possible, or concrete must be put into service as quickly as possible.

There are other types of portland cement available, such as Type IV and Type V. They are special-use cements and are seldom used in exterior residential construction.

Water. All water involved in concrete mixtures should be equivalent in quality to drinking water. In other words, not polluted or contaminated with any oils, acids or excessive sulfates. Water, when mixed with the cement, forms a paste called "matrix". It is this matrix that binds all the aggregates together, and thus the quality of the water is important to the strength of the concrete.

Aggregates. About 75% of the volume of concrete is composed of coarse and fine aggregate. For the best mixture of aggregates, the entire volume should have as few voids as possible. This can be achieved when the fine and coarse aggregates are uniformly graded. Fine aggregate refers to sand and fine gravel pieces that have a diameter no larger than 1/4 in. Coarse aggregate is gravel or crushed stone that is over 1/4 in. in diameter, and yet smaller than 1 1/2 in. in diameter. These sizes are carefully controlled by the concrete batcher. The durability, workability and strength of the concrete will depend on aggregate that is properly graded and free from any acids, dirt or organic residues. Most premixed bags of household cements have a smaller range of aggregates, but still offer excellent strength characteristics.

Admixtures. A material that is added to the concrete (cement, water, aggregate) during the mixing to accelerate or to slow down the curing process, capture small air bubbles, improve the workabil-

Tiers of laminated platforms can be used as steps. The steps lead down to a walkway and patio of aggregate concrete with decorative redwood strips that also serve as expansion joints.

ity, or add color to the mixture, is called an admixture. Most used are "air entrainment" admixtures, which were developed specifically to increase the concrete's resistance to severe frost action and to effects of applications of salt for snow and ice removal. Small amounts of air-entraining agents are introduced into the mixture. Concrete made with this admixture contains small, well-distributed and separate air bubbles so tiny that each cubic foot contains many billions of bubbles. This reduces the potential for surface spalling and breaking up due to freezing. The recommended percentage is no more than 6% of the total volume. Air-entraining agents can be purchased separately and added to your mixture if you are mixing your own concrete.

Reinforcement. Since concrete behaves effectively when compressed, any reinforcement is used only to stabilize the poured section. However, steel reinforcement must be added to the design so the steel can compensate for all conflicting tension forces. A patio slab or floor slab poured on a well-prepared grade requires no structural reinforcement; it does require temperature reinforcement. This type of reinforcement is usually a type of welded wire fabric (WWF) similar to steel mesh, which is inserted into the form before the pour. It counteracts the expansion and contraction of the concrete when there are severe changes in temperature. Without temperature reinforcement, the slab would crack in a very short period of time. Once concrete has cracked, it is almost impossible to repair. Temperature reinforcement is available through most building material suppliers. The following chart is a minimum temperature reinforcement size based on different slab thicknesses.

WELDED WIRE FABRIC

Size and Type	Slab Thickness
6 in. x 6 in. # 10/10 WWF	3 in. or less
6 in. x 6 in. # 8/8 WWF	4 in. or less
4 in. x 4 in. # 8/8 WWF	5 in. or less
4 in. x 4 in. # 4/4 WWF	6 in. or less

Temperature reinforcement for slabs of greater thickness must be figured as layers of several thicknesses. You will probably not require a slab of any greater thickness than 6 in. If you plan an 8-in. slab, use two layers of the steel that is recommended for a 4-in. slab.

Concrete Strength
Concrete strength for exterior use is not as critical as strength necessary for a column or structural beam. The average strength used in most slabs is 3000 lbs. per sq. in. (psi). Concrete strength is determined by the ratio of water to cement. The "water/cement ratio" is critical to the strength of concrete. Too much water can cause poor bonding, or separation of the cement paste and the aggregate, while too little water will result in no adhesion at all. Concrete for patios, walks and walls should have a water ratio — including any moisture in the aggregate — of six gallons of water to each bag of cement. The maximum aggregate size is one inch. The slump from the top of a slump test cone should be 2 to 4 in. This mixture will produce a 28-day strength (time until full strength) of 3500 psi.

One bag of cement weighs 94 lbs. and represents 1 cu. ft. in volume. Most concrete that is batched is available and priced by the cubic yard. Therefore, to achieve a satisfactory water cement ratio per cubic yard, use about 6.2 bags of cement, which would require about 37.2 gal. of water. When you are mixing your own concrete on site, be sure to measure the amount of water you are adding for each bag of cement. In the case where you have purchased a premixed bag of concrete, follow the instructions for mixing in the proper quantity of water.

The proper proportion of cement to aggregate depends on many variables, including the moisture content, size, graduation, and the specific gravities of both the fine and coarse aggregates. Care must be taken for any field mixing that you might undertake. One method used in the past is that of "arbitrary proportions". It specifies a ratio of cement, sand, and coarse aggregate without reference to their characteristics or to the amount of water to be used in the mix. Therefore, a 1:2:4 mix consists of 1 part of cement to 2 parts of fine aggregate to 4 parts of coarse aggregate. The method is neither exact nor economical. In lieu of any other method, or lack of availability of premixed or prebatched concrete mixes, the following cement/aggregate ratio is recommended: 1 bag of cement: 2½ bags of sand: 3½ bags of crushed stone no larger than 1 in. in diameter. This recommendation is again based on a resulting volume of one bag equal to one cu. ft. The water/cement ratio would then be 6 gal. per bag of cement. Be sure to add an air-entrainment agent to the mixture.

Consistency of the Concrete Mixture

More aggregate is used in stiff mixes than in fluid mixes. The stiff mixes are more economical in the cost of materials; however, they require more labor in placing and finishing. A method of evaluating the consistency of the mixture is the "slump" test. When using a prebatched concrete, you will normally be getting material that is well suited for your patio construction. In a premixed bag material when water is added as directed, you will achieve a suitable slump of 2 to 4 in. However, when you field mix your own concrete, you must work with the mixture — adding minimum amounts of water until you achieve the same 2-to-4 in. slump. All concrete should be mixed thoroughly until uniform in appearance, with all ingredients distributed equally.

The slump cone is 12 in. high, with a base diameter of 8 in. and a top diameter of 4 in. Set cone on a firm surface and hold down by placing feet onto cone projections. Fill cone with 3 layers of concrete. Tamp each layer 25 times before adding the next layer.

Level off the concrete when cone is filled. Lift the cone and allow the concrete to settle. Stand the cone next to the concrete in order to measure. A large slump indicates a wet consistency; a slight slump is due to a stiff consistency.

Handling and Placing Concrete

While more specific recommendations will be made for the placing and finishing concrete in Chapter 5, the handling of the concrete mixture should be carefully controlled. This will keep the concrete uniform from batch to batch. In addition, improperly handled concrete will tend to separate. If the location of the building area is too far for a ready-mix truck to enter, how to carry the concrete from the truck to the forms must also be carefully considered. Prepare the path for smoothest possible passage by wheelbarrow or push buggy. This will reduce separation of coarse and fine aggregates.

Placing of concrete into prepared formwork must be undertaken with care. Excessive free fall of the concrete from heights of over 3 ft. can cause segregation of the aggregate. Avoid placing the concrete in layers of more than 6 to 12 in. where reinforcement exists, or more than 18 in. where there is no reinforcement, such as footings or foundations. After placing the concrete into the forms, some type of compaction is needed to consolidate the concrete and to make it denser.

Finishing and Curing Concrete

The surface finishing depends on the use of the deck. A broom finish gives a rougher texture and provides better footing. A smooth or steel trowel finish creates visual uniformity.

The strength of concrete is also affected by the curing process. Because of the curing that must occur, permitting release of excessive moisture during the

Fresh concrete can be imprinted with various types of designs. Be careful not to stand on the wet concrete; you may be able to stand on the pattern maker.

Make concrete look like brick using Wonderbrix. Put tape up, trowel on coloring compound and remove tape. When color compound has hardened, apply grout.

first 7 days will reduce concrete strength by almost one third. To control this, concrete should be continuously moistened (sprinkled) with a hose on a daily basis. If you are pouring in a region that is very hot, protective burlap or polyethylene sheeting should be used to trap the moisture. Never pour the concrete if the temperature is below 50° Farenheit or above 90° Farenheit. If you must pour in very high temperatures, try to pour early in the morning so you will have enough time to finish and install the protective cover. (See also Chapter 5.)

BRICK MASONRY

Brick is the oldest of all artificial building materials. Brick work is adaptable to a great variety of uses, such as exterior walls, interior walls, fireproofing, backing of stone and terra cotta, and for paving and decorative purposes. A masonry construction can provide a multitude of effects, shadows, shades, textures and jointings. Brick used in a vertical construction is almost always set in mortar, which if properly done forms a watertight and durable connection. In cold climates, with the possibility of expansion and contraction, metal reinforcing is recommended to keep the wall intact. Brick is considered a mass material, in that its structural abilities are dependent on its mass or bulk. When combined with reinforcing, brick becomes less dependent on its mass for stability.

All exterior masonry must meet three main requirements for satisfactory operation: strength to carry the loads, watertightness to prevent rain penetration, and durability for wear and weather resistance. Each one of these abilities can be traced to the craftsmanship that went into building. Therefore, while a brick wall may be a desirable architectural element in your design concept, it requires a good level and quality of craftsmanship if it is to survive.

Properties

Solid masonry units (brick) are composed of burned clay, shale, fire clay, silica, alumina with varying amounts of metallic oxides. These are formed into the desired shape and then fired in a kiln at high temperatures. The fusion of the materials during the manufacture results in durability and weathering resistance. This is why chemicals are the only agents that affect

There are many types of patio paving materials. Shown are the most common types: (from left), common block, interlocking concrete paving block, flagstone (quarried limestone), and patio block (1 ft. x 2 ft. but can be split every 6 in.).

This basketweave pattern is one of the easiest to set, particularly if you need to leave space for trees or shrubs. Joints are adjusted as necessary for correct alignment.

the surface of brick. Clay brick is available as waterstruck or sandstruck. These differences are a part of the manufacturing process. The surface finish tends to be smoother in a waterstruck brick.

The natural colors of burned clay are many. Brick color ranges widely: creams, reds, oranges, purples, dark browns, and even black. The chemical composition and the firing temperatures affect the color. The texture is produced by the different molds, cutting techniques, dies and curing. Preferred textures include: smooth or matte with vertical or horizontal markings; rugs; barks; stipples; sandmold; waterstruck, and sandstruck. The type of brick available in

your community will determine the strength range available; it varies from color to color.

Clay absorbs water. Low absorption is a desirable quality; otherwise the brick will pull water in the mortar too rapidly for it to cure properly.

Classification of Brick

The term "brick" refers to a solid clay masonry unit. Cored brick is also classified as solid masonry if the cores do not exceed 25% of the cross-sectional area. The cores are introduced into brick used in wall construction to even the drying and to reduce the weight of the brick. The brick used for patios or paving is a solid

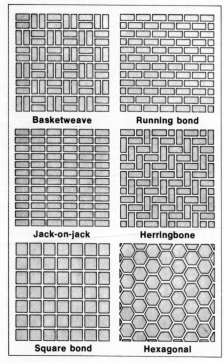

A wide variety of brick patterns is possible, although some are easier and more popular than others.

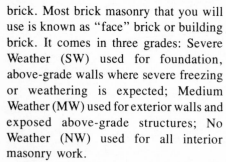

Bed joint refers to surface on which masonry is placed, head joint refers to joint between masonry units, collar joint to joint between wythes.

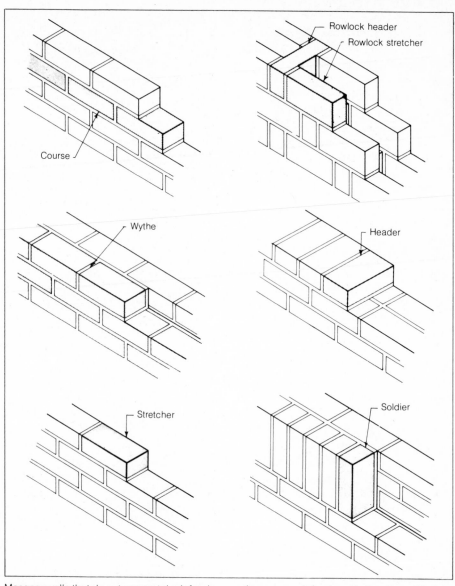

Masonry walls that do not use metal reinforcing need masonry reinforcing. No less than 4% of the wall surface should be composed of full-length headers, with a maximum distance between full-length headers of 24 in., whether the distance is vertical or horizontal.

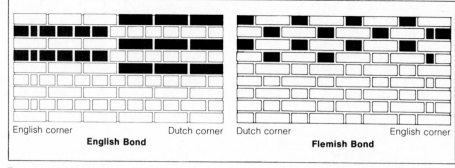

Two traditional bonding methods consist of: English Bond — alternating courses of headers and stretchers; Flemish bond — alternating headers and stretchers within each course.

brick. Most brick masonry that you will use is known as "face" brick or building brick. It comes in three grades: Severe Weather (SW) used for foundation, above-grade walls where severe freezing or weathering is expected; Medium Weather (MW) used for exterior walls and exposed above-grade structures; No Weather (NW) used for all interior masonry work.

Brick used for exterior garden walls will usually be either SW or MW depending on your location. Face brick is used on all exposed surfaces and is often backed by common brick. Glazed brick is another variation that may need to be specially ordered. It can produce unusual color combinations when inserted into the brick pattern, and is designed for SW usage. For barbecues, where brick will be ex-posed to open flame, firebrick is recommended. Your local supplier will be able to furnish you with samples and costs per square foot for each type.

Brick Bonds, Patterns and Joints

Bond, when used in reference to brick masonry, may have three meanings. Structural bond is the method of interlocking or tying together individual masonry blocks so that the entire assembly will act as a single unit. Pattern bond is the pattern formed by the bricks, and the mortar joints on the face of the wall

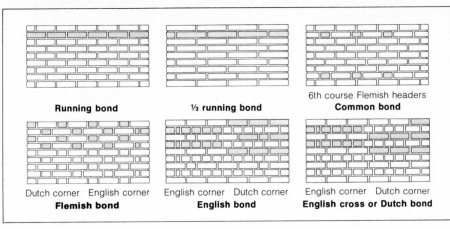

Shown are some of the basic structural bonds commonly used in masonry walls. Horizontal metal reinforcing must be used for running bond since there are no headers used.

This solid concrete block wall offers a smooth, continuous surface; textural interest is created with raked mortar joints.

that may result from the type of structural bond used — or it may be purely decorative. Mortar bond refers to the adhesion between the mortar and the brick or the reinforcing steel.

Brick, depending on the climatic situation, may be set on either a bed of sand or a mortar (or reinforced concrete) bed. In either case, you are free to select from a variety of patterns.

CONCRETE MASONRY

Concrete masonry for decks or patios refers to molded concrete units used primarily in the construction of walls, retaining walls, or decorative screens. They are available in most locations and are moderately priced compared to brick. The range of textures and colorations is less varied, but still very decorative. Screens are available with voids in a multitude of different shapes and patterns.

Concrete paving blocks for patios are also available. They are rectangular or interlocking forms that can be set into a sand or mortar bed. They come in a variety of shapes and patterns and are easy to transport and handle. Other advantages include low cost, high durability, and easy replacement.

Properties

Concrete masonry units are made from a mixture of portland cement, lightweight or medium size aggregates, water, and admixtures. This is molded into a desired shape through compaction and vibration. The blocks are cured either by steam or by air to achieve a 28-day strength.

Concrete block has strength capabilities similar to those of concrete. The strength of concrete block depends on the water/cement ratios, type of aggregate,

fabrication procedures and curing. The normal compressive range of strength is 700 psi to 1800 psi of gross area. The durability and weathering characteristics of concrete block depends largely on the quality of the mixture and the materials used. When used for walls in climates where severe freezing and thawing occur, or there are unusual pressures, we suggest use of steel reinforcement. It will not eliminate all cracking, but will reduce it to hairline fractures. Most screen and wall block are available in a variety of surface textures and colors.

Classification of Block

Concrete masonry units can be classified as: concrete brick, which refers to solid units; concrete block, which consists of both solid and hollow units; concrete pavers, for street or patio use, and special units primarily employed for screens or decorative walls. There are grades to in-

dicate best use of each type. Grade N is suitable for general use. Grade S is to be used for general use, but above grade only. In addition, concrete block will also be rated on its structural capability by type: hollow load-bearing units; solid load-bearing units; concrete building brick. Generally, Grade S is limited to walls not exposed to the weather and to exterior above-grade walls protected with weather-resistant coatings. Grade N may be used below grade as well as above; however, protective coatings are recommended below grade.

Block Bonds, Patterns, and Joints

The similarities between concrete block and brick are very obvious when comparing bonds and patterns. The pattern bonds and decorative screens are only used in wall construction. Each pattern requires a consistency in construction in order to create the desired effect. For walkways or

Concrete block walls can take on unusual textures and designs with application of several layers of stucco plaster.

patio areas, concrete paving blocks or precast paving units can be used in a variety of pattern bonds. The bond patterns can be integrated with other materials. Your local block supplier or fabricator can provide you with a descriptive list of units manufactured in the area; special shapes and forms are available. Make sure you bring your plan (see Chapter 4) so that the correct shapes are selected.

Concrete masonry screen walls provide sufficient visual privacy for many backyards, but do not offer a great deal of acoustical privacy to closely set houses.

Eye-catching screen patterns can be created using concrete masonry units, but you must plan ahead carefully to insure sufficient bonding and structural strength.

Patio Blocks

Patio blocks enable the homeowner to build a patio that works just as well as a concrete one, but costs only half as much. If the patio is built without mortar, settling will never be much of a problem. If one area becomes low or has a problem drainage spot, the homeowner has only to remove the stones, add more sand to the base, replace the blocks, and it will be set for several more seasons. Their main drawback is their tendency to settle unevenly and thus to require frequent adjustment. In cases where mortar is not used, weeds can become a problem. They can be controlled by using a nonselective, granular herbicide (like Triox Crystals). Simply shake the crystals from the container onto the problem spots, spray with the garden hose, and wait. The weeds will be gone within a week. Granular herbicides are better than liquid ones because they are usually stronger and leave no contaminated containers or sprayers behind them.

For most block patios, the best choice is to build them without mortar because this process allows the patio to settle or move naturally without cracking. If weeds are a real problem, or for those who feel that a patio without mortar does not give peace of mind, then you can add to the mortar one of the new latex liquid mixes available. It will not only give strength to the mortar, but will make it more impervious to the elements as well. To give even more protection to that fragile mortar, seal the entire patio with a masonry sealer. Applied with a brush or sprayer, the sealer adds strength and toughness to block, stone and brick faces, and to mortar joints.

Paving Blocks

Long used in Europe, pavers are one of the best materials for a durable patio. Usually manufactured in the shape of a capital "I", they interlock to make an almost solid surface that will rise and fall with frost cycles. The blocks vary in thickness between one and four inches. The best ones have chamfered edges that allow them to "roll" with frost heaving, which prevents cracking.

Pavers can be used for driveways and walkways, and are split in the same manner as a common brick. But their installation is a little different than that of other materials in that the grade is first set in

Concrete pavers provide a working surface from which to lay down the next pavers. The units do not firmly interlock until sand is swept into the joints.

STONE SELECTION FOR PATIOS AND WALKWAYS

Stone	Use	Advantages	Disadvantages
Granite	Steps, Exterior surfaces, walls	High polish, Durability, Weather resistance	Hard to form
Traprock	Paving	Hardness	Lack of grain
Limestone/Sandstone	Building	Finely grained, Easy to form, Strong	Does not weather as well as granite
Flagstone or Bluestone (forms of sandstone split into thin plates)	Paving	Same as sandstone	Many degrees of hardness; select hardest finish available.
Slate	Thick slabs — stair treads, sinks, partitions, blackboards; Thin slabs — used as flagstone	Dense, many colors available, wears well	Difficult to find in sufficient quantity or consistent quality
Marble	Interiors	Good visual appeal	Deteriorates in exterior use.

coarse sand and the pavers are laid on top of it. The workman always adds courses by working on top of the brick he has laid.

STONE

Stone is one of the earliest of all building materials, and has been the foundation of many important architectural structures. It has been thought of as a very permanent building material which may be why most famous monuments were constructed of stone. Since the advent of steel and concrete, the use of stone has been confined primarily to the facing or outer shell of the building, paving of exterior spaces, and to adornment of interior spaces.

Stone offers strength, beauty, durability, good coloration and surface textures. It comes in varying sizes, colors and shapes; its availability is regional. Stone as used in a patio is usually flagstone, sandstone, limestone or slate. These materials are very expensive, and unless properly built, the patio will deteriorate quite rapidly.

Stone Sizes

Stone is quarried; it is broken out from its natural ledge. Big blocks are first cut to the rough size desired using power saws. Hand tools and machinery polish and dress the stone with the chosen finish texture and surface. Unless the supplier has your specific size in stock, almost all ashlar, which is the cut stone, must be ordered. Only flagstone is commonly stocked in many sizes. You must decide

what scale of material you desire as a finishing material and then make your selection of the stone. Always select your stone according to local availability. Its appearance, durability, strength and ease of maintenance are directly related to its price.

Granite provides a sturdier, longer lasting wearing surface than flagstone, but is heavier and more difficult to cut. Flat granite units can be found at many stone quarries at a reasonable price.

Stone Masonry

Stonework may be divided into three general construction types. Rubble work is not truly cut stone, since it is constructed from local stones that are not easily cut but can be split. Ashlar is the cut stone facing used on the outside of a wall, without regard to the stones' finishing or coursing and pattern. Trimming denotes moldings, caps, sills, cornices and all cut stonework other than ashlar.

All ashlar and trimming for exterior trim as a facing should be no less than 1½ in. thick. When ashlar is backed by brick

work or other material and is part of the wall structure, the stone should be no less than 4 in. thick. For flagstone, the thickness varies according to type of stone. However all stone used as a paving material should be set into a well-compacted sand bed or reinforced mortar bed as in brick masonry paving material. Once the material is in place, it will tend to increase in hardness and weather resistance.

Flagstone. While not available in every area of the United States, flagstone can be used to create some striking patterns. For best results, choose stones that are between one and two inches thick.

The main problem with flagstones is setting them correctly. Any large air gap beneath the stone creates a weak spot that can cause the stone to break under pressure. To prevent this, work slowly and carefully, building a sand base beneath each stone before setting it in place. A second drawback to the stones is their irregular shape, which often creates the need for large joints between the stones. The larger sand joints do provide the patio with good drainage, so pitch is not as serious a concern as it is with other materials.

MORTAR

Mortar can be looked at as the glue that binds the individual units into a wall or building structure. To be effective, mortar must satisfy the following conditions: bond the units together, sealing the spaces between them; compensate for the variation in the size of the units; integrate the metal reinforcement within the joint; and provide a visual effect with texture, shadow or color not apparent in single masonry units.

Properties

Mortar is always inserted into the construction in a plastic (soft, workable) form. It has two sets of characteristics — those when plastic and those when it has hardened. Plastic mortar properties include: workability, the cohesive ability of the mortar to spread easily and hold well to the construction; water retentivity, because the mortar must be able to retain moisture when it contacts the absorptive masonry unit and loses its plasticity. The hardened mortar properties consist of: bond strength, which is a measure the adhesion of the dried and cured mortar; durability, measured by the mortar's resistance to repeated cycles of freezing and thawing; compressive strength, the amount of force that can be supported by the mortar in terms of psi (pounds per square inch); appearance, which is the overall visual quality once in the wall and cured. The longevity of the mortar and the construction is completely dependent upon the quality of workmanship. While the usual compressive strength of mortar varies between 75 psi and 2500 psi, improper workmanship can reduce those values by half.

Mortar Components

Mortar is a mixture of one or more cementitious materials, clean and well-graded sand, and water. There are several types of mortars. Lime mortar — a combination of lime, sand and water — hardens at a slow rate, has low compressive strength and offers only poor durability. However, it does have high workability and water retention. Portland cement mortar hardens quickly at a consistent rate and develops a high compressive strength with good durability, while giving low workability and water retention. Portland cement-lime mortar combines the benefits of both types. It is the most commonly used of all the mortars and is available in a premix bag form at your building supplier or local hardware store. Masonry cement mortars are made from mortar mixes called masonry cement. The main advantage of this type of mortar is its convenience in mixing. It is available in premix

It is harder and more time-consuming to set brick into a circular patio than into a rectangular patio, but it can be done. This semi-circular brick patio replaces a smaller rectangular concrete patio.

bag form through your local building materials supplier. To each of the mortars listed above, coloring agents can be inserted into the mix.

Mortar Proportions and Uses

There are five types of mortars recommended for use in construction, of which only three are applicable for use in exterior walls, patios or foundations. Each mortar type is determined by proportion of portland cement, hydrated lime, aggregate, and water. Type M or S is used in foundations, basements, or isolated piers. Type S or N can be used in exterior walls. From the chart, it can be seen that the proportions determine the strength and the ability of the mortar to resist weather conditions.

Mortar Mixing

Mix only enough mortar for immediate use. Use a maximum of water but make sure you do not dilute the mixture. You will find that the mortar becomes stiff quickly due to evaporation. You can add more water, but in that case you should remix the mortar. Use the mixture within two hours of mixing. This goes for both

your own mix and the premix variety. Do not put in too much sand, as this makes for a very weak bond between the mortar and the masonry units.

If you can rent a mixer from your local rental store, you will be a step ahead. For batching in a mixing machine, the following recommendations are made: use three-quarters of the required water with half the sand, and all of the cement. Then add the rest of the sand and mix well, adding the remaining water slowly — a little at a time — until you achieve the correct workability. The machine mix will take about five minutes.

If you are hand-mixing, spread the sand in a mortar box. Spread the cement on top of the sand in a uniform layer. Proceed to mix the dry mixture from both ends with a hoe or similar tool. Blend the mixture well. Add three-quarters of the water required. Mix until all the mixture is equally damp, and uniform in consistency. Add the remaining water slowly until the right workability is achieved. Let the batch stand for five minutes and then remix with the hoe. Do not add any more water.

4 Developing A Site Plan

Design ideas must be translated into a usable form for obtaining the necessary building permit or estimating quantities of materials required to build a deck or patio. The first step is to create a measured drawing. This is a drawing of the site, as well as of the deck or patio and its relative position with respect to the lot lines, underground utilities, water supply, and so on. The procedure is quite simple, but requires a methodical and consistent approach to recording what you see. You will need to buy some 8½x11 in. (or larger) grid paper. The grid is normally a light blue printed on a white background. At the same time, purchase a yardstick or 12-ft. tape in order to measure the positions of the various trees, foundations and other structural features. Once you have the grid paper, put it on a clipboard or similar writing platform so the paper will stay in place. At this point you are ready to start working out your site plan.

(1) Mark, in the upper corner of the page, the North Arrow plus East, West and South. Then locate the direction from which the prevailing summer and winter winds are likely to come.

(2) Select an outside corner of your house, at the foundation line. This will become the reference point for all subsequent measurements. From that corner, consistently measure in one direction, either clockwise or counterclockwise.

(3) Establish a drawing scale. To do this, give each individual grid a scale value of: ¼ ft., ½ ft., 1 ft., or 2 ft. For example; if you measured ten feet, six inches along your foundation wall, this would convert to twenty-one grid boxes if the scale were "one grid equals ½ foot."

(4) Measure the entire foundation, and mark it onto the grid. Note the North, South, East, and West exposures.

(5) Locate the interior room or rooms that will connect to the outside patio or deck. The procedure is similar to that used to measure and record the foundation. Use the original reference point (corner), measuring around the outside of the house until you arrive at an exterior window or a juncture that is also within the interior space. Locate that point on the interior wall and show it on your plan. Then measure and record the room dimensions at the same scale.

(6) From the information gathered from the local utilities, locate the relative positions of all the pipes and wires. You can then see if there will be any conflict

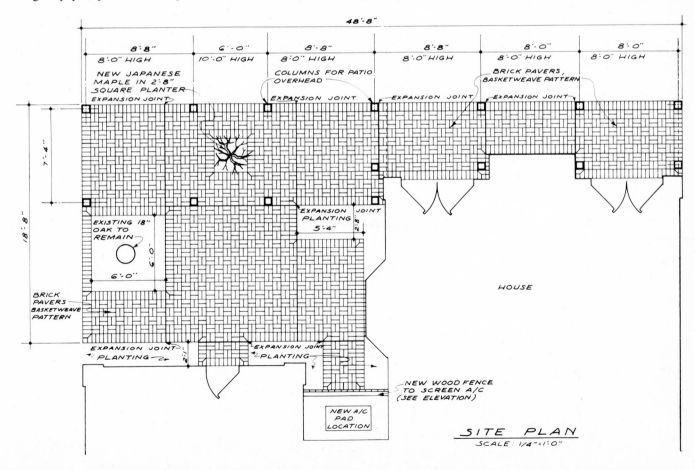

SITE PLAN
SCALE: 1/4"=1'-0"

with underground or overhead utilities.

(7) Once again from the reference corner, locate the boundaries or corners of your property. You may find that you will have to attach several pieces of grid paper together to cover your entire lot to scale. Be sure to include the lot lines. This is important in order to meet the zoning set-back requirements.

(8) Mark the positions of all trees, evergreens, and shrubs in the area; note which will be kept and which will have to be relocated. This will help estimate the amount of work involved, and will indicate shady areas.

(9) Now you can add to your site plan the size and shape of your deck or patio. It's a good idea to make several copies of the original drawing so that you can try more than one design alternative. It is important that you compare several plan arrangements so you can not only see the size and shape possibilities but can begin to estimate quantities and types of materials.

Once you have settled upon your design and are pleased with it, draw up the plan at a larger scale. This drawing will be limited to the area immediately around the deck and the house as well as any trees, evergreens, flower beds, or shrubs. The larger-scale plan will help you visualize the patterns and textures of your materials, as well as giving you a more accurate feeling for the relative size. To accomplish this, simply convert the previous measurements to another scale. For example: if you measured ten feet, six inches, along the foundation wall, this would convert to sixty-three grid boxes if the scale were one grid equals two inches, or to 42 grid boxes if the scale were one grid equals three inches.

Laying out a Deck

In laying out your deck, locate all fences, screens, walls, stairs and roof structures. These will affect the outer boundary of the deck. Once you have decided where the deck should be placed in relation to the house, it is critical that it be laid out square with the house shape. Decks have often been built on a skew when the proper squaring has not been worked out. Your drawing on the graph paper should now be taking shape. The size and pattern should be clearly established. Measurements should be indicated as well as the choice of material.

Patio Layout

You are now ready to lay out the site for your patio. Proper layout of the patio area is necessary before you can accurately estimate quantities of materials and acquire a building permit. It also reduces the difficulties of construction. By following the steps given earlier you should have already measured the exterior space, and have all obstacles and utilities marked. In laying out the patio, locate all trees, bushes, shrubs, and plants that are to be kept within the patio zone. Make sure you have indicated all plantings adjacent to the patio. You will later, prior to construction, want to protect them from damage as you build the patio. If you desire outdoor lighting, locate approximately where those lines must go. Once the patio is down, it is quite expensive and time-consuming to rip it up in the event you forgot to install a line or pipe. At this point on the drawing, you should be able to clearly indicate the depth and breadth of your patio and the material selected. Determine the exact size and location with respect to the foundation of your house or building. In addition, determine how far the site slopes within the area. This will help in setting the level of the patio surface. Plot out carefully the edges or borders. If they are to be specific material, you should indicate their sizes. If your design is to include any screens, walls, fences or trellises, you should locate their position relative to the patio. If building any overhead cover, it is necessary to build the framing structure before the patio. This is because a patio would

interfere with the support posts. Decide now how the materials are to be transported and erected. In most cases the patio surface can be altered to accommodate the structures to be placed over it or near it.

DRAWING THE ELEVATION

At the previous stage you have drawn a complete plan at a large enough scale so that all the particular details have been indicated. Now you can draw an elevation of the large scale plan. Use the same scale as for the enlarged (second) plan.

(1) Measure vertically from a horizontal line of the foundation — or from a floor line that shows on the outside of the building — to locate all the openings, vents, eave lines, etc. On this elevation, draw in the ground level as it exists. This is important, as it will provide the information necessary for the foundation or base preparation.

(2) On the same sheet, superimpose a drawing of the deck or patio. Do not forget to show railings or stairs if you plan to have them. This information is again necessary so you can estimate quantities.

Most building inspectors will accept a well-drawn plan and elevation of this type in order to issue a building permit. In the event that they require a more "architectural" plan drawing, there are several drafting services usually available in most communities, or your local technical school might be able to suggest how to have your plan drawn so it will be suitable for submission.

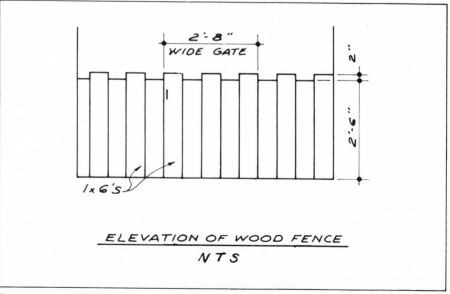

ELEVATION OF WOOD FENCE
NTS

The site plan on the previous page also includes addition of this wood fence.

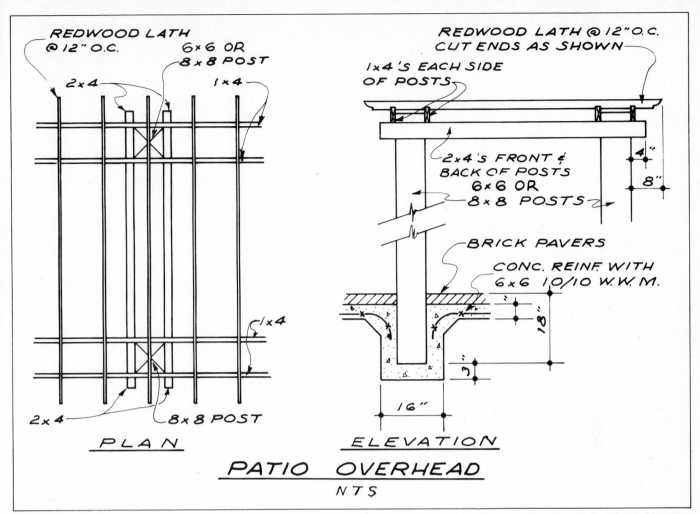

REDWOOD LATH @ 12" O.C.

6×6 OR 8×8 POST

2×4

1×4

REDWOOD LATH @ 12" O.C. CUT ENDS AS SHOWN

1×4'S EACH SIDE OF POSTS

2×4'S FRONT & BACK OF POSTS 6×6 OR 8×8 POSTS

4"

8"

BRICK PAVERS

CONC. REINF. WITH 6×6 10/10 W.W.M.

18"

3"

1×4

2×4

8×8 POST

16"

PLAN

ELEVATION

PATIO OVERHEAD
NTS

This patio overhead is a feature of the site plan on the previous page. The plan gives a view from above; the elevation shows the components in cutaway.

5 Patio Building Basics

Having made the decision to build a patio, you must realistically ask yourself how much time and effort you are willing to invest in the project, as well as what type and quality of material you are will to pay for. Then look into the construction requirements. This section will concentrate on the actual building on a step-by-step basis.

The level of craftsmanship and your assembly skill will determine the final visual quality. Craftsmanship is a desirable quality, but should not be the only consideration. We will present the material so as to simplify construction and to keep the time and difficulty at minimum.

THE PARTS OF A PATIO

Before starting the patio project, it is helpful to recognize all the components that form a patio. The patio is really composed of two main elements: (1) the wearing surface, which is the finish surface of the patio and which can be of a variety of materials; (2) the base preparation, such as gravel, sand, soil, or existing concrete.

To give you a better sense of the relationship between the two elements, any loads or forces that are applied to the wearing surface are immediately transferred through the wearing surface to the base. The base in turn distributes them to the soil. This is an exceptionally efficient combination, and in many ways is much easier to build than a wood deck of comparable size. In order to visualize the two elements working together, we will first evaluate the two separately.

Patio Wearing Surfaces

The major part of the patio is the wearing surface — the surface exposed to the elements. The surface is usually built directly on grade. That is, the surface is not raised above the ground more than 6 to 8 in., in order to reduce the overall cost and to keep the method of construction simple. The surface is usually located one or two feet below the interior floor level. If

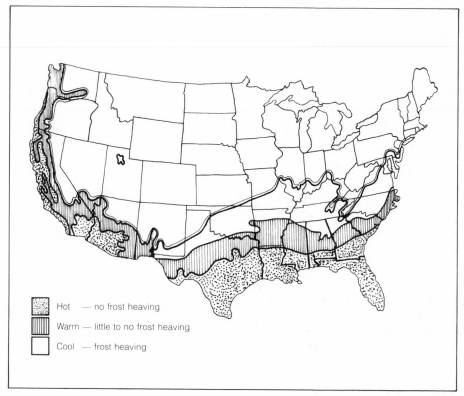

Hot — no frost heaving

Warm — little to no frost heaving

Cool — frost heaving

In most areas of the country concrete footings will be subject to heaving during the winter months.

the patio is adjacent to the house, it is common to have steps or a small platform between the house and the exterior wearing surface. The small platform may be nothing more than a raised surface in a similar material, or a wood platform extending over the patio itself. Since the patio is located on grade, you might want to raise it just enough (pour it thick enough) to eliminate the step or platform between the interior and exterior. This is quite feasible if the distance between deck and house is one or two feet. It is recommended that for anything over that distance there be intermediate steps or a platform. This is also much safer.

If the patio is located adjacent to the foundation of your house or building, and you are in a climate where rain and/or snow are prevalent, the patio surface should be gently pitched away from the foundation at a rate of no less than ⅛ in. per ft. of slab width. This must be consid-

ered a minimum. A more realistic figure is a ¼ in. per ft. For example, if you have decided on a patio width of 12 ft. extending from the foundation of your house, at ⅛ in. per foot the total drop across the width would be 1½ in. This figure is acceptable in climates where the annual rainfall is considered minimal. In a more northern climate it is desirable to use the ¼ in. per ft. which results in a 3 in. drop over the twelve ft. This keeps the water away from the house interior and reduces

A patio wearing surface can be of railroad ties as well as the more common materials such as concrete, brick, block, pavers, or stone.

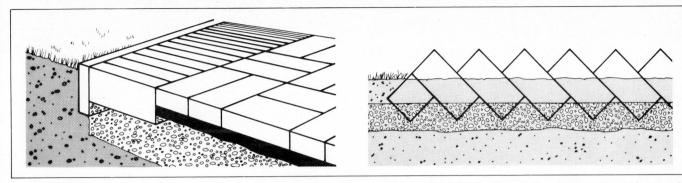

Brick can be set on edge over the gravel-plus-sand subbase to create an attractive edging. Pretreated lumber or railroad ties must be set in a trench if used as edgings — either flush to patio surface or to a minimum depth of 3 in. Brick can also be angled in trench with 2 in. of mortar or concrete. Use a half brick to close off the edging. Extend the concrete or mortar a few inches beyond the last brick.

the possibility of the patio surface being undermined.

The patio wearing surface materials, discussed in Chapters 2 and 3, are quite varied. Your choice will be determined by how much money you wish to invest and the amount of maintenance you can handle. In selecting the patio surface material, remember its use. A slippery surface is not a good choice next to a pool; a rough texture would be best. If you are planning to entertain, select a surface that will be easy to clean and will not stain easily.

Patio Base Preparations

The base preparation is rarely seen. The purpose of the base is to prepare the soil so it will accept the surface material without later settlement, drainage, or heaving problems. The soil on which the patio will be placed must be prepared, compacted, and edged in order to keep the wearing surface in its correct position. Most materials that are placed under a patio surface are there to increase the density of the soil as well as to provide a leveling course. A course is a layer of material. Normally the base courses are composed of gravel, sand or concrete. These materials are readily available in most regions. They

are relatively inexpensive and their unit of measure is most often the cubic yard. Edging or border materials which are most often set into the surrounding soil are metal, brick, or railroad ties.

A slab on grade does not require a foundation; however, an edge stiffener is recommended as part of the design. This is simply an additional thickness of concrete added to the edge of the concrete slab to make sure that the edge keeps its position and shape. It should be used in all concrete slabs on grade. To build an edge footing, formwork is required. In the

same way that an edging is a form for the material to be put within it, concrete also requires formwork. This is often of plywood and 2x4s, or stock lumber. The outline of the concrete is defined by the formwork. Once this has been created, the concrete can be poured into the form.

Patio and Roof Structure

If you desire a roof structure over your patio for shading or privacy, it is important to plan this before beginning any construction. Since the patio is usually located at or a little above grade, the roof

Railroad ties used as edgings can be set either flush to the wearing surface or set at least 3 in. deep in a trench with the widest dimension face down.

When building overhead cover for a patio, plan ahead so that you can install the overhead supports first and then build the concrete forms around the posts.

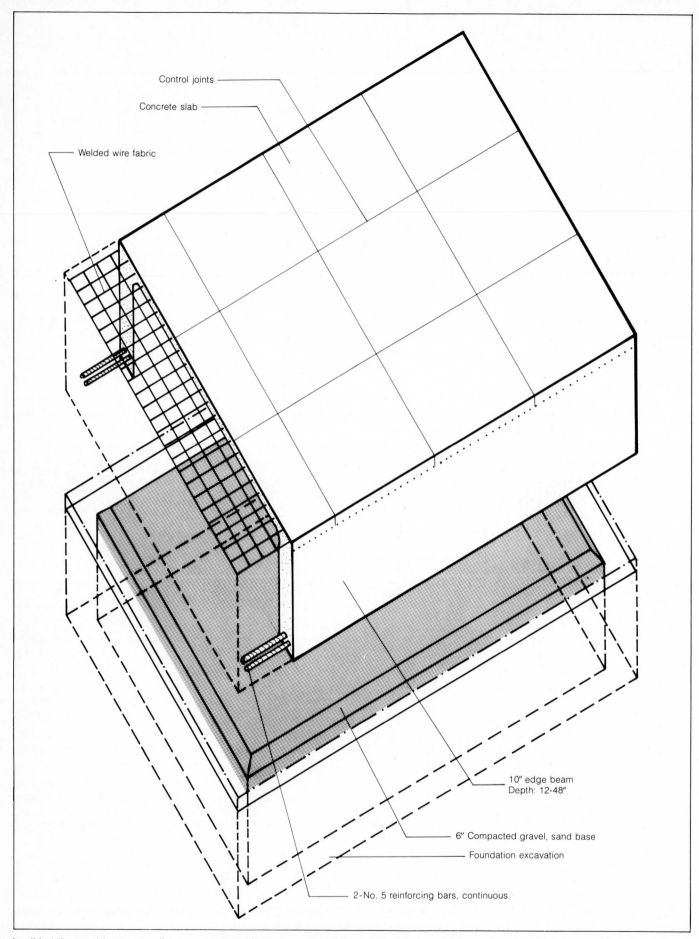

Control joints

Concrete slab

Welded wire fabric

10″ edge beam
Depth: 12-48″

6″ Compacted gravel, sand base

Foundation excavation

2-No. 5 reinforcing bars, continuous

In all but the most temperate climates an edge stiffener is preferred. It anchors the slab and keeps it from shifting and heaving.

structure should be built prior to the patio. If you desire to add overhead protection after you have installed a patio, you will have to place the support columns around the perimeter. This may or may not be possible, depending upon the dimensions of your patio and upon the span between the columns. In Chapter 7, the actual design, fabrication and assembly of a roof structure are described. You should familiarize yourself with this chapter and with the necessary building and layout procedures.

Once any roof structure has been completed, you are ready to undertake construction of the patio area. Try to integrate the posts or columns into the patio material design. This will give the appearance of planning control and unity between the roof structure and the patio area. In most cases, the roof superstructure (framing but not infill) is installed, and then the patio is completed. This allows you to have a solid platform from which to complete the roof infill.

ESTIMATING THE MATERIAL QUANTITIES

Since the base materials are ordered by volume rather than by weight, it is important to make sure that the quantities you order are adequate. To measure for base materials such as sand and gravel, you must know the size and depth of the areas using those materials. For purposes of demonstration, we will give figures for a concrete patio that adjoins the house on one side, and which measures 12 ft. across and is 16 ft. parallel to the house, with edge stiffeners on three sides. You should be able to estimate your quantities based on this design.

Based upon a 4-in. thick slab on grade, the base preparation is composed of three main ingredients: gravel base course, sand cushion, and form work with a 6-in. edge beam.

The gravel base will usually be 6 in. in depth, which will compact into approxi-

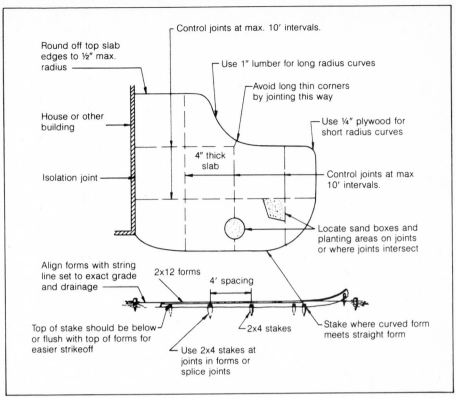

mately 4 in. Therefore, the gravel to be ordered should be 12 ft. x 16 ft. x 6 in. (or .5 foot in depth) divided by 27 cu. ft./yard. This results in 3½ cubic yards of gravel. For the sand: you would require a depth of 2 in. (or .17 of a ft.) x 12 ft. x 16 ft., divided by 27 cu. ft./yard. This equals 1.20 cubic yards. It would be advisable to order 1½ yards of sand, as any excess can be tamped down into the gravel or used elsewhere.

The last ingredient is the formwork. For our example, a 2x12 will be used as an edge stiffener. To hold the 2x12 securely in place, 2x4s that are 24 in. long and placed as stakes at 16 inches o.c. will be required. Therefore, for the 2x12: 12 ft. + 16 ft. +12 ft. (edges of three sides) is required — 40 ft. of 2x12. There will be a total of 62 ft. of 2x4 required (see sketch). The concrete needed will be 1½ cu. yd. for a 6-in. edge beam and 2½ cu. yd. for a

4-in. slab. A 12x16 ft. area of welded wire fabric will be required: 6x6 #10/10 type. In addition, 40 linear ft. of No. 5 reinforcing bar will be required for insertion into the edge beam. These quantities apply to the actual patio construction. If you plan a walkway or retaining wall, additional quantities of the materials will be needed.

If you were to build the slab so that the wearing surface ended up flush with the ground level, you would follow the same procedures and measurements as above but would simply excavate the additional 4 in. for the slab itself.

If building a patio higher than 4 in., the sand and gravel calculations would be the same but the concrete and formwork ingredients would increase. The concrete would simply require the additional volume due to the increased height; the formwork would have to be built up to handle the additional concrete. The form would be built of 2x12s plus additional pieces of lumber, as necessary for the height. This form should be staked every 10 in., with bracing in two directions (meeting at 90° angles) for each stake. This ensures that the form will hold up to the pressure of the concrete as it is placed. The edger and excavation remain the same as previously described. If the patio

Forms for a free-form patio are not much harder to lay out than forms for a rectangular slab, but they are more time-consuming. Control joints can be as close as 4 ft., but no further than 10 ft.

ESTIMATING CUBIC YARDS OF CONCRETE FOR SLABS BEFORE ADDING IN EDGE STIFFENER

Thickness inches	Area in square feet (width x length)					
	10	25	50	100	200	300
4	0.12	0.31	0.62	1.23	2.47	3.70
5	0.15	0.39	0.77	1.54	3.09	4.63
6	0.19	0.46	0.93	1.85	3.70	5.56

The edge stiffener rims the slab and anchors it in position.

is sufficiently high, you may need to use the edge beam as a retaining wall near the house. This means that the slab would not need to be solid concrete throughout. It could be only 4 or 5 in., of concrete overall, but the edger that rims the slab would be high enough to give the additional height and also anchor into the ground. The edger forms would be boxes that were staked, braced, and bolted to hold the rim of concrete. The interior area could be filled with compacted dirt or fill. Since it is difficult to guarantee that the dirt or fill has been properly graded and tamped, and that it will not settle over time, for this type of patio you should seriously consider consulting or partially contracting with a landscape contractor.

Remember that for a 6-in. slab, the lumber you would use is "dressed", which means it is surfaced to give smoothness and uniformity. This procedure reduces the size of the lumber. The 4-in. dimension of a 2x4 is actually between $3\frac{1}{2}$ and $3\frac{9}{16}$ in.; the 6-in. dimension of a 2x6 will be between $5\frac{1}{2}$ and $5\frac{5}{8}$ in. This means that the ground level grade you set up may need to be slightly lower than the bottom of the form. Backfill a little outside the forms to prevent the concrete from running out from underneath. The concrete should be placed just a little higher than the desired final surface height, to allow for shrinkage and settling. If you are in doubt about the specific quantities for your design, check with your local building materials supplier for assistance.

BUILDING PERMITS

Once you have completed your drawing and estimated your material quantities, but prior to placing your order, submit your plan for a building permit. Refer to the sections on "Building Permits" in the previous chapters for additional information. Most communities will not permit you to proceed with your construction without a permit. In some cases, building inspectors have requested that work already completed be undone and corrected according to building code standards.

CONSTRUCTION OF A CONCRETE PATIO

To help you in the construction process of building your patio, a 12x16 ft. adjacent concrete patio, 4 in. thick situated on

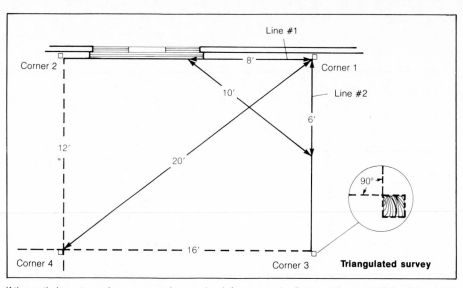

If the patio is rectangular, you can always check for square by first creating a multiple of the 3-4-5 triangle; the diagonal will always be the corresponding multiple of 5. You may also wish to nail up a 3-4-5 right-angle triangle from lumber to doublecheck the corners.

grade, will be used to illustrate the necessary steps. Every attempt has been made to simplify the sequence so that any similarities and differences will be very clear between this design and yours. There may be parts of the construction procedure that you may wish to subcontract out. In this event, pick up where the subcontractor left off. It is recommended that you have another person assist you in pouring and finishing the concrete, because it is difficult to carry out those steps without aid.

Step One: Site Preparation

Remove all the topsoil and sod within the area you have designated as the patio area. Drive several stakes around the perimeter, allowing at least one foot (or more) beyond the actual edge of the proposed patio. Rake the ground, removing any large rocks, glass or debris in the excavation area. The depth of the excavation will depend on the thickness of your slab, and whether the patio wearing surface will be above ground or flush with the ground level. For our example, the excavation will be 6 in. deep before grading for drainage. After you have levelled the site, and while you are excavating, you will have to grade the earth so that the corners of the patio furthest from the house will be lower (in this case 3 in.) than the point closest to it. Once this has been accomplished, smooth out the surface as much as possible by raking. In many cases you can grade just by moving the earth from low spots to the desired high areas.

If your site slopes steeply away from or toward the house foundation, try to level and grade it as much as possible. To do this might require additional excavation beyond the depth of the topsoil. It may be necessary to call in a landscape grader if the grade requires much earth fill.

If fill is required, determine the quantity by figuring the height to be achieved over the area to be covered. This figure should then be doubled as the fill will compact to almost one half of its original volume. To fill a site, put the greatest amount of soil where the greatest void exists, spread it around, and tamp. The tamping may be done by a large roller or by a mechanical tamper that can be rented. Continue to infill in 4-in. layers. Keep the soil moist but not wet. The soil will absorb the moisture and swell, which will be its natural state when covered by the concrete slab. To check for the desired level, pick one of the straightest 2x4s. Lay it down over the area placing on it a 48 in. carpenters level, on edge. You must find the level before you can create the pitch. This will tell you which areas need more fill or stripping. Check for levelness on the diagonal as well. Always tamp down thoroughly.

Step Two: Staking Out the Patio

To ensure that the patio will be square to the foundation, and to the edges it adjoins, the perimeter edges must be located accurately. A triangulated survey method will be used to make sure that all dimensions and corners are square.

Drive a wood stake at the foundation,

For very large patios it is a good idea to give additional strength to the form by supporting every other 2x4 stake with a 2x4 set at an angle.

You can either tack the string to a stake, or wrap it around to prevent its slipping or becoming loose. Be sure that the wrap-around is at the same height for each stake.

Stake the form boards with 2x4s to keep the form stiff during the concrete placement. Note how the string follows the top of the form board.

where the concrete slab will meet the foundation (Corner 1). Measure along the foundation wall a distance of the length of the patio, in this case 16 ft., and locate another stake at that point (Corner 2). String a line between the two stakes. Make sure that the line is parallel to the house foundation. From the first stake driven (Corner 1), measure along the line 8 ft. and drive another stake. This will be a reference point. Again from the first stake, measure out 6 ft. perpendicular to the wall line. If you are exactly perpendicular, the diagonal from the six ft. point and the 8 ft. point that you had staked would measure exactly 10 ft., creating a right triangle. If it is not exact, move the six ft. measure left or right until it coincides with the ten-ft. diagonal. Measure 6 ft. further from this point to find Corner 3. Now measure out 12 ft. from Corner 2 and 16 ft. from Corner 3. Where the two measures intersect, stake that point as Corner 4. You have now created your rectangle. Once you have located the two exterior corners, check the two diagonal measurements. They should be the same (in this case, 20 ft.). The tops of all the stakes should all be exactly the same height at the time, which means that the two exterior corners (3 and 4) will have stakes that are 3 in. longer to compensate for the pitch. Once you have staked the entire patio, you are ready to proceed.

Now you must mark the height of the patio deck onto the exterior foundation. Using a carpenter's level, continue this line across the length of the foundation between the stakes. This will be your ref-

erence point for footings, formwork, and the gravel/sand base. Mark this height on the stakes you have set up. String up lines running from mark to mark on the stakes. Because the grade will slope down 3 in. at the furthest corners, the marks on Corner Stakes 3 and 4 should be 3 in. lower in actual height than the reference point line on the foundation.

Step Three: Formwork

From the corners where the patio meets the house, dig trenches out to the furthest corners. The trenches should be just outside the patio excavation area. They should be as deep as the edging form (11¼ in.) and 2 in. wide. In one trench place a 2x12 that has been cut to a length of twelve ft. Stake the corner end closest to the foundation. Using a carpenters level, level the edge board until it is level with the mark on the house foundation (this will also be the height marked on the interior stake). At the furthest corner, move the beam down 3 in. to match the mark you made earlier on the stake; this should be following the pitch you graded for drainage. The top of the form board should align with the string lines. Now attach the first stake to the board with 16d nails. Make sure that the stakes are on the outside of the board and that your square has not changed. Repeat this operation for the second board on the other side of the patio. Then take the remaining 16-ft. 2x12 and connect it to the outside corners of the two side pieces. Stake the 2x4s around the entire perimeter you have laid out. The stake height should be just below

the top of the 2x12. The stakes at the two farthest corners will be the same height relative to the foundation as those nearer the house, but will actually be 3 in. longer due to the grade. Cut all stakes off just below form height. Having staked the perimeter on 16-in. centers, you have set the exterior formwork. With the dirt that was removed during initial excavation, fill in around the outside of the boards. Make sure the dirt is tamped against the forms; this will prevent unwanted movement of the form boards. On the inside of the form, tamp the earth so it is level with the bottom of the form board; if necessary, relevel and regrade the entire area within the form, compacting or filling.

Permanent Forms. You may want to use decorative divider strips, left in place permanently, to act as control joints and to give texture and pattern. These forms should be made of 2x4 redwood, cypress, or cedar; you will have to prime these forms with clear wood sealer (or buy already-primed wood). You should mask the top surfaces with tape to protect them from staining and abrasion during concrete placement. Because these forms will be permanent, assemble them carefully. Corner joints should be neatly mitered, and intersecting strips should meet in neat butt joints. Anchor the outside forms to the concrete with 16d galvanized nails by driving them into the wood at 16-in. intervals at mid-height, horizontally, before pouring the concrete. Interior divided strips will take nail anchors similarly spaced, but driven from alternate sides of the board. All nail heads should be driven flush with the forms; do not drive nails through tops of permanent forms. Any stake that will remain in place

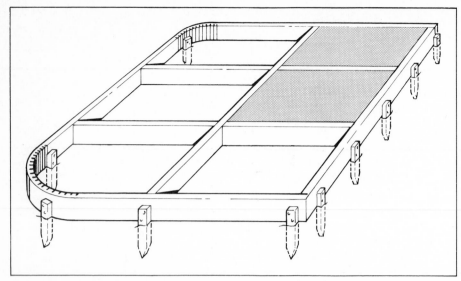

Stakes should be set closer at corners and on curves. The interior forms shown are treated wood that will be left in the concrete when the exterior forms are pulled; they also serve as control joints to prevent cracking.

Railroad ties set into the concrete as permanent interior forms add a rustic texture and also act as control joints. They combine particularly well with aggregate concrete, as shown.

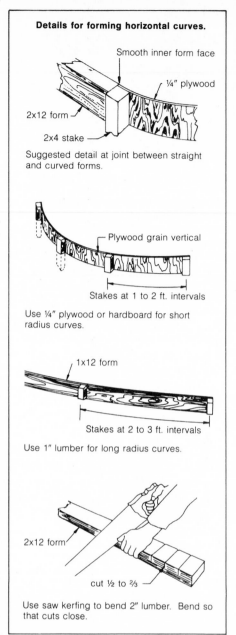

Details for forming horizontal curves.

Smooth inner form face

¼" plywood

2x12 form

2x4 stake

Suggested detail at joint between straight and curved forms.

Plywood grain vertical

Stakes at 1 to 2 ft. intervals

Use ¼" plywood or hardboard for short radius curves.

1x12 form

Stakes at 2 to 3 ft. intervals

Use 1" lumber for long radius curves.

2x12 form

cut ½ to ⅔

Use saw kerfing to bend 2" lumber. Bend so that cuts close.

permanently should be driven or cut off 2 in. below the concrete surface.

Curved Forms. Your patio design may call for curved forms. If so, you can use one-inch lumber rather than two-inch. You may also use ¼–to–½ inch thick plywood, sheet metal, or hardboard. Gentler, short-radius curves can use two-inch thick wood forms that have been saw-kerfed and then bent until the kerfs are held closed; or you can bend plywood, with the grain vertical. Wet lumber will be easier to bend than will dry lumber. For very tight curves, use ⅜ in. redwood or plywood bender boards. Sandwich together two or three boards against the stakes, and nail into position. Vertical curves can also be formed by saw kerfing. Another option is to bend the 2x4s during

staking. When the slope changes sharply, shorter lengths of forming are best.

Lay out the curve with a string line that is tied to temporary stakes. Then adjust the line up or down on the stakes to give a smooth curve. Short lengths of the forming are then set to the string line and are staked securely. To keep forms at proper curvature and grade, set the stakes closer on curves than on straight runs.

Forms for Steps. There are several possibilities for the arrangement of the steps in relation to the patio. If you are building a patio which uses existing access to a back door, then you will already have steps in place and will simply have to set up the forms using the existing concrete steps as part of one side of the form. In this case, lay an isolation joint (expan-

sion strip) where the bottom step will meet the patio.

If you are adding a patio and do not already have steps leading to it — for example, you have installed a sliding glass door to give access to a new patio area that is below the interior floor level — the procedure is a little more complicated. You will need to form, place and partially cure the concrete steps before placing the concrete for your patio. This is because you will have to brace the step forms; you will want to remove the step bracing and forms before placing the concrete for the patio. You should place an expansion strip at the base of the top riser, and where the bottom step will meet the patio.

Footings. You will need footings un-

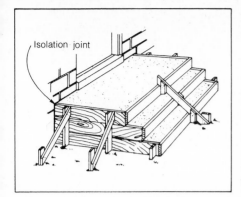

Steps leading down from the house to your patio should be formed and poured before placement of the concrete for the patio. Bevel the form boards for the risers so you can finish the treads under the forms.

Level from left to right risers and position them so the back of each tread will be ¼ in. higher than the front. Concrete placement begins with the bottom step.

Edging along a riser form gives a smooth, gradual curve to the edge of the tread. A ¼-to-½-in. radius tool is usually used; the first troweling follows soon after.

One finishing method calls for early stripping of forms so that risers and treads can be finished before concrete sets firmly. Finishing starts at the top: the landing is struck off, darbied, and edged, then hand-floated and given its first troweling.

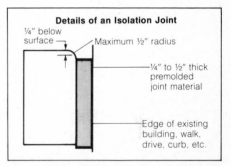

Isolation joints are used when dissimilar materials meet. Brick adjoining concrete, and old concrete butting against new concrete, are a few such cases.

derneath the steps. The footings should be 2 ft. deep; or, in regions of hard frost, the footings should extend 6 in. below the frost line. Tie the steps to the foundation walls using anchor bolts or tie rods. One economical measure that will act as footings and prevent the steps from sinking, is to dig two or more 6-to-8-in. diameter postholes beneath the bottom tread and fill them with concrete. The depth of these would be as noted above. Tie the top step or landing into the foundation using at least two metal anchors.

The step forms will take a coat of oil to aid in removing them. Once the forms are built, put large rocks or broken concrete or bricks inside so you will not need to fill the whole volume with concrete. Keep this fill well away from the edges and the top so it will not be exposed. For concrete steps, use gravel that is no larger than 1 in. in diameter.

If you are building a raised patio even with the interior floor, you will need steps leading down from the patio to your yard. These steps use the same forms as those leading from the house, but do not require footings. You would want to place expansion (isolation) strips at the base of the top

riser and the base of the second-to-the-bottom riser.

Dimensions: Check your local building codes to find any minimum or maximum dimensions set. For flights of more than 5 ft. (which is unlikely), a landing should be provided. A top landing should be no further than 7½ in. below the threshold. If the flight is less than 30 in. high, the minimum tread width is usually 11 in. and the maximum step rise 7½ in. For higher step flights, the minimum tread width may be 12 in. and the step rise may become 6 in. For design purposes, steps with treads as wide as 19 in. and rises as low as 4 in. are sometimes built. One rule of thumb has it that the riser and tread should add to 17½ inches; however, patios and decks will often take more generous dimensions.

Easier Alternative. If you decide to buy precast steps and to bolt them to the house, place the steps in position before pouring the patio. You will need to dig posthole footings, place the steps and anchor them, and then put an isolation (expansion) joint between the steps and the patio.

Oiling the Forms. You can now oil the

interior part of the form. Use an inexpensive grade of motor oil or an oil spray. This helps later in the removal of the form. Along the foundation wall of the house, install a preformed expansion material. This material comes in ½ in. by 4 in. strips. It is used to separate the concrete patio slab from the foundation of the house. To place it, lay it loosely along the foundation line. Once the concrete is poured it will remain in place. You are now ready for the next step.

Step Four: Preparing the Base

You are now ready to prepare the base with the gravel and sand. Your reference point will be the top of the form board. Place the gravel over the entire area. Lay it down in two layers of 3 in. each. Make sure that each layer is tamped thoroughly until firm. The 6-inch depth of the gravel should be tamped down to 4 in. You are now ready to place the sand over the gravel course. To do this, place the sand uniformly over the entire area in a 2-in. layer. Tamp the sand down. If the gravel shows through, do not be alarmed. Place enough sand so that a difference between the top of the sand and the top of the formboard will be approximately 4 in. If the space is less, remove some sand.

At this point the edge beam must be created. To do this, remove the earth from the inside perimeter of the formboard for a width of 6 in.; this 6-in. trough all

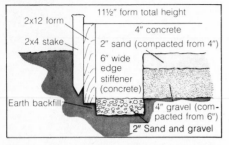

This is a side view of the edge stiffener and the base preparation. Because dressed lumber is slightly shorter than its nominal dimension, some backfill is required under the form.

Mask the tops of divider strips and outer forms that will remain in place so they will not be stained or abraded during concrete placement.

Pretreated strips may be stained to match your deck, fence, or screen.

around the perimeter should be about 6 in. deep after leaving about 2 in. of gravel and sand on the bottom. It will be excavated to just below the bottom edge of the formboard. Moisten the area so the shape will hold. Having done this, check that the corners of the forms are braced and tightly connected, and that all alignments are still square and correct.

Step Five: Setting the Reinforcing Steel

Reinforcing comes in two forms. The first type used in the slab will come in rolls or sheets of 4x8 ft. This welded wire fabric is visually similar to wire mesh, but has a larger spacing and is welded at each intersection of the wire. It can be placed into the form in two ways: formed metal "chair rails" can be purchased to be placed in the sand on which the welded wire fabric sits. This ensures that the fabric will be in the middle of the concrete when it is poured. Another method is to place two-to-three inch stones inside the form; the fabric is placed on the stones. The chair rails allow for the fabric to be tied to them; the rocks are less stable. Either method will suffice. The main idea is to keep the fabric in the middle of the concrete, or 2 in. from the top of the slab. The second type of reinforcing is the #5 straight deformed rod, which comes in a variety of lengths. The rods are placed in the form in the perimeter trough you have created. To elevate them above the bottom of the trough, drive a wooden 2x4 into the bottom of the trough every three or four feet around the perimeter. This will keep the rod elevated. If the 2x4 is left unattached, it will float when the concrete is poured. Keep the steel as clean as you possibly can. Once the reinforcing steel has been placed in the forms, the concrete can be poured.

Step Six: Pouring the Concrete

As was previously recommended, ready-mixed concrete is without a doubt the most desirable, since it is delivered mixed and ready for placement when you are at the right stage. If you are planning to mix the concrete yourself, please refer to the section on Concrete in Chapter 3.

Prior to pouring the concrete, prepare the ground area so that the truck can back in as closely as possible. This way the delivery can be directly into the form rather than having to barrow it in from

some other location. It is strongly recommended that you have a helper to assist you in this phase of the operation.

As you fill the forms, make sure that you place the material evenly over the entire area. Allow some overage, since you will want to work the concrete down into the forms by filling all the voids. Be careful not to let the material drop over 3 ft. in height, which would cause separation of the aggregate from the cement paste. After adding each layer, compact by pushing the end of the shovel into the crevasses or corners. Start in a corner and continue laying each successive pour against the previous one until the entire form has been filled. When the form has been filled to overflowing, the truck will be ready to leave — your work, however, must continue. A truck's capacity is usually 12 to 20 yards of concrete. That means that you will be able to pour a 12x16 ft. patio in one pour.

As you spade concrete by pushing the spade vertically and pulling it out, do not overdo it. The material could separate — causing water to float to the surface, which would cause spalling at a later date. Work it uniformly, treating each square foot equally. It is possible that your reinforcing will bend while the load settles to the bottom. If so, get a couple of coat hangers and pull the reinforcing up as you work that particular area. Once the entire form has been worked over, you will be ready to finish the concrete.

Step Seven: Finishing the Concrete Slab

Having placed the concrete as quickly as you can, making sure it has been properly compacted in the forms, you are ready to finish the material. There is a tendency for the concrete to "bleed". This is the water rising to the surface due to the heavier materials settling on the bottom. The placing, screeding and darbying should be accomplished as quickly as possible to prevent this from occurring. If a large amount of water does rise to the surface, try to remove it by drawing a length of garden hose across the surface. "Bleeding" can cause future scaling or spalling of the surface.

Screeding. Screeding is the process of taking off any excess concrete from the poured slab. It must be done immediately after you have poured the entire area. It is also a way to attain your desired level.

Select a very straight 2x4 or 2x6 board that is at least 18 ft. long. This is a two-person operation. Place the 2x4 across the upper edge of the concrete along the house foundation. Beginning at that point, slide the screed back and forth moving slowly down toward the exterior edge of the slab. Make sure that all high spots are leveled and that low spots are filled in. When filling in the low spots, go back and rescreed the area. Continue the operation until the entire slab has been leveled.

Darbying. The next step in the finishing procedure is darbying of the surface. This means that it is smoothed with a darby to level any raised spots and to fill depressions. Long-handled floats of either wood or steel are used, which can be rented or purchased from your local supplier. This is part of the process during which the final surface of the patio is set.

Edging. When all the bled water and surface water sheen have left the concrete, the concrete has begun to harden. You can now begin to perform the final finishing operations. Use an edger to round off the perimeter edges against the forms. This will prevent chipping or damage to the edge of the slab. Run the edger around the edge, forming a uniform curve. Work the material back and forth. If your first run does not work very well, try it again.

Jointing. Immediately after edging, put the joints into the slab. While a slab without any joints may look very nice, a slab without joints will begin to crack. These joints allow the cracks to occur in the joint and not in the wearing surface. The depth of the joint should be one-fifth

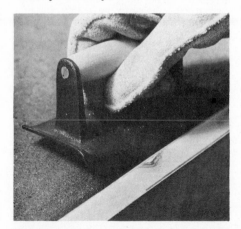

Before edging the patio slab, cut between the form and the concrete edge to a depth of 1 in., using a mason trowel or margin trowel. Do not edge until the concrete is sufficiently set to hold the shape of the edger tool.

to one fourth of the thickness of the slab. Usually, all joints are put into the concrete at 4-to-10 ft. intervals in each direction. In our sample slab, three joints will be required for the 16 ft. direction and two joints will be required for the 12 ft. direction. For putting in joints, it is good practice to use a straight board as a guide, and a tool with a ¾ in. bit. Exercise the same care in placing the joints as you did when edging. Set the board up on the 4-ft. spacing. Place the jointer into the concrete and pull towards you over the distance. You can use other boards to kneel on if you cannot reach across.

Control joints are made with a hand tool, sawed, or formed by using wood permanent divider strips. It is good idea to indicate the location of each joint with a string or chalkline on each side of the form.

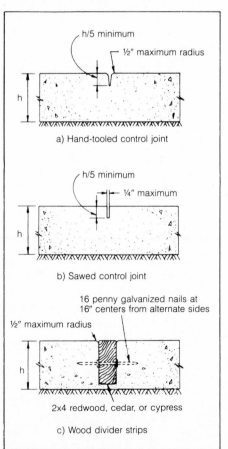

h/5 minimum

½" maximum radius

h

a) Hand-tooled control joint

h/5 minimum

¼" maximum

h

b) Sawed control joint

16 penny galvanized nails at 16" centers from alternate sides

½" maximum radius

h

2x4 redwood, cedar, or cypress

c) Wood divider strips

When possible, control joint panels should be square. The joint should be a minimum depth of one-fifth the height of the slab — and preferably one-fourth, but no deeper.

Floating. Floating immediately follows jointing. There are three reasons to float the concrete: to embed large aggregate just below the surface; to remove slight imperfections, and to consolidate the cement paste at the surface to prepare for troweling. Use an aluminum or magnesium float. Work the float gently back and forth over the slab. Work within the 4-ft. joints; that way you can compare uniformity. Remove all marks made by the jointer.

Troweling. Troweling produces a hard, smooth surface. A steel trowel is moved back and forth across the surface of the concrete. Keep the blade as flat to the surface as you possibly can. If you tilt it, a washboard effect will be visible. After you have completed all the squares between the joints, take a break for a half an hour before you start the next pass. This will allow the concrete to set further. After the surface stiffens, each successive troweling should be made by a smaller trowel so that adequate pressure will be transferred to the concrete. At least two to three passes with the trowel is recommended.

Broom Finishing. After you have completed two passes with the steel trowel, it is usually a good idea to surface your concrete slab with a rougher texture. By pulling a brush or stiff bristle broom across the surface, you will end up with a nonslip surface. Alternate the pattern in each of the squares between the joints.

This completes the steps necessary to place and finish a concrete patio slab. While the finishing steps appear to be time-consuming and demanding, the better the finish, the more long-lasting your patio will be. There are many other options available to you to achieve special surface finishes.

Finishing Air-Entrained Concrete
Because of the microscopic air bubbles, there is less water in the mixture. Since there is less water, there is less tendency to bleed. As a result, the floating and troweling can be done sooner, with less difficulty in arriving at a good surface. Better results are almost always achieved with air-entrained concrete.

Exposed Aggregate Surface
A surface of exposed aggregates is an extremely elegant surface for a concrete patio. The visual texture that can be had

with an exposed aggregate surface is determined in the selection of the aggregate itself. Colorful aggregate should be uniform in size — ranging from ½ to ¾ in. diameter. Select aggregate that is round or pear shaped, not flat or sliver-shaped. For exposed aggregate surfaces a relatively stiff concrete mixture must be used. Immediately after the slab has been screeded and darbied, the aggregate should be sprinkled over the entire area of the slab. Cover every portion of the slab, otherwise it will look uneven. This can be done by hand. Pat the aggregate down into the slab with a 2x4 or a darby tool. After all the aggregate has been embedded, and as soon as the concrete will support you on

After spreading aggregate evenly, embed by tapping with wood hand float or straightedge. Float again for final embedding, until the slab surface appears similar to that of a normal slab.

Wait to begin brushing until the slab can bear the weight of a person on kneeboards, with no indentation. Then remove excess mortar by lightly brushing the slab with a stiff nylon-bristle broom.

Brush and fine-spray the slab simultaneously. Exposed-aggregate brooms often can be rented. If aggregate becomes dislodged, stop and wait a while longer. Continue until water runs clear and no apparent cement film is left.

knee boards, hand-float to get the stones well covered with the mortar. Shortly after the floating has been finished, but not before the concrete has begun to harden, you can expose the aggregate. This is done by brushing the surface of the floated slab and hosing the surface with water. If the aggregate is dislodged, you are probably hosing off too soon. Brush gently over the entire area, exposing the aggregate uniformly. Wash the area continuously to remove the mortar, as well as to inspect for uniformity. Once this step has been completed, edge and joint the slab — but no more than 4 hours later.

Colored Surfaces

There are four ways to color concrete: (1) mix dry concrete color into the concrete while the material is being mixed; (2) add a layer of colored concrete to the top of uncolored fresh concrete; (3) dust the fresh concrete with a "dry shake" powdered concrete color before it hardens; (4) paint after the concrete has hardened and cured.

Dry Mix. The most expensive way to color concrete, and perhaps the easiest, is to pour the color into the concrete while it is being mixed. For cleaner and brighter colors, use white Portland cement instead of the gray type you usually find. Blend the dry color into the dry concrete mix for 4 or 5 minutes before adding water, to prevent streaking and to give an even color. Mix for an additional 5 minutes after adding the water, to ensure even distribution of the color throughout.

Colored Topping. Coloring the top layer of a concrete slab is cheaper than coloring the entire surface, but it takes a little more time and effort. As soon as the slab has hardened slightly and the surface water has disappeared, put an additional layer of concrete on top, mixed as described above.

Dry Shake. Dusting the color on hardening concrete is one of the cheapest methods. The major problem is even color distribution. After the slab has been floated several times, apply "dry shake" onto the slab by hand, using about two-thirds of the total quantity. Then float the surface. Put down the remaining dry shake over the whole area. If too much dry shake is put in any one area, the color will not be consistent. Spread as evenly as possible or the color will end up more intense in some areas than in others.

Paint. Cement-base paints may be applied to damp concrete and to surfaces that will be exposed often to water. Most other paints should be put down once the concrete has cured and is dry; if not, blistering and peeling can occur. Remove any dust, dirt, grease, or oil from the surface before painting. This can be accomplished by scrubbing, brushing, or hosing, or washing with solvent. Thoroughly stir the paint just before applying, to give even distribution of color. Do not thin except following the manufacturer's instructions. You may apply paint with either a roller, spray, or brush. Two coats will be necessary for almost any type of paint.

Portland-cement paint is a little different in its requirements: the concrete must be thoroughly wet to prevent surface suction and to help in hardening paint. It needs damp-curing, which can mean sprinkling or spray. The curing is begun once the cement-base paint has hardened enough so it won't be harmed by the spray — about 12 hours after being applied. This type of paint calls for stiff-bristled or whitewash brushes, instead of the usual paint brushes.

Placing and Curing Colored Concrete. The concrete should be placed while still somewhat stiff; the slump should measure 4 in. or less. The techniques for placing and finishing are the same as for uncolored concrete, but take extra care. Usually, a little less trowelling is necessary, and a broom finish can be substituted.

Curing is an important step for colored concrete. Although you must be sure to keep the moisture from evaporating too fast from the surface, too much water can hurt the evenness of the color. Burlap, plastic sheets and waterproof paper present similar problems because they can cause splotches on the surface or condensation that results in dripping and discoloration. Spray-applied curing compounds may also harm color uniformity. For all these reasons, colored concrete is best just air-cured, which means less strength and surface hardness. Many manufacturers that produce coloring agents for concrete recommend the particular products that can be used to cure the concrete. Color-matching curing wax is one alternative, and is quite popular.

Here are some tips that will be helpful for preventing moisture evaporation:

SOLAR POWER OF YOUR PAINT COLOR

Color	Percentage
Black	1-5
Browns	5-20
Reds	5-20
Medium gray	15-30
Dark blues	5-10
Medium blues	15-20
Oranges	15-30
Medium greens	15-30
Light greens	40-50
Cream color	55-90
White	70-95

Shown are the percentages of light reflected back from various colors. The most absorbent, hottest colors are listed first, followed by the cooler colors.

COLOR CHART

Color	Pigment
Buff, ivory, cream	Synthetic yellow iron oxide
Blue	Cobalt oxide Ultramarine blue Phthalocyanine blue
Brown	Brown iron oxide Raw and burnt umber
Gray or black	Black iron oxide Mineral black Carbon black
Green	Chromium oxide Phthalocyanine green
Red	Red iron oxide

(1) apply a clear sealing compound;

(2) place 2 in. of sand — very clean — over the surface and keep sand moist;

(3) water-cure by continuous flooding — no alternate wetting and drying allowed. The same is true for applying wet, clean burlap or cloth that is kept flat and smooth and continuously wet.

The Easier Alternative: Colored Cement. There are three types of colored cements available, for which the color is usually consistent: (1) pigmented cement with pigments already blended into white cement; (2) a cement made specifically for color, as a special cement; (3) a standard portland cement with a light tint such as gray or tan.

Curing

Concrete attains its strength through curing. The curing must be a gradual process, otherwise the strength and durability will be affected.

Once the concrete has been placed and finished, it must be kept moist. Sprinkling with a hose, or a steady fine spray is desirable. Do not flood the slab with water. Keep the forms in place during the curing period. If you are curing in very hot weather (over 80°F) cover the moist slab with plastic sheeting or wet burlap. This procedure can also be used in colder areas. Continue to moisten the slab for a minimum of three full days from the day the concrete was poured. The concrete should be hard enough after the three-day period for you to pull the forms. Try to keep off the deck for at least 7 to 10 days after placing the concrete. This ensures that the surface will harden properly.

BRICK PATIO CONSTRUCTION

Once you have decided to use brick as the surface material, you will need to select the pattern, color and texture, as well as the size of the brick. The range of brick paving sizes is enormous. You must also decide if you wish to have a patio with or without joints. The joints between the bricks can be used very effectively for pattern purposes; a brick patio where the joints are not accented can create a uniform appearance. The number of bricks you need will depend upon the size of brick and the patio pattern chosen.

To help you in the construction process, a sample brick patio on grade will be discussed. The support material will be a sand and coarse gravel base over compacted soil. There may be parts of this process (excavation, perhaps) that you choose to subcontract out. If so, simply pick up the steps where the subcontractor left off. In most cases a brick patio can be built by one person. Steps One (Preparation) and Two (Staking) are the same as for a concrete patio, so we will begin with Step Three. The example will again be 12 by 16 ft.

Step Three: Formwork

While most of the procedure established in Step Three of "Construction of a Con-

crete Patio" is applicable, there are some additional operations for a brick patio. Since the brick design will rest directly on the sand and gravel subbase, a permanent treated wood edger will be required. For purposes of demonstration, a 2x10 board that has been treated for below grade will be used. Measuring against the house foundation, measure the 12 by 16 ft. patio area and mark the desired height of the brick surface. Place the treated 2x12s into the excavated area but on the outside of the 12 ft. and 16 ft. dimensions. In addition, place another board against the house foundation. The *inside* dimensions of the forms should be 12x16 ft. Nail the corners together and recheck all dimensions. The bracing stakes can be eliminated, since the brick and the earth infill will be enough to stabilize the edging boards. The boards will follow the graded pitch so that water will run off away from the house. Having set the boards around the perimeter of the patio area, infill and tamp the soil against the formwork. You may want to string a line from the corner stakes to act as a patio height guide.

If you use a temporary edger, it need not be treated wood — or, excavate deeper and set the top of the brick flush with ground level, using no form other than undisturbed earth.

Expansion Joints. In severe winter areas, expansion joints will reduce frost heave. Put joints every 8 to 10 ft., preferably as squares, and where dissimilar materials meet. Do a paper pattern first, to find location of joints.

Step Four: Preparing the Base

Having set the exterior wood edger and maintained the desired level around the perimeter of the patio, you can place the gravel. Since the brick, if placed flat on its side, is only 2¼ in. thick for a standard modular brick, you will need to place the gravel in the form until it is 4 in. from the top of the form. If you will be placing the brick on edge, 6 in. must be allowed from

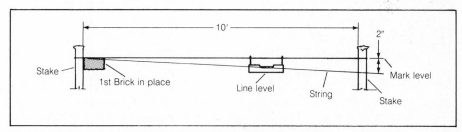

You may wish to string a line across the patio area from stake to stake. This will give you a height guide as you lay bricks from one side of the patio to the other.

the top of the form to the top of the compacted gravel.

After placing the gravel and tamping or compacting it in the form, the surface is then ready for the next course. For a brick patio with a gravel base, a 2-in. course of stone screenings should be used instead of the sand. These stone screenings are very fine stones that have been uniformly graded, specifically for this subbase application. (Check with a local gravel supplier.) Place the stone screenings over the entire surface. You can use a rake to level out any uneven portions of surface. Make sure the surface is true to the exterior form board. Having completed this step, you are now ready to place the brick.

Step Five: Splitting the Bricks

Edgings, or the size and shape of your patio, may require that you split some of the bricks. For example, if you choose a running (staggered) pattern — as in a brick wall — start the first row with a whole brick and the next one with a half brick. To split bricks, use a bricker's chisel and a heavy hammer. (A three pound sledge with a 10-in. handle works well). Set the chisel across the middle of the brick and strike hard. The brick will split neatly. You may substitute brick edge blocks or railroad ties for the treated wood edger to keep the bricks in place.

Level the brick as it is set. Otherwise the patio will appear wavy. Level just two or three units at a time, and then be careful not to jar them.

Tap the face of each brick as you set it in the sand, using the butt of a hammer. This gives a firmer wearing surface.

Several types of brick patterns require partial bricks. Score the top of the brick using a brick chisel.

Be sure to strike squarely when splitting the brick. Give a quick, forceful tap to avoid splintering the edges.

Asphalt expansion strips come 4 in. wide by 4 ft. long, but you can trim them with a razor. Use a buffer block to pound them into control joints. Fill joint with mortar, using a thin tuckpointing trowel.

Step Six: Placing the Brick

Once again, make sure that the stone screenings are uniformly placed over the entire area. In this example, the brick will be placed on edge so that the difference between the top of the form and the stone screenings should be 4 in. Over the screenings, lay down a 15 pound building felt. This material is asphaltic in composition, and will not deteriorate. It is used over the screenings to provide a suitable base for the brick. Overlap the felt at least 6 to 8 in. Lay the felt as square and as flat as possible. If you position the felt properly, the lines over the surface will help you place your brick in correct alignment. The brick example we will use is a basketweave pattern; the brick has dimensions of 3⅝ in. by 7⅝ in. long by 2¼ in. thick. Each three bricks, with ⅜ in. joints between, equals 7⅝ in. This means that a basketweave pattern will be 7⅝ in. square each time a group of three bricks is placed.

Beginning in one corner, place three bricks, leaving a ⅜ in. joint between each brick. Place the next three bricks at right angles to the first three bricks. The important point is that three bricks placed side by side equal the length of the brick. If not, adjust the brick until that dimension is achieved. This check will help you lay out the entire area. The size of the joint would have to be adjusted if the thickness of the brick were not 2¼ in. Always work from a corner outward. Try not to go back to an area already worked on, as you may disturb the spacing. All the brick should be placed on edge in an alternating basketweave pattern. If you had chosen a basketweave utilizing two bricks placed flat instead of three placed on edge in each direction, the crucial factor would be that two bricks with the joint equaled the length of one brick.

Step Seven: Finishing the Brick Patio

Now that you have put all the bricks in place, you must add another material to the joints to keep the brick in position. To add sand, gently place it over the brick and down into the joints. Again, start in a corner and move outwards. Do this about a quarter of the way and then start at an opposite corner. This provides even distribution. Having worked the joints with sand to the edges, complete the center. Place the sand over the brick and sweep it into place. Do not force it, or it will cause the brick to move. Gradually fill all the joints by sweeping the sand over the surface into the joints. Moisten the brick periodically with a hose to increase the stability of the sand.

Bricks can be used to create laminated (on edge) stair tread design, on either brick, concrete, or wooden stair risers.

Use about half a sack of very fine sand to fill in brick patio joints. Sweep sand into the joints; sprinkle with water to pack sand down. Sweep in more sand, sprinkle, and continue until joints are full.

Once all the joints are full, you can finish the top of the joints in the following manner. Mix a bag of cement with at least a double amount of sand. Spread the mixture over the surface of the bricks and work it into the joints. After the material has been completely dispersed into the joints, pack the joints if you have to. Wet the area down with a gentle mist. Continue to do this for a half an hour. The cement will bond with the sand and form a hard joint. Over the next few days, continue to wet the surface. This method produces an effective joint for a brick patio on gravel. Renew the joint bond each year and you will have a very satisfactory wearing surface. This same procedure can be applied to a variety of patterns with joints. In the event that you have selected a brick or pattern which results in a flush fit, you can eliminate this procedure.

Brick Paving Options

There are a number of options available to you for brick paving construction methods.

Using Brick Pavers over Existing Concrete. If the area has an old concrete slab that is no longer desirable or is unsightly, brick pavers may be put down over the concrete. The pavers can be placed with or without a mortar. Between the concrete slab and the brick pavers, place a 2-in. sand bed.

Using Brick Pavers over a Sand bed. This procedure is often used in areas where there is little rain and very low water tables. The brick paver is placed over a 2-in. sand bed that has been well compacted. Between the sand and pavers a 15 lb. roofing felt is placed. The pavers are then set in place.

Once the brick has been set in place, it can be cleaned periodically by washing it down. Do not use any coatings or paint. These will reduce the effectiveness of the material as a surface. In cold climates, avoid the use of ice-melting agents such as salt. They will cause deterioration of the brick and mortar if used. Use sand instead. If you shovel the snow, use a rubber edged shovel or snow plow. Your brick patio, if properly maintained, can last a lifetime.

PATIO BLOCKS

Since the patio blocks usually measure 1 ft. by 1 ft. by 1 in. (1 ft. sq.), calculating how many of them are needed is no real problem.

It is always best to order some extra

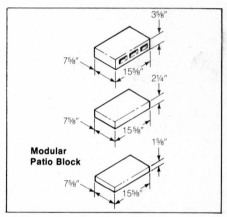

Patio block comes either in 1 ft. x 1 ft. x 1 in., or in sizes similar to brick, or in modular units nominally called 16 in. x 8 in. (15 ⅝ in. x 7⅝ in.) in depths of 2 in. or more.

blocks. Since patio blocks (as well as bricks) must be cut to fill in at the edges, there is a chance that some of the blocks may be broken incorrectly and will need replacing. What is more, you may have a block or two crack in severe weather or under stress. You should have at least 20 extra blocks on hand for these situations. The building steps are similar to those for a brick patio, but with a few adjustments.

Step One: Prepare the Base

Some guide books will tell you to dig out enough soil for a 2-in. bed of sand beneath your blocks. In a hard frost area, this is not enough. You will need to dig out at least 4 in. below the bottom of the block. For proper drainage, a block patio should drop 2 in. for every 10 ft. A 10-ft. sq. patio, for example, would be 2 in. lower at one end than at the other. If you are using standard patio blocks, which are

1 in. thick, you would need to remove 5 in. of soil in all at the highest point and 7 in. at the lowest. Measure the boundaries of your patio and set up edger boards and corner stakes, using the same methods as for the brick patio. The ideal base for a block patio is 2 in. of fine limestone gravel (called "tailings" or "traffic mix") at the very bottom of the patio bed. This mix compresses well and when wet actually binds together to form a base similar to concrete. In parts of the country (like New England) where it is not available, any fine gravel will do.

Tamp the gravel down firmly, using either a vibrating compactor (which can be rented from local garden centers), or a hand-compactor (available for about $15 at many local hardware stores).

Step Two: Lay the Sand Base

To lay the actual base for the blocks, you will need 2 in. of sharp sand. Note that the correct type of sand for a base is torpedo sand — not the finer, mason's sand used in mortar mixes. When spread evenly, the torpedo sand provides excellent drainage and will stay in place. Finer sands tend to wash away or shift in heavy rains. Add the layer of sand, following along the top of the edger board, which follows the slope that you set when removing the soil. This will achieve your grade for drainage. By measuring from the top of the edger board to the top of the sand, you will have a space 1 in. from the top of the sand for the blocks. The top of the edger board will indicate the position of each block as you move along. You should periodically re-check the grade with a carpenter's level.

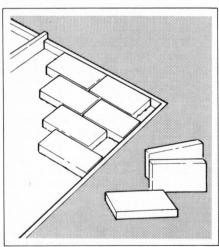

When placing concrete block (and also brick), begin in the corner and shift the block as necessary to create previously planned pattern.

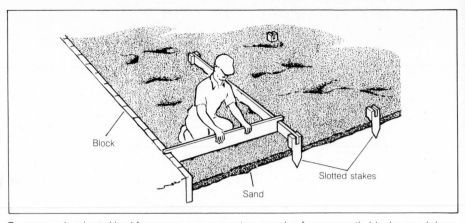

To ensure a level sand bed for pavers, you can set up wooden forms or patio blocks as edgings, add sand, and then put up temporary wood strips fastened to 2x2 stakes every 4 ft. Notch a 1x6 at ends to same thickness as edging, and use to level sand, resting one end on edging and other end on wood strip.

Step Three: Place the Blocks

Begin placement in a corner, working from the highest point to lowest. Check frequently for correct grade.

Step Four: Sweep in Sand

When all the blocks are in place, carefully sweep mason's sand (the fine type) into the cracks between the blocks. Wet the sand thoroughly and let dry. Then spread more sand across the blocks, sweep, wet and let dry. For added strength, mix the sand with portland cement on a 1:1 ratio and sweep into the cracks. Wet and let dry for two or three days before using the patio.

You may wish to finish the edges of the patio off by either using sod, railroad ties or heavy blocks to keep the edges in place. If you cannot find suitable concrete edge blocks at the local concrete specialty yard, you can make your own out of mortar mix. For 1½-inch-thick end blocks, build a mold out of two five-foot 2x4s nailed to a 2x6 or 2x8 (see sketch). Caulk the joints carefully with any ordinary household caulk, and oil the mold with motor oil.

Next, mix a 40 pound bag of mortar mix in a wheelbarrow to a stiff consistency. Pour the mortar into the mold (you can add steel rods or welded wire fencing at mid-height for extra strength) and let dry at least 10 hours. Remove the end block from the mold and let it cure under wet burlap for at least three days before setting in place.

For added color, spread marble chips on the bottom of the mold before casting. Then, when you turn the mold over and remove the block, use a stiff wire brush and the garden hose to scrub off the outer

layer of mortar and reveal the chips in the surface of the block.

PAVERS

Pavers can be used for patios and walkways and are split in the same manner as common brick. However, their installation is a little different than that of other materials in that the grade is first set in coarse sand and the bricks laid on top of it. The workman always adds the next rows by working on top of the brick he has laid.

For those interested in the process, excavate 4 in. for the gravel and sand, plus the depth of the paver plus 2 in., all the way across to allow for grade. Add the gravel layer. Then spread a base of torpedo sand at least 2 in. thick across the entire patio area. Check the grade in the sand using a level and a long, straight 2x4. If you need to adjust the grade, add more sand. Once the grade is set, do not step back on the sand. If you must step on the sand again, regrade it. Tamp the sand thoroughly.

Starting from a corner, lay four or five pavers in line and work straight to the next corner, standing only on the blocks you have laid and not on the sand. (See sketch.)

When complete, sweep fine mason's sand onto the paving stones and wet the sand. The pavers will now interlock to form a continuous, firm surface. Repeat this process. Do not use portland cement mix on the pavers. When the patio is done, finish the edges with railroad ties or end blocks. Some paver manufacturers make special end stones for the purpose.

Finally sweep the patio well, wash it down with the garden hose, and apply a good coat of cement sealer to extend the patio's life.

Pavers, depending on their shape, are usually needed at a rate of 2½ per sq. ft. So, for a 10x10 ft. patio (our example), you would need approximately 250 stones.

STONE PATIO CONSTRUCTION

If you have selected stone as your paving material, you have chosen a material that is durable and weathers well. If using flagstone, check with your supplier about the quality and hardness of the flagstone available. In northern climates, it is recommended that the flagstone be set in mortar. This reduces the potential for lifting up or settlement of the wearing surface. Because the material is not uniform in shape and texture, it requires a little more planning in the beginning, primarily in laying out the patio. The joints between the material should be kept at a minimum in order to reduce the area of the joint. If too many joints occur, crevassing or dips between the material could cause a very uneven and imperfect wearing surface. There are several methods for setting the stone into the ground.

Stone Patio Over Earth

We have already discussed how to lay out the patio and find the perimeter measurements. The preparation of the soil for placement of stone is the same as for brick. A layer of gravel from 6 to 8 in. must be placed and tamped in the formwork once the base soil has been compacted and tamped. The formwork can be the edge of the excavated soil, or a more rigid board similar to the one described in the brick patio construction. Having compacted the gravel course, a 2-in. sand bed is then placed over the gravel. Keep compacting this layer until a minimum amount of settlement can be seen. Remember, the denser the base, the more stable the patio surface. Moisten the sand slightly and place the stone, starting in one corner. Try to select the shapes that best fit together with the least amount space between them. As you proceed, fill all the joints with sand. Complete the entire area of the patio. Try to use stones that are large. The smaller the stone, the greater the tendency for the stone to yield under pressure when you step on it. Once the entire patio surface has been completed, mix a bag of cement with two

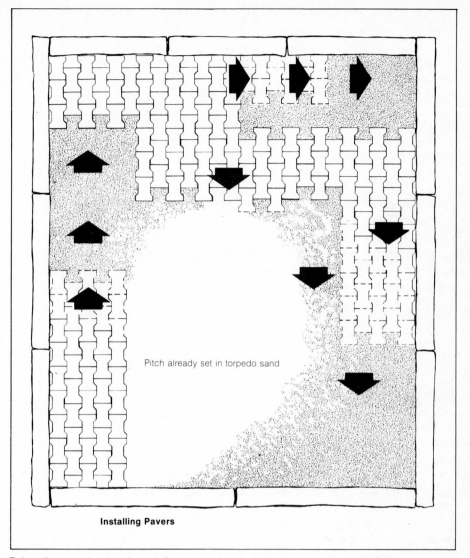

Pitch already set in torpedo sand

Installing Pavers

To install pavers, begin at lower left corner and work clockwise around the patio. Use the pavers as a surface from which to work as you lay the units.

MATERIALS LIST FOR SEVERAL TYPES OF 10 FT.X10 FT. PATIO

Material	Number Needed*	Gravel	Coarse Sand	Fine Sand
Brick	470	1 yard	1 yard	3-4 bushels
Patio Block	110	1 yard	1 yard	3-4 bushels
Paving Stones	270	1 yard	1 yard	3-4 bushels

(No figure is given for flagstone because its size varies from quarry to quarry)
*Extra blocks should always be purchased at the time of installation to ensure later color and texture match of repairs.

equal parts of sand and cover all the joints, hand tooling if necessary to get the mixture properly distributed. Moisten the area for at least half an hour. Continue this procedure over the next few days to provide a hard and durable wearing surface. This type of construction will not stay level where frost occurs; it is not, therefore, recommended for very northern climates.

Stone Patio on a Concrete Slab

To minimize any heaving in cold weather,

it is recommended that the stone be placed on a concrete slab that is below grade or whose top surface is flush with the ground. The concrete need not be finished beyond simple floating of the surface. The concrete must cure before the stone is laid. Generally, a 3- or 4-in. reinforced concrete slab is recommended. (Refer to concrete patio construction for procedures.) Once the concrete slab has cured approximately seven days, you will be ready to start laying the stone.

First you will have to buy several bags

of cement mortar of the premix variety. This will reduce the amount of time necessary to lay the stone. Mix carefully according to the instructions. Over the top of the concrete slab, in an area of about 4 x 4 ft., spread a layer of mortar ¾ in. thick. This is called the setting bed. Place the stone according to the pattern selected, pushing each stone into the setting bed until it feels solidly in place. Fill in the joints with the cement mortar, making sure the joint is as flush as possible to the surface of the stone. As you finish the first 4x4 area, start the procedure again, working in adjoining areas. Complete the entire patio in this fashion. After the stone has set for a day, use a very light brush and a hose to clean the area.

For convenient access, precast concrete (wooden rounds will also work) can be used to create a pathway across a gravel patio or backyard.

Gravel patios should have a raised edging to keep the gravel from spilling out of patio boundaries. Railroad ties set in trenches offer a suitable edging.

A stone patio, if maintained properly, will provide years of service. As in brick patios, try not to use any salt or ice-melting agent, as it will deteriorate the mortar joints and cause scaling of the stone.

GRAVEL PATIO CONSTRUCTION

The gravel patio is the simplest to build of all the patios. It requires little base preparation. Excavate about 6½ in. and prepare the soil base as previously described. The gravel for the patio should be contained within a metal or wood edging strip, which can be placed in the excavated area or staked. If staked, use stakes that will be concealed under the gravel wearing surface. The size and type of the edging, and the patterns that can be generated by you, are unlimited. Once the area has been prepared and the soil base has been tamped, place a river-washed gravel or peastone gravel in the forms; a depth of 4 top in. is recommended. The gravel should be a little lower than the edging so it will not spill over. Once poured into the form, rake the gravel to make sure that the depth is uniform. If your edging is properly placed at the desired level, it can act as a leveling guide. Gravel must be replaced on a regular basis. Find a source that will be constant over the years so that when you do add gravel, it will be close in size, color and shape.

USING RAILROAD TIES AROUND THE PATIO

In the previous section on paving without mortar, we mentioned railroad ties as a good material for end caps on mortarless patios. They have several other decorative and utilitarian uses in the patio environment, although they do not offer a solution to every problem.

True railroad ties, measuring 6x8 in. x10 ft., are heavy, bulky pieces of hardwood that are awkward to handle — especially for one person working alone. Their density (most ties are oak) makes them prone to cracking, especially in areas where winters are hard.

A number of substitute ties have come onto the market since railroad ties originally gained popularity with home patio builders and landscapers. The quality of these ties varies, from solid oak ties which have been soaked in preservative for several hours, to more inferior woods that have been simply brush-painted with

cheap stain. Used in your patio, these cheaper ties will soon lose their color and can often bring with them a host of unwelcome insects.

How can you get true railroad ties? Buy them either directly from the railroad (you will have to haul them yourself) or from a contractor who has purchased them from the railroad. True railroad ties can be spotted by their rough, used look and by the telltale spike holes in either side. Those spikes were used to hold pieces of rail to the ties.

Unfortunately, few of us want to drive spikes with the large hammers used by railroad crews, so we are faced with another difficult problem in the use of railroad ties — fastening and connecting them. The largest nail usually available at the local hardware store is a 20-penny (20d), which measures 5"x¼". It is too short for use with railroad ties for all but diagonal nailing. The best fastening method is with long carriage bolts, reinforcing rods, or nuts and washers (for best appearance, countersink the hole for the nut). The process is often a long one, since holes must be carefully drilled with long drill bit and extension before the ties can be fastened together.

Cutting a tie can also be a difficult task. Most circular saws penetrate only 2 in., and so must be used on all four sides of the tie to complete the cut. If any one of the four lines does not match up, the tie will have an uneven end. For that reason, it is best to butt cut ties up against others, where such uneven cuts won't show.

Still, ties can perform well when used to edge raised beds around the patio and can even be used as steps, either by themselves or in combination with brick, stone or rock. (See also Chapter 9.)

For extensive projects, however, it might be best to use cedar landscape ties, which usually measure 4x6 in. Although they lack the weight and staying power of the larger railroad ties, they are much easier to cut and handle. Additional handling instructions are given in Chapter 9, under "Railroad Tie Planters".

Railroad ties can be used for a rustic stairway leading down from a raised patio area. Bracing principles are similar to those for planters (Chapter 9).

This chapter will concentrate on the actual building of the deck. While the level of craftsmanship and assembly skill will vary from person to person, we will provide information that is fundamental to all skill levels. In addition, the process of construction will be simplified in order to keep the time necessary for construction to an absolute minimum.

PARTS OF A DECK

Before actually starting the deck construction, it is necessary to identify all those pieces that ultimately will be part of your finished deck. A deck is composed of two major elements: (1) above grade components such as decking, joists, beams, ledgers, railings and deck furniture; (2) below grade or supporting elements such as posts, footings, piers and foundations.

All weight or loads that are imposed on the deck are first supported by the decking itself. While the decking might be decorative, its main function is to transfer all the weight and load to joists. Joists are the primary structural element supporting the floor. They are best described as closely spaced structural members that support the deck and in turn are supported by the beams. The beams are larger and more massive. Their function is to gather the

load and weight of the joists and transfer it to the supporting posts. The posts are spaced at an appropriate interval to transfer all the load from the beams directly into the ground through footings. Footings, which bear the entire weight of the deck, are set into the soil to distribute the weight uniformily. In very low-profile decks, where the deck is situated very near the ground, the beams may simply rest on the footings, eliminating the need for posts.

Decking

The major visual element of a deck is the surface that you stand on. The decking is the most interesting part of the deck because of its size, pattern, coloration and detailing. The decking also determines the spacing of the supporting joists, which in turn affects the beams and foundation. Therefore, the pattern selection should be determined in order to develop a suitable structural framing plan. Most wood decking can be applied in many ways, the most common being: parallel, diagonally, diamond, parquet and radially. The most-used grades of material are: Common Construction, Clear, or Select. The most popular species for decking are redwood, cedar, hemlock, fir, and pine. In order to meet the building

code requirements for exterior decks, all decking should be supported by joists no more than 24 in. on center. In the event that you plan to have heavy loads resting on the decking, the spacing should be reduced to 16 in.

Almost all decking is laid flat. Thus, the 2 in. nominal dimension of the deck will be its depth, and the 4 or 6 in. dimension will be the wearing surface. For a finer-lined, narrower-patterned deck, set the 2x4 on edge instead of on the side; however, a greater amount of material is used. All decking is generally spaced about an ⅛ to ¼ in. apart. This allows rain and dirt to flow through the deck onto the ground underneath. Because the decking determines the general layout of the supporting structure, first choose the deck pattern desired, the grade of material and the type, and then determine the spacing of the joists.

Joists

The joists bear the full brunt of the load from the decking. They span from beam to beam (refer to illustration) and their spacing is more often dictated by their spanning and material capacity than by spacing imposed by the decking. For typical joist span limits for different sizes of joists, see Chapter 3 under wood materials. Most joists are 2 in. material — 2x6, 2x8, 2x10 represent the most-used sizes. Joists are attached to the beams by nails, mechanical connectors, joist hangers or a ledger strip. Joists are capable of being cantilevered out beyond each supporting beam a distance of one quarter of the span. This flexibility allows you to derive maximum use of the material. For example: joists spanning a distance of ten feet from support to support can be increased in length to fifteen feet overall (two times the 2½ foot extension, since there are two beams, still spanning the same distance from support to support. This can be done with no increase in size of joist or spacing. We suggest that you

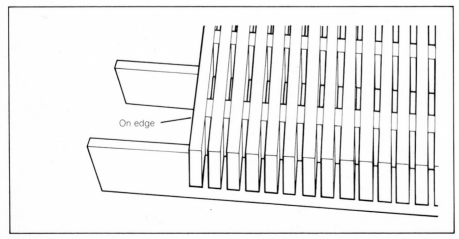

On edge

Although decking is usually set flat, it can be set on edge in order to achieve a narrower-lined pattern.

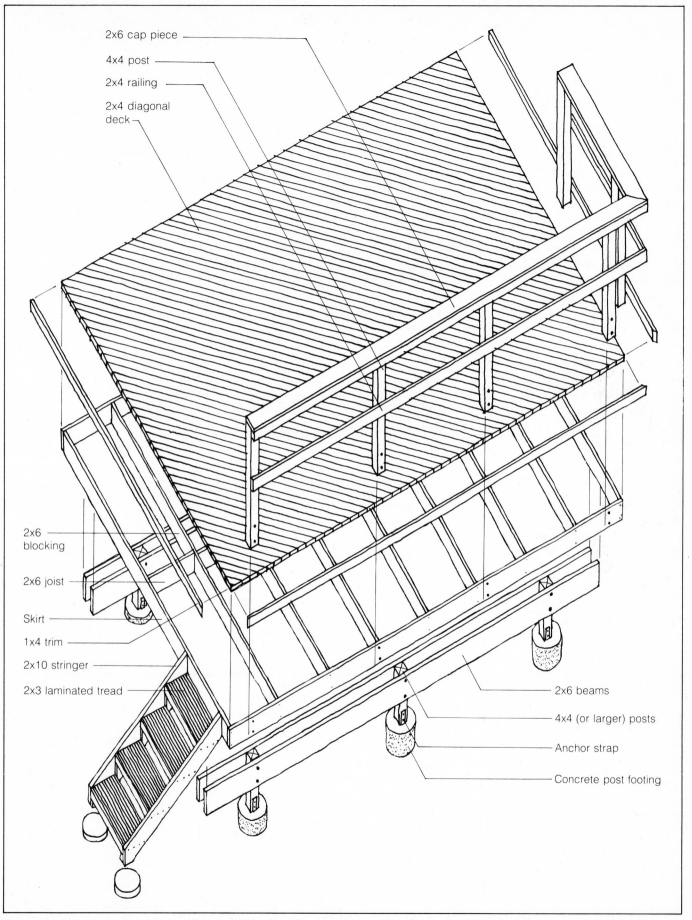

2x6 cap piece

4x4 post

2x4 railing

2x4 diagonal
deck

2x6
blocking

2x6 joist

Skirt

1x4 trim

2x10 stringer

2x3 laminated tread

2x6 beams

4x4 (or larger) posts

Anchor strap

Concrete post footing

Here are the components for a free-standing deck. This plan utilizes laminated stair treads, and a partial railing. Blocking and/or bracing should be added for large or two-story decks.

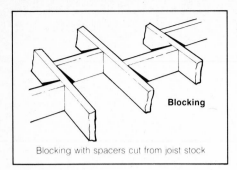

Blocking should be installed between staggered joists to provide extra stiffness.

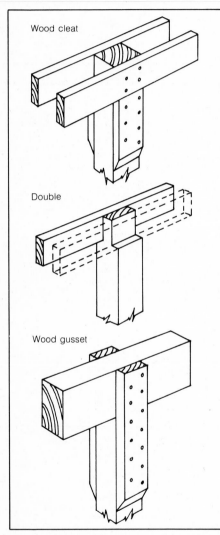

Subtract deck board thickness, joist, and beam to find correct level for bottom of beam. Fasten beam as shown. If using post as support for rail or overhead, fasten beams to side of posts instead of on top.

insert cross-bracing between the joists, since it increases the overall stiffness of the joist and decking assembly. Some local codes stipulate the use of cross-bracing or bridging.

Beams

Beams are those structural elements that support the joists. The size of the beam

Deck Variations

When setting decking on a diagonal, reduce joist spacing to compensate for longer span. Where a change in decking direction occurs, reinforcement of a double joist and blocking must be added. If changes in direction are made over joists or beams, additional blocking is added only for changes that are perpendicular to joists or beams.

required depends on the spacing of the beams and the spacing of the beam supports. In general, the trade-off between beam thickness and the number of supports is as follows; it is less expensive and time-consuming to have a thicker beam than it is to have many posts and footings. Often, beams are constructed from the same smaller or thinner-sized materials as joists, and are bolted or nailed together in order to create the increased size. This form of built-up beam is standard. Beams are fastened to the footings or posts by metal connectors or cleats. These are available at most lumber yards or material suppliers. Beams can also be cantilevered

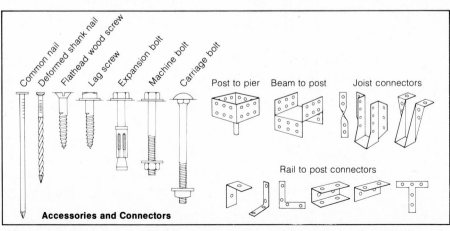

Accessories and Connectors

Different connectors are required for varying methods of attachment.

in order to achieve an overhang. The same limit, ¼-span per support, applies.

Ledgers

Where the deck is to be framed into the side of your house or building, the method of framing uses the existing building as one support. Joists are connected to the house and supported by a ledger strip. Usually a ledger is a 2-in. thick material (normally wood but occasionally steel) that is attached to the house by bolts, nails or mechanical connectors. Another way to attach the joists is by using a metal angle of a minimum size, normally 3 in. x 3 in. This is attached to the house by bolts or a similar device. It is important that the ledger strip be set so that the joists and the finish decking are at least one to two inches below the interior floor level. This will reduce the possibility of rain or snow entering into the house. The minimum recommendation is one inch. Where climatic problems are not likely, the decking can be located flush with the interior floor level.

Posts

The posts transfer the weight of the decking, joists, beams, and the user loads into the footings or foundation. Most posts are 4x4, but this must be increased when the posts are supporting a structure over 6 ft. above grade. The larger size is also required where the site is sloping away from the house, or high loads are expected. In addition, posts that will also support overhead cover or roofing must be larger. Check your local building code for requirements.

Posts are connected to the foundation or footings either through direct embedment or by mechanical connectors. If your construction is high off the ground, diagonal bracing will be required to increase the stability of your deck. The cross-bracing can be effectively integrated into your design by extending the pieces up to the height of the railing or by creating a diagonal lattice work around the base. Local building codes often dictate the bracing requirement.

Footings

The footing is the final destination of all the loads and forces supported by the decking, joists, beams, and posts. You will find that your local building code is very specific about the foundation re-

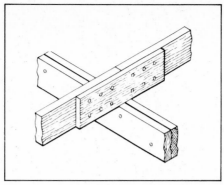
This is one means of splicing a beam to achieve additional length: use a butt joint over post and tie two beams together by fastening a cleat to each side.

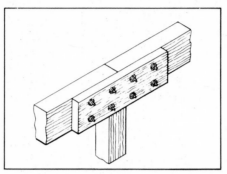
To create thicker joists beams, build them up from thinner members by fastening pieces together with bolts or lag screws.

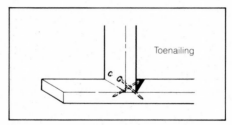

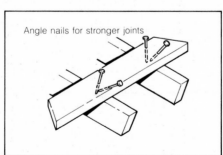

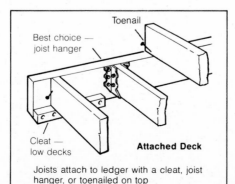
Joists attach to ledger with a cleat, joist hanger, or toenailed on top

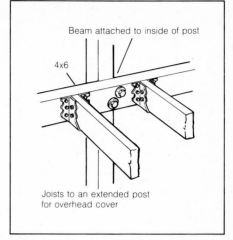
Use joist hangers when connecting beams to a post that also supports overhead cover or a railing.

To fasten beams to tops of posts, use cleats and metal connectors.

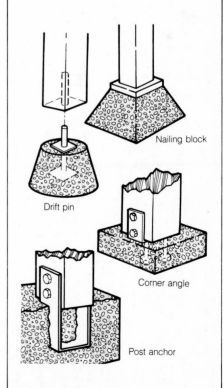
There are several ways to connect post to footings. It is easier to place anchors before concrete sets.

quirements. Most footings should be constructed on undisturbed soil or rock, which is difficult to achieve. The footings must extend to below the frost line in your area. Generally this ranges from 24 in. minimum to 48 in. maximum; however, local conditions may require special consideration. Footings are usually of poured-in-place concrete. They can be rectangular, circular or square, depending on the connection required and on the formwork. Most footings extend out of the ground about 2 to 6 in. so that the post will not come in direct contact with the soil. This also lets the water drain rapidly from the area. Where the posts are embedded into the concrete, rather than attached with mechanical connectors, the

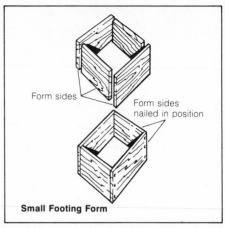

Form sides

Form sides nailed in position

Small Footing Form

Although it is simpler to use packed earth as forms whenever possible, small footing forms such as these are easy to build.

MINIMUM BEAM SIZES AND SPANS

Species Group 1	Spacing between beams, ft.								
Beam size	4	5	6	7	8	9	10	11	12
4x6" x	6	6	6						
3x8" x	8	8	7	6	6	6			
4x8" x	10	9	8	7	7	6	6	6	
3x10" x	11	10	9	8	8	7	7	6	6
4x10" x	12	11	10	9	9	8	8	7	7
3x12" x		12	11	10	9	9	8	8	8
4x12" x			12	12	11	10	10	9	9
6x10" x					12	11	10	10	10
6x12" x						12	12	12	12
Species Group 2									
4x6" x	6	6							
3x8" x	7	7	6	6					
4x8" x	9	8	7	7	6	6			
3x10" x	10	9	8	7	7	6	6	6	
4x10" x	11	10	9	8	8	7	7	7	6
3x12" x	12	11	10	9	8	8	7	7	7
4x12" x		12	11	10	10	9	9	8	8
6x10" x			12	11	10	10	9	9	9
6x12" x				12	12	12	11	11	10
Species Group 3									
4x6" x	6								
3x8" x	7	6							
4x8" x	8	7	6	6					
3x10" x	9	8	7	6	6	6			
4x10" x	10	9	8	8	7	7	6	6	6
3x12" x	11	10	9	8	7	7	7	6	6
4x12" x	12	11	10	9	9	8	8	7	7
6x10" x		12	11	10	9	9	8	8	8
6x12" x			12	12	11	11	10	10	8

Beams are on edge. Spans are center to center distances between posts or supports. Grade is No. 2 or Better; No. 2, medium grain southern pine.
Species Group 1: Douglas fir, larch, southern pine. *Species Group 2:* Hemlock fir, Douglas fir, south. *Species Group 3:* Western pines and cedars, redwood, spruces.
Example: If the beams are 9 ft. 8 in. apart and the species is Group 2, use the 10 ft. column; 3x10 up to 6 ft. spans, 4x10 or 3x12 up to 7 ft. spans, 4x12 or 6x10 up to 9 ft. spans, 6x12 up to 11 ft. spans.

posts must be treated for rot and insect damage. Old telephone poles make very good posts for embedding in concrete. In low-level decks, concrete block or precast footings may be used by placing them on compacted soil. This method does not guarantee that settlement will not occur.

Railings

Although railings are usually considered a decorative part of a deck, building codes often dictate that they not only must be provided, but at a required height. Railings can be built to the extended posts or be attached to the decking. Railings should all be stable; people lean against them, as well as push furniture against them. They must be able to support a high load. Therefore, we recommend that the

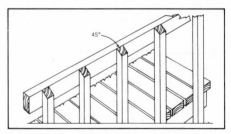

Cut off tops of railing infill at 45° angle for a neat appearance.

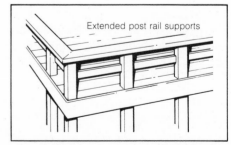

Extended post rail supports

Railings can use deck posts for support to conserve wood and give extra strength. Horizontal rail at mid-height is required on all but ground-level decks.

railings be tied in with the posts or beams, as discussed later in this chapter.

Grade

The position of a deck with respect to the house, and its general form, were discussed in Chapter 1. Accurate identification of the location of the deck is necessary to figure quantities of materials and specific building requirements. The position of the ground in relation to the deck is also very important. Chapter 1 discusses decks in relation to ground level.

A Combined Deck and Roof Structure

In most cases, any desired overhead cover will be situated over the deck. To determine your specific requirements, you must first determine if the roof is to be supported by the columns and posts attached to the deck, or if the roof structure will be supported outside of the physical area of the deck. In both cases, it is important to recognize that the roof structure should be built first. In the case of a roof structure that is to be supported by pre-existing walls or span from house to garage, the roof structure need not be built before building the deck.

In Chapter 7, the actual building and assembly is discussed. You should familiarize yourself with this chapter and the necessary procedures. If you plan to have your deck located under, and supporting, the roof structure, the roof structure posts become the support for the deck. The beams will still frame to the columns as discussed in Step Five of this chapter. The procedures are identical to those described except that the decking will be placed around and fitted to the posts. The posts now extend up through the decking. No other modifications are necessary.

In the case where the roof structure is to be supported outside the limits of the deck area, it is important to build the roof first in order to eliminate any conflict between the construction of the roof and the deck. Size limitations (since you will not have any support beams inside the patio area) may mean that you can provide only portions of the patio with overhead roofing rather than total coverage. If absolutely necessary, posts can rest on an on-grade deck, as illustrated in Chapter 7.

Building Permits

Once your drawing has been completed (as discussed in Chapter 4) and drawn on the graph paper, you are ready to seek a building permit. While most communities have a standard form to be filled out, they also require a copy or several copies of your proposed design. Once you have submitted the form and the drawings with the necessary fee, your building inspector will review your proposal. Any changes to meet your local requirements will be indicated. If all is satisfactory, you will receive a building permit for a construction period not to exceed a period of 3, 6, 9 or 12 months. This is done to ensure that the construction will take place during that time period. If you find yourself exceeding the allotted time period, you may request an extension, which is usually granted. During the period that you are building the deck, the inspector may wish to review in place the various parts of construction. Normally, the inspector will review the foundation prior to its being covered over, and conduct a final inspection before giving you an occupancy permit. This procedure varies from community to community, so it is very important that you check your specific local requirements.

CONSTRUCTION OF A DECK

To assist you in developing and constructing a deck of your design, the sequence of events to be described refers to a basic deck design, from which you can adjust for the variations of your own design. Every attempt has been taken to simplify the steps so that you can see the similarities and differences between the designs. There may be parts of the construction procedure that you may wish to subcontract out. In the event that this oc-

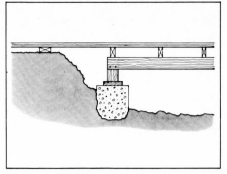

A deck can extend out over a slope.

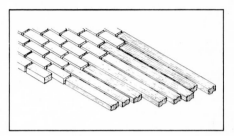

The transition from brick or grass to decking is easy. Locate deck framing so its surface will be flush with the edge of the other material. Where a pool uses the last available level ground, a deck can provide the accessory area.

MINIMUM POST SIZES (Wood Beam Supports)

Species Group 1	Load area beam spacing x post spacing, sq. ft.									
Post size	36	48	60	72	84	96	108	120	132	144
4x4" x	12	12	12	12	10	10	10	8	8	8
4x6" x					12	12	12	12	10	10
6x6" x									12	12
Species Group 2										
4x4" x	12	12	10	10	10	8	8	8	8	
4x6" x		12	12	12	10	10	10	10		
6x6" x						12	12	12	12	12
Species Group 3										
4x4" x	12	10	10	8	8	8	6	6	6	6
4x6" x		12	12	10	10	10	8	8	8	8
6x6" x				12	12	12	12	12	12	12

Grade is Standard and Better for 4x4 in. posts and No. 1 and Better for larger sizes.
Species Group 1: Douglas fir, larch, southern pine. *Species Group 2:* Hemlock fir, Douglas fir, southern fir. *Species Group 3:* Western pines, western cedars, redwood, spruce.
Example: If the beam supports are spaced 8 ft. 6 in. on center and the posts are 11 ft. 6 in. on center, then the load area is 98 sq. ft. Use the next largest area, 108 sq. ft.

Parquet Deck 12′x 12′

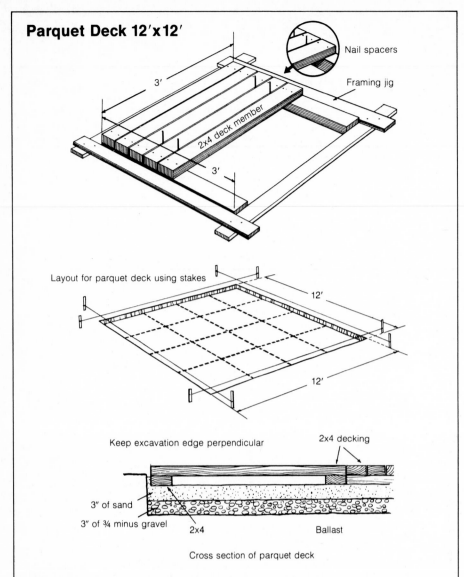

Nail spacers

Framing jig

2x4 deck member

3′

3′

Layout for parquet deck using stakes

12′

12′

Keep excavation edge perpendicular

2x4 decking

3″ of sand

3″ of ¾ minus gravel   2x4   Ballast

Cross section of parquet deck

Frame a nailing jig using scrap lumber; inside dimension will be 36 in. x 36 in. Precut 76 pieces of 2x4 lumber, 3 ft. each. Ease (sand off) raw edges of each piece. Use pretreated wood or heart cedar. Assemble 16 parquet blocks, using jig. Leave 7/16 in. space between parallel deck members. Nail each end of the deck member using two 10d nails, countersunk. Lay out deck site. Excavate 6 in. with perpendicular edge. Fill with 3 in. gravel; level with hand rake. Cover with 3 in. sand; level and tamp.

Lay parquets in place. Alternate direction of decking. When all squares are in place, fill outside edge of excavation with sand to ground level; tamp firmly. You may toenail for rigidity.

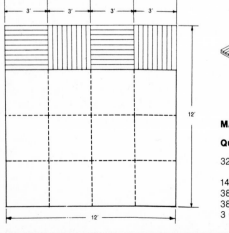

3′ 3′ 3′ 3′

12′

12′

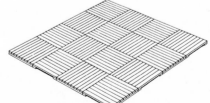

MATERIALS LIST: 12 ft. x 12 ft. DECK

Quantity	Dimension	Use	Length
32	2x4	Nailing Cleats	3 ft.
144	2x4	Decking	3 ft.
38 cu. ft. Sand			
38 cu. ft. Gravel			
3 Gallons Penta or Alternate Wood Preservative			

curs, simply pick up where the subcontractor has left off. The purpose of this section is to provide you with many of the construction tips that carpenters use in the building of a wood deck.

Step One: Preparing the Site

Before ordering all the building materials, clear the area that you will be working in. Remove all shrubs, rocks or other obstacles that will not be included in your design. Strip the area of any grass or similar ground cover. Since the ground under the deck will not be exposed to the sun, any plant material left will deteriorate. Make sure that the ground slopes aways from the house for proper drainage. This can be done by building up the soil near the foundation wall of the house and tapering it away for positive drainage.

Step Two: Staking Out the Deck

Start by pacing out and laying out the deck on the ground. Even if the deck is to be free-standing, square the deck to the house. Locate one corner of the deck adjacent to the house or, if your design calls for one corner any distance from the corner or face of a wall, mark that spot by driving a wood stake into the levelled prepared ground. Using a triangulated survey method to make sure that all dimensions and corners are exact and square, you can lay out and stake all the corners. From the stake that has been driven into the ground, run a line parallel to the foundation of the house measuring the length of deck desired. Drive another stake at the point measured. String a line between the two stakes. Exterior foundation walls are often imperfect, making measurement quite difficult, so check that the first line is as parallel as possible to the wall. Next, measure along that line 8 ft. and drive another stake at that point.

From the first stake driven measure out 6 ft. perpendicular to the wall line. If you are exactly perpendicular, the diagonal between that 6 ft. point and the 8 ft. stake will measure exactly 10 ft., and thus will create a right triangle. If it is not exact, move the 6 ft. measurement left or right until it coincides with the 10 ft. measurement. Stake that point. You have now created a square. From this point all other deck dimensions can be laid out. Make sure that your stakes are in the ground solidly or your dimensions will be off, causing problems later on. Accuracy of

A two-story deck is a feasible solution to the problems of sloping terrain.

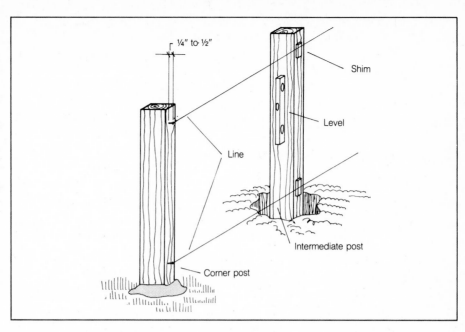

the four points of your deck layout can be verified by measuring the diagonals between the opposite corners; they should be equal. Whether the deck is free-standing or attached, the procedure for staking out the deck is identical. Some people like to drive an 8d finish nail in the top of the stakes and connect the string from nail to nail. This increases measurement accuracy.

Step Three: Footing Hole Layout

Having located all the corners of the deck, you can now stake out all the locations for the footings. Most posts are set back from the leading edge of the deck by 18 to 24 in. If the footing location coincides with an underground utility, it is advisable to relocate the footing into another arrangement. The size and number of footings are determined by the size of the deck and the load expected to be placed on it. In the example deck to follow, there will be 3 lines of footings. Having staked the footing locations, the type of footing will dictate the actual size of the hole and depth.

Step Four: Footings

There are several types of footings available to you. The one most effective for your specific design depends upon the type and consistency of your soil. If it is a soft clay or similar spongy material, you should use a mass form concrete footing. This is simply an oversize hole dug to the required depth, filled with concrete and capped with a wood form in which is set an anchor strap. Another type, which can be used in soils composed mainly of sand and gravel or equally dense material, is the Sona Tube. It is a cylindrical wax paper form that can be purchased in lengths up to 24 ft. and is available in a range of diameters. The tube is cut off a

little above the desired elevation and placed into the posthole. The soil is then compacted around it to make sure that it is stable and will not shift. If in doubt, brace it using 2x4s attached to the top.

There are two ways to set the posts. The preferred method is to end the concrete several inches above the grade. To do this, simply mark the desired elevation on the inside of the Sona Tube. After filling the tube with concrete to the desired height and smoothing it off, a post-strap or post-seat is inserted into the concrete until it is flush with the top of the footing. Use a carpenters level to make sure it is perpendicular. Another method, if permitted by local codes, is to embed the post in the tube and then pour concrete around it, making sure that the post is plumb and in alignment with all the others. Check each post or post-seat twice. This will reduce the possibility of error. Brace the posts with 2x4s set into the ground, and brace in two directions at 90 degrees from each other. In northern climates where extreme freezing occurs, the Sona Tube may crack. The cracks can be reduced by purchasing some steel reinforcing rods. A number 5 bar is sufficient. Once put in the center of the tube, just short of the desired height, the rods lower the chance of cracking. A minimum diameter of 12 in. is recommended for 4x4 posts sitting on top of the footing. Where the post is to be embedded, a minimum of 16 in. is recommended for a 4x4 post.

After all the footings have been poured, allow three days before removing any of the framework or paper from the

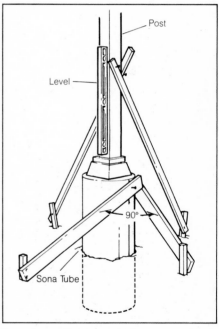

Brace in two directions with braces meeting at 90° angles.

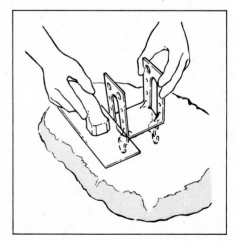

Here is another method of embedding the post support in the cement.

concrete. When the footings have been stripped and the ground surface has been compacted to level, put down a 4 mil or 6 mil sheet of polyethelene and cover the sheet with 2 to 4 in. of river washed gravel. This will give a clean and maintenance-free area under the deck.

Step Five: Setting the Posts and Beams

Having established the foundation, it is now time to erect the posts, and to square them if you have embedded them in the concrete footing. The posts are critical to the overall design since they must not only be level, but plumb. They should be checked at least twice to be sure that they are plumb and in alignment. If you have not already attached the posts to the post-seat or post-straps, now is the time to do so. Try to select metal straps and bolts as well as nails that are high-quality galvanized material. This will prevent rusting, which could stain the wood deck or post. Attach the post to the post-seat, or strap, with bolts. Drill the hole the same size as the bolts. Generally two bolts per connection will be satisfactory. Your posts should be higher than that height required by your design. If they are too short, you will probably have to lower the deck and introduce a step down from the house, since the posts determine the overall height of the deck. Where there is some slope to your site, always take the longest elevation as the reference and then measure every other dimension to that. This will help in meeting your height requirement. No matter where the deck is to be located, the height of the post is the height to the level of the deck, minus only the thickness of the deck material, the width of the joists, and the height of the footings. If the post will extend up to support overhead cover, then the post height would be the height to the level of the roofing you have planned, minus the thickness of the roofing beams (if the beams cap the posts rather than fitting flush) and the height of the footings. The thickness of the deck and the width of the deck joists would be included in, not deducted from, this figure. Prior to attaching the post to the foundation, dip the end, after drilling, into a water-repellent solution. This is a good idea even if using pretreated wood.

With all the posts in place and braced in order to maintain plumb and alignment,

TIPS FOR DECK CONSTRUCTION

Fasteners

1. Use nonstaining fasteners.
2. Always fasten a thinner member to a thicker member, unless clinched nails are used.
   (a) A nail should be long enough to penetrate the receiving member a distance twice the thickness of the thinner member but not less than 1½ in. (i.e., for a ¾ in. board, the nail should penetrate the receiving member 1½ in. Use at least a 7d nail).
   (b) A screw should be long enough to penetrate the receiving member at least the thickness of the thinner (outside) member but with not less than a 1 in. penetration (i.e., fastening a ¾ in. member to a 2x4 would require a 1¾ in. long screw).
3. To reduce splitting of boards when nailing:
   (a) blunt the nail point;
   (b) predrill (three-fourths of nail diameter);
   (c) use smaller diameter nails and a greater number;
   (d) use greater spacing between nails;
   (e) stagger nails in each row;
   (f) place nails no closer to edge than one-half of board thickness and no closer to end than board thickness;
   (g) In wide boards (8 in. or more) do not place nails close to edge.
4. Use minimum of two nails per board; i.e., two nails for 4- and 6-in. widths and three nails for 8- and 10-in. widths.
5. Avoid end grain nailing. When unavoidable, use screws or side grain wood cleat adjacent to end grain member (as a post).
6. Lag screws:
   (a) use a plain, flat washer under the head;
   (b) use lead hole and turn in full distance — do not overturn.
   (c) do not countersink (reduces wood thickness).
7. Bolt use:
   (a) flat washers under nut and head of machine bolts and under nut of carriage bolt;
   (b) in softer woods, use larger washer under carriage bolt heads;
   (c) holes should be exact size of bolt diameter.

Outdoor Wood Use

1. When a wide member is required, use edge grain boards. They will shrink, swell, and cup less during moisture changes than flat grain boards.
2. Do not use wood in direct contact with soil unless members are pressure-treated.
3. Provide clearance of wood members (fences, posts, etc.) from plant growth and ground to minimize moisture content. Bottoms of posts, when supported by piers for example, should be 6 in. above the grade.
4. Use forms of flat members that provide natural drainage (a sloped top of a cap rail, for example).

Shown are beam and joist placement for an extended post.

attach the beams. The most effective method of attaching the beams to the posts is to tack nail one beam to the outside of each post within a row. To do this, first attach the beam closest to the house. Make sure it is level — using a carpenters level — as well as straight and at the proper height. Do not cut the post yet, or the beam. Continue to attach the rest of the beams in the same manner, leveling them to the first beam you installed. Once you have completed this procedure get a very straight and true 2x4 and lay it over the beams. Put a level on it to make sure that everything is level. Check the diagonal level as well. Adjust if necessary until all are level. Lag screw all the beams into the posts using ¼x3 in. galvanized lag screws. Use at least two and preferably four per connection. You can now cut the posts flush with the top of the beam if you will not be extending the posts for nailing or overhead cover support. Repeat the sequence with another set of beams, but install them on the inside of the posts. Level them to the other beam and attach in a similar manner. Having done this you have assembled the most critical part of the structure, although the ends of the beams are still out of alignment. Measuring from a constant point on the deck, locate the cutoff mark on the end of each pair of beams. This can be verified by

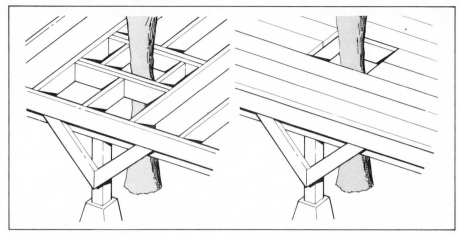

Use doubled joist lumber and blocking to box in the tree and provide support.

using a chalkline from one end to the other to make sure all the ends will be cut off at the same point. Cut off the ends of the beams. Before cutting, double-check to make sure that all measurements are as you want them.

Step Six: Installing the Joists

Once you have cut all the beams to the desired length and attached them, you are ready to install the joists. Since the joists rest on the beams, it simplifies the construction and assembly procedure if you build the "skirt" first. The skirt is simply the outside joist that spans across the beams. It is also the joist that caps the ends of the joist which meet it perpendicu-

larly. Toenail the skirt to the beams, as well as where it crosses the beams. On the inside of the skirt, which has now been nailed to the beams, put down the joist pattern, on 24-in. centers. Lay down one joist; the distance from the center of that joist to the center of the next will be 24 in. Measure from center to center to check spacing.

Begin at one end of the deck and work to the opposite edge. Do not be alarmed if the last two joists have a space of less than 24 in. Using the inside dimension from skirt to skirt, cut each joist and locate it in place, crown side up. Cut the joists accurately. If too long, the skirt will bow outwards. Install the blocking as necessary

Even a ground-level deck requires support posts at regular intervals to provide support for the joists that support the decking material.

between the joists. Blocking will be required if your decking pattern is a diamond, herrigbone, or zig zag. Blocking is the same size of material at the joist, located on 24 in. centers but running perpendicular to the joists. Once all the joists have been put in place, nail each joist with two or three 16d galvanized nails. Where you are unable to nail the joists to the skirt because of its proximity to a wall, use joist hangers and nail the joist in place. Cut the blocking and install at intervals of 2 or 4 ft. The spacing of the blocking is determined by the spacing and size of the pattern. Toenail all joists to the beams using at least two 16d galvanized nails per joist/beam connection. Another method for attaching the joists to the beams is with metal straps. These are available, as are the joist hangers, from your lumber yard.

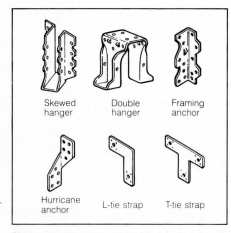

These are the connectors best suited for attaching joists to beams.

Step Seven: Putting Down the Decking

Your decking pattern is now ready to be installed. Always make sure that the curved end grain of the wood faces downward. This will eliminate any cupping of the decking boards. All boards are to be placed bark side up. Use 12d box nails or 16d casing nails. The nailing pattern must be uniform and symmetrical. To ensure that all the nails line up, first lay a chalkline along each joist span. Drive two nails in at each joist, along the chalkline. The butt joints of the decking should line up over the joist and be centered. After attaching the first 2x4 or 2x6 deck board, leave ⅛ to ¼ in. space between boards to allow moisture to pass through and to speed drying of the deck surface. For accurate spacing, place a wedge or large nail between the boards. Space

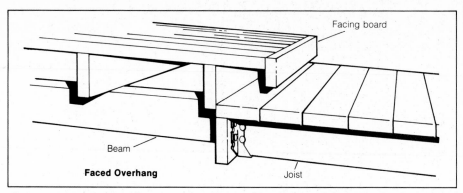

Faced Overhang

When using stepped decks, you can extend the decking on the upper level 6 to 12 in. further than the juncture of the decks. Finish off edges of extended joists or decking by adding a facing board.

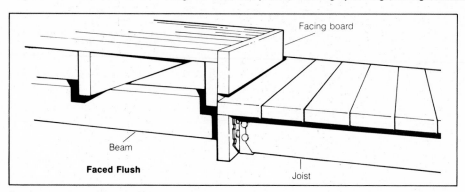

Faced Flush

Stepped decks can be used instead of stairs. Attach joists either to existing beam of the upper deck, or bolt on another beam to support the joists of the lower deck. This will depend on how much of a stepdown you desire.

evenly between the remaining boards. Keeping all the boards parallel and true is difficult. If you find the boards are not exactly parallel, do not try to correct all of the problem by adjustment of the next board. Adjust gradually over the next two or three boards. Keep checking dimensions, based on the first board, and your chances of misalignment will be less. When you are about 6 to 8 ft. from finishing, you will have to plan out how to make sure the last piece of decking will fall over onto and fit flush to the skirt. To figure this out, space the remaining boards to coincide with the edge of the skirt. If in

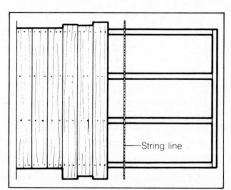

Use string lines to verify measurements in both directions. When you have progressed to about 6 ft. from the skirt, start adjusting the space between board so the spacing will be even and last board will fall flush with skirt.

doubt, lay out the boards to fit to the skirt before nailing them down. You are now ready to trim the deck to its finished dimensions.

Step Eight: Trimming the Decking

Trimming the deck is the last major step in the finishing of the structure. When you trim, make sure that you have verified all the dimensions and the square. Small discrepancies in dimension can be absorbed in the trimming. The framing plan allows ¾ in. overage of the decking on each end of the deck. This can be trimmed flush or, to adjust dimensions, simply trim as required. Trim from the house outward. When sawing, try to keep the saw away from the skirt; if you come too close you could mar the surface of the skirt. Use a

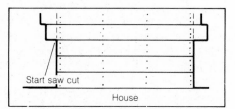

When laying decking, plan according to the direction the saw will travel when making final trim cut. Always precut the first four boards before nailing down at any spot where saw will not be able to start a cut, such as next to house wall.

chalkline to help you see the cut line. To cap the end of the cut decking, as well as to provide an edging strip, install a molding piece around the edge of the decking. This gives an attractive finish.

Step Nine: Installing a Railing

Railings add the final finishing touch to the deck. There are many patterns to choose from, offering both beauty and safety. Be sure to check local building codes for the required height. Normally, any deck over 24 in. above finished grade will require a railing. A railing built of 4x4 posts and 2x4 rails is an excellent combination. Besides being economical, this arrangement allows you to infill in any way you desire.

These are cutaway views of low built-in railings. The posts either attach to the supporting joists or come up through, and are securely connected to, the skirt.

There are several methods used to support a railing. The first is to extend the posts up through the deck to the desired height of the railing. All it requires is a longer post than that used in Step Five. You would attach the beams and joists in the same fashion, the difference being that you would have to fit the decking around the protruding posts. The second method, and probably the best, is to attach railing posts directly to the exterior skirt of the deck. For this method, measure the post size from the bottom part of

the skirt to the desired rail height. Laying out the location of all the posts depends upon the spacing of the posts, normally 48 in. o.c., and the length and type of railing material used. Alternatives are shown in some of the accompanying drawings. At corners, locate a post on each face of the corner, about 4 to 6 in. back from the corner. This will simplify the mitered corner connection of the railing. Once you have marked all the dimensions on the skirt, install the posts using galvanized stove bolts, or similar connectors with washers. Keep the head of the bolt to the outside. Having attached the posts to the skirts, the horizontal railings can be installed. When you dimension the posts, take into account that you will be placing a 2x6 over the end of the post. This capping works very effectively to

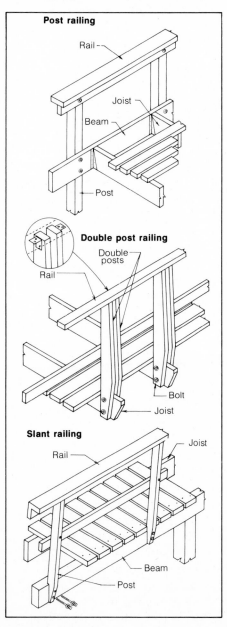

Post railing

align the posts and provides a good nailing surface. Install a side rail around the outside of the posts flush to the underside of the cap rail. This side rail can then be bolted in using two stove bolts per post. A lower side rail at the desired height can be installed in the same fashion. Make sure that the side railings butt flush with each other at the corners, or the job will look unfinished.

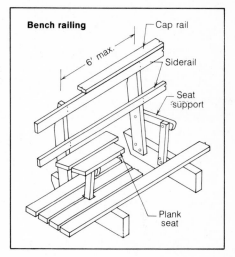

Bench railing

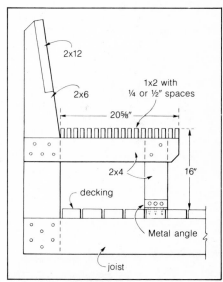

A bench may serve as a railing. It should be 15 in. wide and 15 to 18 in. above deck floor.

Support for Benches. It is also possible to build in benches about 16 in. high, with seats 18 to 24 in. deep. You can use the railing as a support for the seating, with 2x4s on the inside to support the other face.

Step Ten: Building Stairs

Stairs should be used to connect the deck with the ground, particularly if your deck is more than 12 in. above the ground. Stairs can be 4, 5 or 6 ft. wide. If you plan to install a stair in your design, it is best to postpone the installation of the decking in the area of the stair until the stair has been installed. This will allow you to build from above rather than from the underside. This section will present a method of construction for a laminated stair.

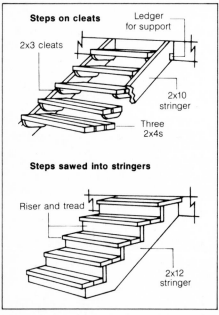

The stairway at the top uses an open stringer; the treads rest on cleats and are nailed to the cleats and the stringers. The stairs below use cut stringers to support the treads.

The sides of the stairs are called "stringers", and must be strong enough to support the heavy loads imposed by people walking on the treads. Each step consists of a tread, which is the horizontal piece, and the riser, which is the height between treads. For deck use, a rise of 6 to 7 in. and a tread of 10 to 12 in. is quite workable. To determine the number of risers, measure the distance from the finished deck surface to the ground. If the ground falls away, measure to the lowest spot possible. Divide the distance in inches by 6 or 7 in. of rise. If you get a whole number, then that is the number of risers you need. In the event that the

number is not even, round off to the nearest whole number. Then divide the original distance by that number to find the height of each riser. Try to keep this height around 6 or 7 in. For example, if your deck-to-ground measurement were 48 in., you would require eight risers of 6 in. each or seven risers of 6⅞ in. To determine the total run of the treads, multiply the tread width times the number required. In the previous example, since eight risers were required, you would need eight treads of 10 in. each, for a total of 80 in. (6 ft., 8 in.) measuring from the face of the skirt down to the ground. The stringers for your stair should be very strong. Use 2x10s or 2x12s for short runs — less than 6 ft. If longer than 6 ft., use 2x12s and reinforce the notched stringer with an additional, unnotched 2x12.

Now that you have decided on the tread and rise, you can begin marking your pattern onto the stringer. You will need a pencil and a carpenters square. Mark the tread horizontally on the stringer and then the riser, vertically. Repeat the procedure so the end of the square for each rise coincides with the adjacent end of the tread you have just marked. For each tread and riser, reposition the carpenters square and continue marking until you have completed the number required. Make sure that you leave at least four additional inches remaining on the end of the stringer for attaching it to the footing or ground. Following the lines you have marked onto the stringer, cut the marked pieces. Your cuts must be square and true, otherwise you could have an irregular tread. If you need to double up because the run is over 6 ft., attach another stringer that has not been cut to the outside of the one already cut. This will give you an extension to which you can nail the next notched stringer, and provide the additional stiffness.

It is time to connect the stringers to the skirt. The most effective, secure method is to use metal hangers or framing straps. This will guarantee that your stringers will be stable and tight to the skirt. Before attaching the stringer, you may want to position a concrete footing under the stringers; this will prevent shifting. Angle irons and bolts can be used at the ground connection. To find the location of the first tread, measure down the height of the riser, after subtracting 1½ in. for 2x4 decking, e.g., if the riser is 6 in., mark off 4½ in.

Then move down 2⁹/₁₆ in. — the dimension of a 2x3 on edge, which will be laid across the stringers to form the tread. If your tread is over 3 ft. wide, 2x4s laid on edge must be used. This would then require that the top of the stringer be 3½ in. below the top of the decking. If not using a laminate stair, adjust this dimension so that it equals the height of the tread. The top of the stringer can be trimmed to allow for this adjustment. Making sure that the studs are cut to length accurately, insert them one against the other, nailing as you go. Make sure you use galvanized nails. When you arrive at the end of each tread, finish it with a uniform pattern of nails. This end piece, called the stair "nosing," is the most visible. One variation is to introduce a ⅛ to ¼ in. spacer between the studs laid on edge. This will create a pattern similar to that of the decking. Once all the treads have been installed, nail the sides of the studs through the stringer.

Exit to the Ground. When the last step down exits to the ground rather than to another deck surface, nail on the lowest cleats 2 in. from the top edge of the stringers, flush with the cut on the end of the stringers, and square from the cut. Beneath each cleat tack a piece of 4x4 on end (like a short post), flush with the cut on the stringers. Tack spacer to cleats. Square the stringer at the deck skirt, level the spacer, and plumb the stringer cut. Finally, set the 4x4s in redi-mix concrete, or use pier blocks.

Variation: Plank Stairway. In this stairway version the treads are flat pieces of 2x6, rather than pieces placed on edge. It is easier to build and will be as long-lasting, as long as you take care to place the bark side of the board up when building the treads. Begin this stair construction the same way as for the laminated stair: measure the drop from the deck to the ground level and find the number of risers required.

Measuring on the Skirt. Mark the skirt for the overall width and for the inside width. Follow the instructions in the laminated stairway section for connections of the last step, installing inside stringers, and squaring the decks.

Cleats. For plank stair treads, we are using a double thickness of 2x6s. This means the cleats must be measured a little differently. For a 4 ft. outside width (3 ft. 6 in. inside width) mark a 4½ in. distance down on the stringer. Then measure down

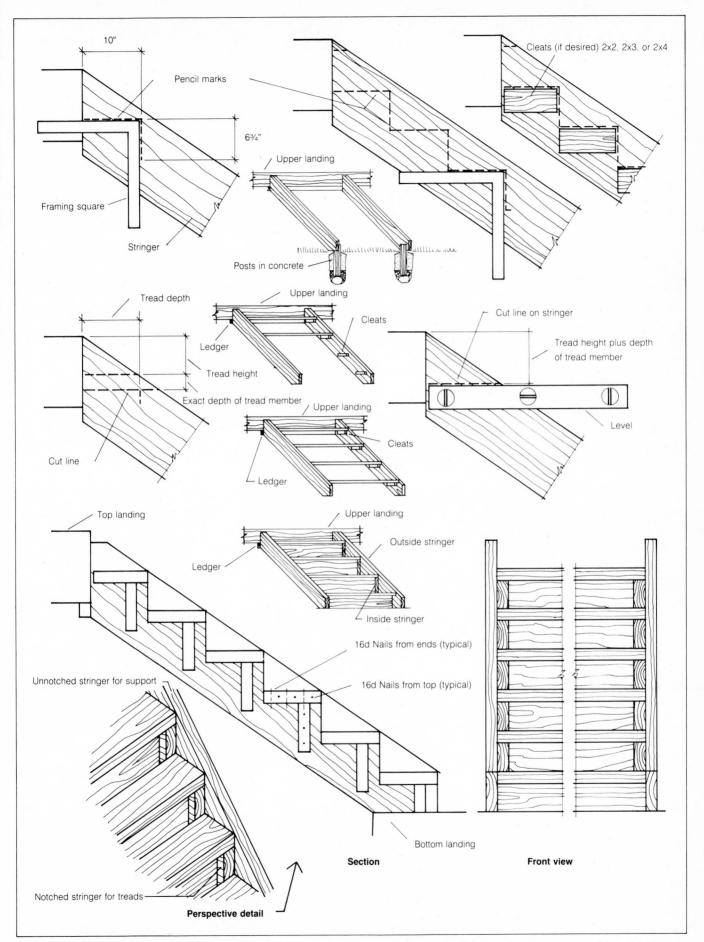

10″

Pencil marks

6¾″

Framing square

Stringer

Upper landing

Posts in concrete

Cleats (if desired) 2x2, 2x3, or 2x4

Tread depth

Upper landing

Ledger

Tread height

Exact depth of tread member

Cut line

Upper landing

Cleats

Cleats

Ledger

Cut line on stringer

Tread height plus depth of tread member

Level

Top landing

Upper landing

Ledger

Outside stringer

Inside stringer

16d Nails from ends (typical)

16d Nails from top (typical)

Unnotched stringer for support

Notched stringer for treads

Perspective detail

Section

Bottom landing

Front view

Whether using cleats or notched stringers for tread support, measuring procedure is the same. Stairs receive heavy use; provide good support.

Cut stringers support two-piece treads in these stairs. Because the stairs are less than four feet wide, and the run under six feet, only two cut stringers were used. A safety railing is used on one side. Local codes may require handrails on both sides of the stairs.

and mark another 3 in. distance (the thickness of two 2x6s laid flat) from the first mark on the stringer: The first cleat will be attached a total of 7½ in. from the top of the stringer. Mark a line from your lowest mark.

For a 12 in. tread, measure, out 12 in. on the scribed line near the top of the stringer. Then measure 6 in. down and 12 in. out for each succeeding tread. Using a square, attach 2x3 cleats (cut 11 in. long) with ¼x3 in. lag screws with washers.

Placing the Treads. Place treads on cleats in the same way as attaching decking, using 2x6s cut to 3 ft. 6 in. You will need four of these boards per tread, but don't put the boards together yet. First, nail two adjacent 2x6s to the cleats (20d noncorrosive nails) to form a single-thickness tread. Then nail a 2x6 to the top of each of the two boards that are attached to the cleats (use 16d noncorrosive nails for this step). Nail into the flat 2x6s through each side of the stringer. Last, nail on fascia piece with 16d noncorrosive nails.

An Attached Deck

The deck presented in the design in Steps One through Ten was free-standing. If your house will support one end of the deck, you will eliminate posts and beams

along one wall, which saves time and money. In addition you will ensure that the two will work together over the years. However, some of the disadvantages are: (1) the connection to the house requires careful attention, even to the leveling of the deck in relation to the house; (2) the deck may settle at a faster rate than the house. If the deck is to be located in a northern climate, the wood may expand and contract, causing minor structural failure of the joists attached to the house wall.

If you decide that attaching the deck to the house is desirable, the procedures outlined in Step One to Step Ten apply with the following modifications.

Step Three: Footing Hole Layout. Because the house offers some support, you will not need to put footings next to the house. You will probably only require two lines of footings instead of three. The setting of the posts and beams will not be changed, however.

Step Six: Installing the Joists. The skirt adjacent to the house must be supported, since the joists are framed into it. This means the skirt must be framed into the house. If you have a wood house, the house rests on a header, which rests on a single or double sill. By keeping the skirt in alignment with the exterior header, the

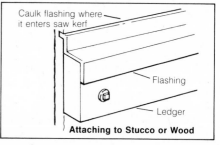

Whether attaching the ledger to stucco or wood, flashing will help keep the connection secure and prevent moisture seepage.

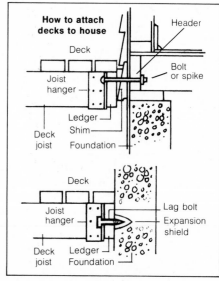

To anchor to a wood house, you can bolt or spike the ledger; for masonry, use expansion shields and lag bolts.

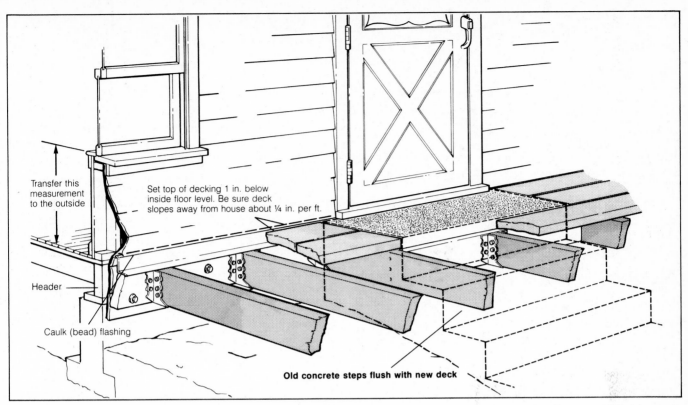

Transfer this measurement to the outside

Set top of decking 1 in. below inside floor level. Be sure deck slopes away from house about ¼ in. per ft.

Header

Caulk (bead) flashing

Old concrete steps flush with new deck

A window makes a good reference point from which to measure evenly down to the house header and ledger board. This arrangement keeps the landing from existing concrete steps as an entry to the deck.

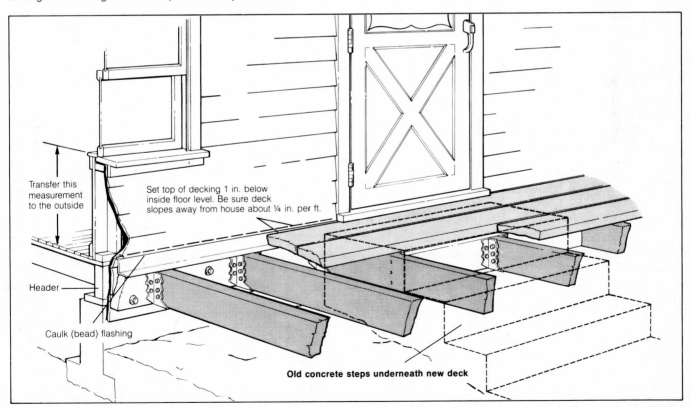

Transfer this measurement to the outside

Set top of decking 1 in. below inside floor level. Be sure deck slopes away from house about ¼ in. per ft.

Header

Caulk (bead) flashing

Old concrete steps underneath new deck

A deck can be placed over existing steps to hide them completely. Whether hiding or using the landing from the steps, the joist support, at both sides of the steps and in the middle, is essential.

two can be bolted together. To do this, drill at 24-in. centers, through the skirt of the deck, then through the siding, sheathing, and header (found just above the house foundation). Keep the head of the bolt to the outside. Make sure that the bolts are long enough to go the full distance with some room to spare. Having set the skirt into the house header, make sure that the joists resting on the beams are firmly attached. Another common method, although it requires more attention to detail, is to install a "ledger beam" along the foundation at the desired height. To do this, you select a steel (galvanized)

Use Construction Heart for posts, skirt, and joists, as well as any wood that touches ground or is within 6 in. of ground. Construction Common can be used for decking.

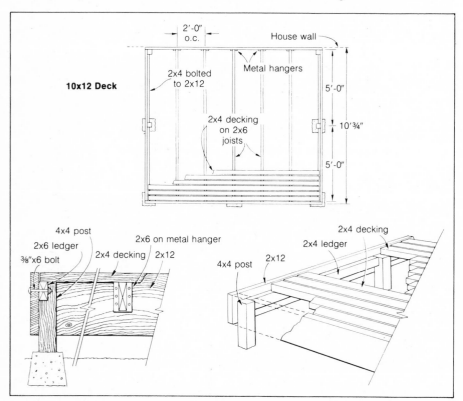

10x12 Deck

2'-0" o.c.

House wall

2x4 bolted to 2x12

Metal hangers

5'-0"

2x4 decking on 2x6 joists

10'3⁄4"

5'-0"

4x4 post
2x6 ledger
3⁄8"x6 bolt
2x6 on metal hanger
2x4 decking   2x12

2x4 decking
2x4 ledger
4x4 post   2x12

The drawings show posts supporting the deck because posts may be necessary if the deck is to meet a high doorway or if the ground slopes. However, when the interior floor level is between 12 and 25 in. above ground and the ground is level, posts can be eliminated. Skirtboards would attach directly to the footings. Anchor skirtboards to the house studs or concrete foundation with 6 in. lag screws into the studs, or expansion bolts into holes drilled in the concrete.

If posts are used, post lengths will vary with level ground. For accurate measurement of the posts, extend a board out from the anchored skirtboard and even with its top. Level it with a carpenter's level. Measuring the height from the top of the footing to the top edge of the board. Subtract 15⁄8 in. (measure for exact height of deck lumber) and cut post to that length.

Attach skirtboards to posts with 3⁄8 by 6 in. lag screws, and toe-nail to nailing blocks in the footings. Once the skirtboards are level and in place, nail them together with 16d nails. Predrill nailholes that fall near the ends of pieces to prevent splitting.

The deck will accommodate 32 2x4s, using a 16d nail as a spacer. (Select lumber to equal 400 lineal ft.)

angle 2 in. longer than the length of the deck, or a 2x6 (or larger) either 2 in. longer than or a little shorter than the length of the deck. If you are using joist hangers with the angle or with the 2x lumber, you will need the extra 1 in. at each end to nail the outer sides of the hangers to the ends of the angle or lumber. Or, if you are using the 2x lumber for the ledger, you can also cut the ledger shorter — less the widths of the joists at each end. You can then butt the end joists against the ends of the ledger, and bolt them into position.

Locate the angle or 2x next to the foundation and bore holes into the concrete foundation through the steel angle or lumber. Insert lead expansion shield or plastic expansion plugs, and attach the ledger with galvanized lag bolts. Flashing is sometimes desirable over the ledger, to keep water from seeping down and causing damage. Remember to make sure that the level of the finished deck is at least an inch below the interior floor level. This reduces the likelihood of flooding.

A Two-Story Deck

While everything covered in Step One through Step Ten is applicable to the two-story deck, there are other considerations for which you must plan. If the deck extends above the ground more than 4 ft., it is recommended that the deck be attached to the house — primarily for stability reasons. If your site is sloping away or up to the house, the deck extending outward will be supported by a series of posts, as has already been discussed. However, on the exterior posts, diagonal corner-bracing should be used. This requires 2x4 or 2x6 members attached from the post to the inside of the skirt. The bracing is placed on both axes of the corner post so that the deck will not sway outward or sideward. All bracing connections should be bolted with at least two bolts per connection.

For a deck that rests on more than two columns which are over 4 ft. high, cross-bracing should be used from post to post. This is built from 2x4 or 2x6 depending on the distance between posts (2x6 for over 8 ft.) and bolted to the post. Try to keep the bolt hole to 1⁄2 in. in diameter. Make the connection just below the beam on one post, and carry that brace down to just above the top of the foundation on the other post. If you have three exterior posts, simply extend the brace on the outside across all three. Keep the connection high on one end and low on the post on the other end. The one in the middle should be connected, if possible, where it crosses the post. Repeat this procedure on the inside face. You can hang many different plants over the diagonals, or install a lattice work to cover it. If the deck has been built over a lower exterior patio or deck, the bracing can become a screen or wind break if vertical boards are placed across it. The decking can run parallel or perpendicular to the house. If the decking is parallel, the beam support must also be parallel.

To connect the deck with the ground, stairs are used and built in the manner described in Step Ten. Because of the height above ground, railing is required. In some zones it may be 42 in. finish height, as opposed to the 36 in. discussed in the previous example. In this case, order the additional length between the railing and the skirt depth. It is advisable to order longer pieces than you might

normally require, since it is easier to cut the piece to size than replace it entirely because it was a little too short.

There is no doubt that the steeply sloping site is the most difficult to build on, but it often results in a spectacular deck with an excellent view and maximum pri-

vacy. Even though the design is difficult to build, selection of the proper tools and materials will make building the project easier. Scaffolding can be rented for a very small fee. It will help in reaching places that are difficult, and will speed deck construction.

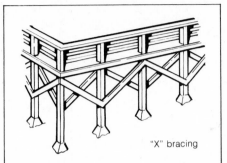

"X" bracing

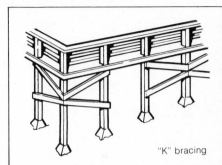

"K" bracing

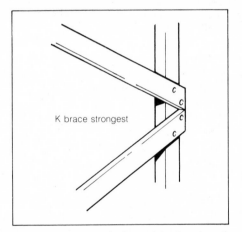

Large or two-story decks require bracing. A K brace is the preferred choice.

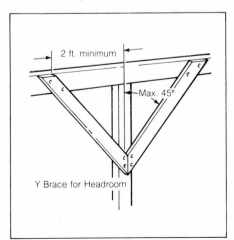

When a K brace does not provide enough headroom, use a Y brace.

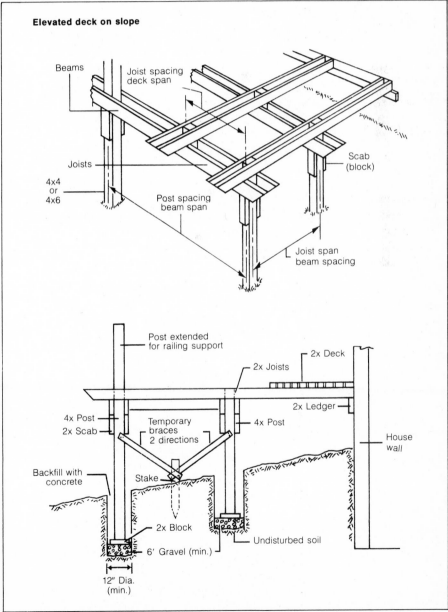

An elevated deck can take advantage of otherwise unusable, sloping ground. Support posts should be set deep into the ground.

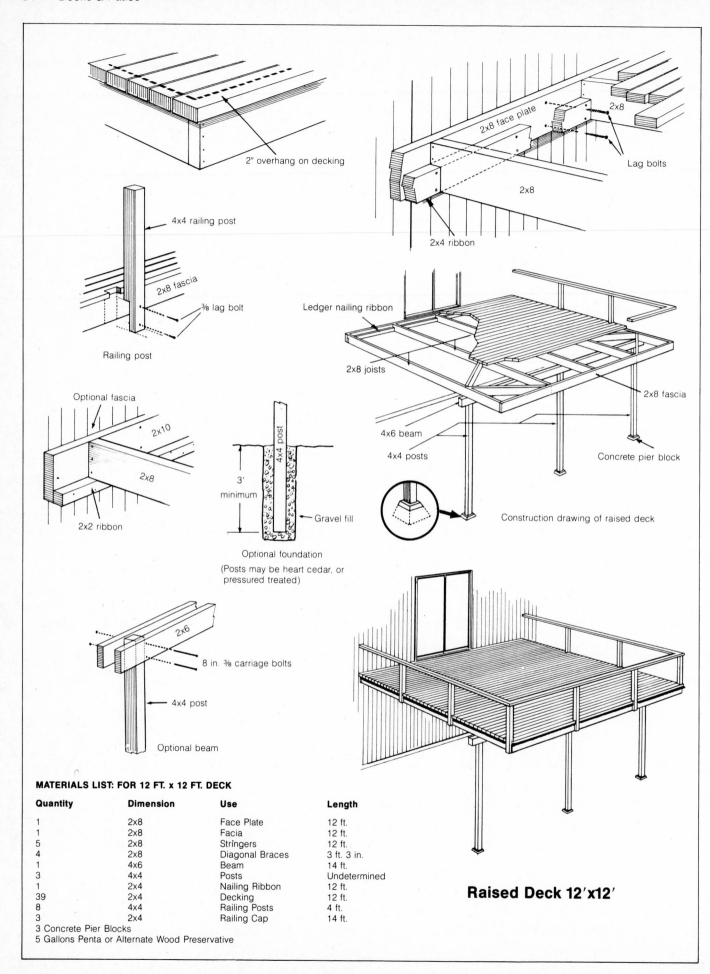

2" overhang on decking

2x8 face plate

2x8

Lag bolts

2x8

2x4 ribbon

4x4 railing post

2x8 fascia

⅜ lag bolt

Railing post

Ledger nailing ribbon

2x8 joists

2x8 fascia

Optional fascia

2x10

2x8

2x2 ribbon

4x4 post

3' minimum

Gravel fill

Optional foundation
(Posts may be heart cedar, or pressured treated)

4x6 beam

4x4 posts

Concrete pier block

Construction drawing of raised deck

2x6

8 in. ⅜ carriage bolts

4x4 post

Optional beam

Raised Deck 12'x12'

MATERIALS LIST: FOR 12 FT. x 12 FT. DECK

Quantity	Dimension	Use	Length
1	2x8	Face Plate	12 ft.
1	2x8	Facia	12 ft.
5	2x8	Stringers	12 ft.
4	2x8	Diagonal Braces	3 ft. 3 in.
1	4x6	Beam	14 ft.
3	4x4	Posts	Undetermined
1	2x4	Nailing Ribbon	12 ft.
39	2x4	Decking	12 ft.
8	4x4	Railing Posts	4 ft.
3	2x4	Railing Cap	14 ft.

3 Concrete Pier Blocks
5 Gallons Penta or Alternate Wood Preservative

Raised Deck 12'x12'

Lay out position of columns and install pier blocks by: digging down to solid ground; leveling bottom of hole; dropping in block; surrounding with gravel.

Locate 2x4 framing studs beneath house siding. Drill holes through the ledger and into studs from both ends of the ledger and into every fourth stud. Attach nailing ribbon to the ledger with 16d galvanized nails, two at a time at 16-in. intervals. With beveled siding, use furring strips between face plate and house. (See optional face plate illustration for alternate construction method.)

(Note: See the optional ledger illustration for alternate construction method.) alternate construction method.)

Notch stringers and attach to nailing ribbon and to beam. Check plumb, level and measurements before nailing. Measure cut and nail four diagonal beam braces in position.

Install decking. Use 10d nail for spacing guide between deck members. Nail deck member to each stringer with two 10d nails. Countersink nails. Check alignment every five or six boards. Adjust alignment by increasing or decreasing width between deck members.

Notch railing posts and decking as shown. Predrill railing posts and stringers and facia and attach posts with two ⅜ in. x 3 in. lag bolts per post. Install railing cap with two 10d nails per post.

SCREENING IN

Usually problems caused by the sun, wind, rain, or insects lead people to think about screening their patio or deck. If you will be going to the trouble of enclosing the area with screens, you must first be sure that you have a solid floor. It makes little sense to screen walls, or perhaps even the roof, and then have insect infiltration from between wooden flooring slats. Before you decide on screening as the answer to an insect problem, check to see if the new electronic insect-killing machines would do the job as well. If insects are the reasons for screening rather than weather conditions, avoid using insect lights on your patio or deck in an attempt to repel them, since this will only attract more insects. Instead, place the lights a distance away from your outdoor area, in order to distract insects from your deck or patio.

If you conclude that screening is definitely needed, first find ready-made wooden or metal frames of the correct size and then stretch the screen yourself.

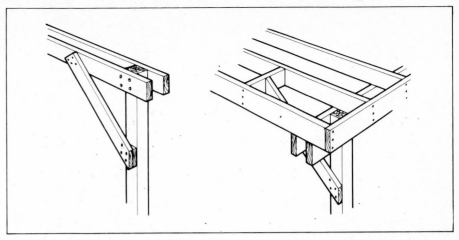

At corners, use what is essentially the top half of the K brace. Tie it from the post to between the joists (in which case you will need blocking between the joists) or to the joist.

Stretching the Screens

Fiberglass is probably the easiest screening material to use; however, it has the disadvantage of being easy to tear or cut and is not suggested if you have a pet with sharp claws or a small child. These instructions apply to both metal and fiberglass screening.

Lay your screen fabric across your frame. You should have enough excess on all sides for easy handling. If your frame is wood, you will staple the screen to the frame. Start at the center of the top of the screen and staple once. Then go to the bottom of the frame and pull the screening tight and staple once at the bottom center. Repeat this procedure at both sides, stapling once at the center of each side. Go back to the top and pull the screen tight again; put in one staple on each side of the first one. Repeat at bottom and sides, pulling the screening tight before you put in each staple. This method provides even stress to the screen and gives a smooth finish. To complete the screen, cut half-round molding, mitering the corners to fit, and nail over the frame to cover the staples. This helps to keep the staples in place, as well as making the screen more attractive. Trim any excess screening fabric edges and paint or stain the frame.

If you are using a metal frame, there is a "channel" around the frame into which you force the screen. When you have done this, you insert a rubber or elastic plastic strip to hold the screen firmly in place. You will need a splain tool to force the screen and the strip into place. Check with your dealer when you buy the frames for the splain tool. The manner in which you stretch the screen is basically the same as for the wood frame. You work from the center of each edge in sequence, so that the screen fabric is pulled tight.

Installing your Screens

You may wish to install your screens permanently — this is a natural choice if you live in a mild climate area. First, toe-nail the screens to the floor from each side, as well as at the top where the screen meets the roofing structure. Then nail the screen frame to the post it touches. Where several screen frames fit together to fill the space between the posts, you will have to connect the screen frames where they touch by covering the joint with 1x3 on one side. If possible, plan the building of your screens and the spacing of your posts so that each screen fits snugly between two posts. You may also install intermediate posts, which will not be load-bearing but will attach to the framing, to support the screen frames.

If you live in an area where a screened-in porch is only a seasonal necessity, you may prefer to install your screens so that they can be removed for storage. In this case, the screens will be attached to the posts with any of several types of hardware fastenings made for this purpose. If you have two screens which together fill the space between two posts, you may want to hinge them together permanently. They will fold together for storage, and the hinges will provide good stability while the screens are up.

Your outdoor area will become more of an outdoor room when overhead cover is added. The roof structure — such as for a trellis or awning — can define the space while still allowing freedom of movement and a feeling of openness. In regions where wind and rain are troublesome, the addition of a protective overhead structure will make the patio or deck usable for more months out of the year. The roof structure will increase privacy when combined with a wall or fence. A roof structure can tie separate elements together, such as the carport and the house, or become a transition space between the house and the garden. The roof structure, if desired, can also operate independently of the deck or patio to visually extend the amount of space devoted to the deck or patio.

Most roof structures for decks and patios are built of wood because wood is strong and yet lightweight enough to be manageable for the home builder.

PARTS OF A ROOF STRUCTURE

Every roof structure is composed of three basic parts: (1) the foundation; (2) the superstructure; (3) the infill. The forces that act on a roof structure — such as wind, snow and rain — are transferred to the superstructure from the infill. The superstructure, which is composed of beams, rafters and columns, distributes the loads and forces to the foundation. The overall stability of a roof structure can be achieved in several ways: (1) by attaching part of the spanning elements, such as beams and rafters or the infill, directly to the eave line or the soffit of the house; (2) by embedding the columns in the foundation to minimize movement; or (3) by making the joints between columns and the beams rigid enough with bracing or a similar device. The decision as to whether you should use a free-standing roof structure or an attached one should be based on your functional and aesthetic needs, rather than structural ones. Both

This raised patio has an unusual roofing arrangement. Brick columns have been set on each side of the patio to support a wooden overhead that attaches to the house with a ledger board. A beam spans the two brick columns.

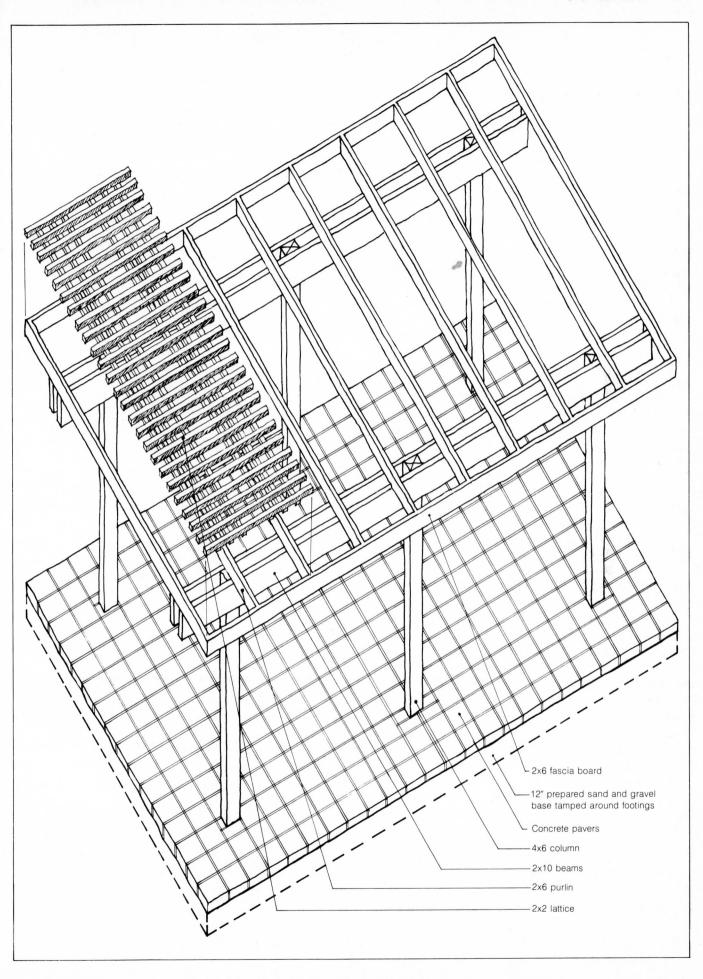

2x6 fascia board

12" prepared sand and gravel
base tamped around footings

Concrete pavers

4x6 column

2x10 beams

2x6 purlin

2x2 lattice

methods are within the abilities of the homeowner.

The Superstructure

The superstructure is composed of two main elements: the columns and the spanning elements (the beams). The columns are embedded in the ground to a depth suitable for rigidity (a minimum of 36 in.). The columns are generally not placed more than 12 to 16 ft. apart in any direction. This is to reduce the difficulty of construction by reducing the weight and length of the beams and other components. While the loads are generally not a controlling factor, the sizes that are recommended take into account a minimum roof load of 30 lbs. per sq. ft. All columns should be at least 4x6 lumber when used 6 to 8 ft. apart. If you plan to have the columns between 8 to 16 ft. apart, or will be extending the columns to support overhead cover, use 6x6 or 8x8 posts.

When laying out the columns, allow for a minimum of 2 to 3 ft. overhang all around the structure. This is true for the attached roof structure as well as the free-standing. This overhang permits closer spacing between the columns while still providing overhead covering. Normally, the area to be covered is not an exact square but is rectangular in form. If you find that the area exceeds recommended column spacing, add another pair of columns in between the end columns. For example, a standard size area is 12 by 18 ft. The area covered by the overhang would be included. The column spacing would be as follows: allowing 2 ft. for overhang on either end, this reduces the distance between columns to 14 ft. Use three columns in a row spaced 7 ft. o.c., which covers the 14 ft. remaining. In the 12 ft. dimension, after the 2 ft. of overhang are deducted, the center to center distance between columns would be 8 ft. You would, therefore, need only two 6x6 columns. A variety of sizes and arrangements can be combined to produce the shape you desire (also see Chapter 6).

The beams span between the columns. Usually they are 2x10s or 2x12s that are firmly attached to both sides of the column. The 2x10 beams can span up to 8 ft. between columns; 2x12s must be used for distances of 8 to 14 ft. They are attached to the columns by galvanized bolts that can be exposed or concealed, depending on the overall look you desire. It is desir-

Parquet units can be arranged to accommodate placement of columns. In this case, posts are placed around perimeter at one end of the patio. Curved plastic panels are used as infill between rafters.

able to have the beams all of one piece (continuous) if possible, including the overhangs. The maximum material size normally available is 18 to 20 ft. in length. If you desire a longer beam length, you must special-order that additional length, or you can "scarf" the beams together by using an intermediate beam between two continuous ones. If the space between the beams were 4 in., then you would need an additional piece 4 in. wide and 10 or 12 in. deep, depending on the size of the beams you have chosen. The beams are then bolted to each other to maintain continuity.

The Infill

The infill spans the spaces between the beams to provide both shade and protection from the rain. For a trellis, the materials are generally lightweight and modular. Usually, 2x2 wood strips of redwood, spruce, fir, cedar or pine are used to span between the "purlins" (intermediate beams). The purlins span between the beams that are attached to the columns. This type of open roofing creates a very light and airy feeling when placed over a deck or patio. A lattice effect can be achieved by placing the 2x2s perpendicular to each other. This gives a denser sensation of light and space. The use of heavy canvas with reinforced edges that fits over or between the purlins is another effective infill method. Corrugated or perforated panels on units of 2 in. lumber can be inset between or over the purlins; plastic or aluminum panels are two examples of the types available.

Wood boards set into the purlins, such as 1x4 or 1x6, result in a louvered effect if set at a diagonal to the span of the purlin.

The Foundation

The foundation for a roof structure is primarily concrete. Embedding the columns in a concrete Sona Tube or a similar device is the most common setup because it is economical and quick to build. A minimum diameter Sona Tube of 16 in. is recommended. The depth varies according to climatic location; however, a minimum depth of 36 in. is recommended. If your area is subject to freezing, increase the footing depth to 6 in. below the frost line. The posts can be treated with a bituminous coating to prevent deterioration. If freezing is likely, the addition of reinforcing bars (#5) is recommended. Another method is to excavate a hole 8 in. in diameter using a posthole digger or similar device, and to fill the hole with concrete.

PRELIMINARY STEPS
Laying Out the Roof Structure

Before you can build the roof structure, you must lay out the exact position of the columns in relation to the deck or patio. There are several requirements that must be pinpointed: (1) the position of the roof structure relative to the house or building; (2) the height of the structure in relation to both the patio or deck and the eave line of the house or garage; (3) the slope of the ground that will support the roof structure; (4) the overall shape or form of the structure; (5) the type of infill desired. All of these considerations will affect the way you will build the roof structure, and the amount it will cost. Once these decisions have been made, it is important that you lay the structure out on paper. Refer to "Drawing Your Plan" in Chapter 4 for assistance.

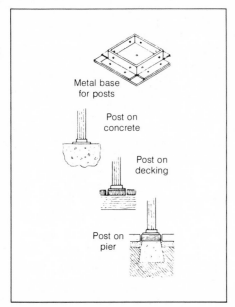

When attaching posts to piers, or whenever building with redwood, cedar or other exterior wood, use noncorroding stainless steel, aluminum, or high-quality hot-dipped galvanized nails.

Integrating Overhead Cover with Patio Deck

If at all possible, it is desirable to build the roof framing structure before installing the deck or patio. The deck or patio can then be fit around the support columns of the roofing. In the case of a patio, it simply means pouring the concrete around the already placed roofing support posts. For a deck, the layout of the deck support posts can be planned to also serve as the roofing supports. The columns will just extend up above the surface of the deck to whatever height is required for the roofing. The decking is placed around and filled to the posts.

Support columns for roofing can be placed around the perimeter of the patio or deck — this is the best option if the patio or deck has been built before construction of the overhead cover. In this case, there are limitations on the spans that can be covered. Planning ahead is absolutely necessary in order to coordinate the layout of the support for the overhead cover with the deck or patio.

If building above an existing concrete patio, you can secure the bottom of the post in a metal post base. Use a masonry bit to drill holes into the concrete; secure the post with noncorroding screws. You can use the same kind of base to anchor the post to a wood deck. To install above brick, remove enough bricks and dig out sufficient soil to enable seating of a pre-cast concrete block to which you can anchor the post. If the block has a wood nailing block at the top, a metal post base can be nailed to it using 8d nails. If the concrete block is the drift-pin type, drill holes into the bottoms of the post to secure it on the drift pins. These measures are less desirable than preplanning before building the deck or patio; however, they will work.

Building Permit

A building permit is normally issued for the entire project rather than for the roof structure. If you are planning just a roof structure, a drawing must be submitted for review. It should show overall height, type of materials, location of columns, location of structure from the lot line, its position relative to your house, and the type of foundation. Once the permit has

ROOF STRUCTURAL REQUIREMENTS

For roof to be supported by house on one or more sides, without overhang.

Roof Area	Rafters Spacing	Size	Beams Number	Size	Posts Number	Spacing
8'x16'	12" o.c.	8' 2"x4"	2	8' 2"x8"	3	8' o.c.
	16" o.c.	8' 2"x4"	2	8' 4"x6"	Same	
	24" o.c.	8' 2"x6"	1	16' 2"x14"	2	16' o.c.
	32" o.c.	8' 2"x6"	1	16' 4"x10"	Same	
8'x20'	Same		2	10' 2"x10"	3	10' o.c.
			2	10' 4"x6"	Same	
8'x24'	Same		2	12' 2"x10"	4	8' o.c.
	Same		2	12' 4"x6"	Same	
			3	8' 2"x8"	5	6' o.c.
			3	8' 4"x6"	Same	
10'x16'	16" o.c.	10' 2"x6"	2	8' 2"x8"	3	8' o.c.
	24" o.c.	10' 2"x6"	2	8' 4"x6"	Same	
	32" o.c.	10' 2"x8"	1	16' 4"x10"	2	16' o.c.
10'x20'	Same		2	10' 2"x10"	3	10' o.c.
			2	12' 4"x8"	Same	
10'x24'	Same		2	12' 2"x12"	3	12' o.c.
			2	12' 4"x8"	Same	
12'x16'	12" o.c.	12' 2"x6"	2	8' 2"x10"	3	8' o.c.
	16" o.c.	12' 2"x6"	2	8' 4"x6"	Same	
	24" o.c.	12' 2"x8"	1	16' 4"x12"	2	16' o.c.
	32" o.c.	12' 2"x8"	Same		Same	
12'x20'	Same		2	10' 2"x10"	3	10' o.c.
			2	10' 4"x8"	4	8' o.c.
12'x24'	Same		2	12' 2"x12"	3	12' o.c.
			2	12' 4"x8"	4	8' o.c.
16'x16'	16" o.c.	16' 2"x8"	2	8' 2"x10"	3	8' o.c.
	24" o.c.	16' 2"x10"	1	16' 4"x14"	2	16' o.c.
	32" o.c.	16' 2"x10"	Same		Same	
16'x20'	Same		2	10' 2"x10"	3	10' o.c.
			2	10' 4"x8"	Same	
16'x24'	Same		3	8' 2"x10"	4	8' o.c.
			3	8' 4"x8"	Same	
			2	12' 2"x14"	3	12' o.c.
			2	12' 4"x10"	Same	

VINES SUITABLE FOR ROOF TRELLIS COVER

Name	Northern-most Survival Zone	Requirements	Description
Virginia Creeper *Parthenocissus quinquefolia*	Zone 3	Full sun to total shade, good soil and fertilizer.	Height to 30 ft., deciduous, medium green leaves, bluish-black fruit, red fall color. Grows rapidly, needs pruning, drapes over walls, trellises or as ground cover.
Boston Ivy *Parthencissus Tricuspidata*	Zone 4	Good garden soil, half to heavy shade. Young plants need regular watering.	Height to 60 ft., shiny 3-lobed leaves with small, blue berries (attracts birds), Scarlet in fall, deciduous, rapid growth. Clings to stone.
Japanese Honeysuckle *Lonicera Japonica*	Zone 4	Sun to heavy shade. Any soil, preferably porous or fertile. Water during dry spells.	Cream-color flowers in late spring and early summer, fall fruits attract birds. Evergreen in mild climates. Prune to control growth.
Wisteria *W. Floribunda*	Zone 4	Full sun to partial shade, roots planted deep, garden soil. Water young plants regularly. Stake, prune each year.	Deciduous, fragrant, pendulous flowers (white, lavender or purple) profuse in early summer. May take several years before first bloom.
Ivy *Hedra*	Zone 5	Light to heavy shade, good garden soil. Prune yearly.	Evergreen in milder climates, dense, shiny leaves. Grows vigorously once established.
Jackman Clematis *Clematis Jackmanii*	Zone 5	Same as ivy. Prune in spring.	Height to 12 ft., rich purple flowers in July on new growth. May be planted with roses.
Sweet Autumn Clematis *Clematis Paniculata*	Zone 5	Same as above	Height to 30 ft. Fragrant white flowers in autumn, then fruit. Dependable.
Anemone Clematis *Clematis Montana*	Zone 6	Rich, slightly alkaline soil. Cool, moist location. Water to establish and during drought. Mulch base to keep roots cool.	Deciduous, height to 20 ft. Leaves and flowers like full sun, base likes shade. Grows well under right conditions, will grow on trees, hedges, posts, walls or arbors. Prune for shaping after flowering.
Carolina Jessamine *Gelsemium sempervirens*	Zone 7	Sun to partial shade (shade roots). Frequent watering needed.	Shiny leaves, fragrant yellow flowers. Evergreen in southern range, not hardy north of North Carolina. Easy to train. *Poisonous to animals.*
Common Jasmine *Jasminum Officinale*	Zone 7	Full sun to light shade, frequent light watering, good garden soil.	Height to 30 ft., semi-evergreen (warm climate). Fragrant white flowers. Grows easily in southern areas.
Passion Vine *Passiflora caerulea*	Zone 7	Full sun, loose sandy soil. Frequent heavy watering, less in cooler seasons.	Grows rapidly in warm, tropical climate. Hardiest of passion flowers, fragrant blossoms. (Blue to white), may bear seeded fruit (some edible), leaves resistant to insects.
Bougainvillea	Zone 10	Full sun, southern exposure, rich loamy soil. Water frequently while growing.	Height to 20 ft. Evergreen in warm climate. Bracts around small flowers give yellow, purple, magenta color in spring and early autumn. Can be *espaliered* (trained) against wall if desired.
Roses	Various, depending on species.	Depends upon species.	Discuss choice with trained nurseryman to determine proper rose for climbing or for borders.
Grapes	Various, depending on species.	Full sun, well drained soil. Needs annual pruning.	Will provide thick cover of leaves and fruit. Plant 6 ft. apart for good arbor cover. Deciduous. Discuss choice with well-trained nurseryman.
Silver Lace Vine *Polygonum Aubertii*	Any	*Annual,* soak seeds to encourage germination. Tolerates dry soil.	Any height, rapid growth which may choke out other plantings. Long flowering period. Does well in adverse urban conditions.
Trumpet Vine *Campsis radicans*	Zone 5	Ordinary soil. Tolerates dryness.	Large orange or scarlet blossoms that attract hummingbirds. Rampant growth, needs little attention to grow, but must be constantly cut back.

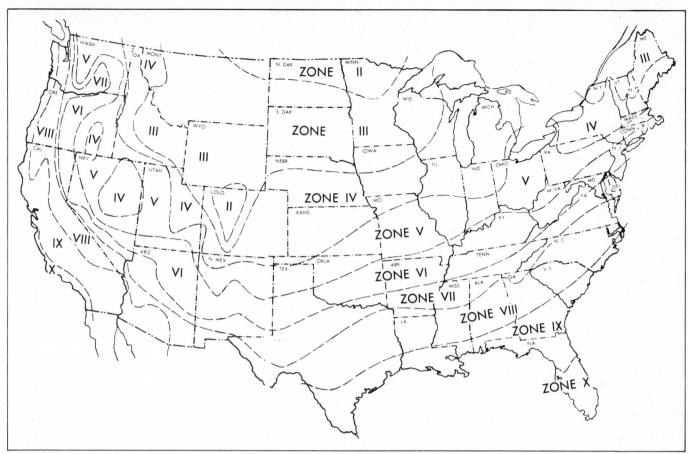

The zones shown here refer to those in the accompanying chart, which indicates survival areas for vines that add shade and greenery to your overhead cover. Zones are based on the average yearly minimum winter temperatures (1895 to 1935); This map was published in the "Atlas of American Agriculture," U.S. Department of Agriculture.

been issued, the inspector will want to look at the deck construction as you build it. Be sure to notify the inspector's office in order to schedule the inspection. This procedure may vary from community to community.

ROOF TRELLIS CONSTRUCTION

This section will provide you with the construction procedures and carpentry tips necessary to build a free-standing roof trellis. Alternatives and variations will be offered after these basics have been covered. If you desire a roof trellis that is attached to the house, the procedures will be the same with one exception — attaching the interior posts. Any differences between the free-standing and the attached roof trellis will be discussed after the step-by-step sequence.

Step One: Preparing the Site

If you have built or are preparing to build a deck or patio, the clearing of the site has already been accomplished. If you are building only overhead shelter, clear the area of any shrubs or bushes that would interfere with the excavation or with as-

sembly of the roof trellis. Stake the approximate area that will be covered by the trellis. Check that any overhead wires or electrical devices are well out of the work zone. If there are any wires within the work area, contact an electrician or your power company for assistance. If you plan to locate the roof structure next to the house, make sure that any obstructions or protrusions from the house will not interfere with the work. A shutter or outswinging door could cause havoc during assembly of the columns and beams.

Step Two: Staking out the Foundation

To find the positions of the columns you must first locate the columns in relation to the building, house or patio area. If the roof trellis will be adjacent to the house, use the triangulated survey method discussed in Chapters 5 and 6 to determine the correct line. If the structure will be free-standing, the columns *may* be parallel to the wall of the house. For an attached structure, the column line *must* be placed parallel to the house wall.

Start at a known corner and stake the

column locations. If the roof will be attached to the house, the column line should be no more than 12 ft. from the wall line. This dimension is determined by the length of the purlins that will span from the house across the exterior beam line. If the roof structure is to be free-standing, figure on at least 2 to 3 in. distance between the edge of the trellis and the house proper; remember that 2 ft. on each side can be an overhang. In this example, the columns will be spaced 6 ft. apart along the beam line and 8 ft. apart from column line to column line. This will cover a 12x16 ft. area. Check your accuracy to assure that the lines are parallel and that the columns are located exactly 6 ft. apart. Drive an 8d finishing nail into the head of one stake, and string lines between all stakes. Check the diagonal measurements. They should be equal.

Step Three: Footing Hole Excavation

Having staked the positions of the columns that support the trellis, it is time to dig the postholes. For additional information regarding the types of footings, refer to Step Four in Chapter 6. For the purpose of demonstration, a 16 in. diameter Sona Tube will be used as the foundation support. If you do not use a Sona Tube, you can make a form from a 16x16 in. wooden box or a large can. These forms will have to be removed from the ground after the concrete has hardened, unlike the Sona Tube. Oil the forms before placing the concrete. Use a posthole digger to excavate the hole 18 to 20 in. wide and at least 36 in. deep. When you excavate, make sure that you are digging at the right spot. If you are unsure, drive in two stakes perpendicular to the column line, several feet on either side of the column stake. Then tie a line across from which you can hang a plumb bob, to check the plumb and location of the hole. Once all the holes have been dug, put the Sona Tube in place and allow several inches from the top of the tube down to the projected ground level. This will keep the column out of contact with the ground. Recheck alignment and plumb of each tube. Once checked, fill around the tubes with the excavated soil. Compact tightly around the tubes; you do not want them to move when pouring the concrete. The shell of the tube can remain buried.

Step Four: Setting the Columns

Once the Sona Tubes or the postholes are in place, you are ready to set the columns. When setting the columns, remember that it is better to have a column that is too long rather than too short. If you are in doubt as to the exact length of the column, allow extra length to determine the length of the column, add the depth of the footing to 36 in., plus the height of the column above grade. For this example, the dimension will be 7 ft. to the underside of the beam plus another 10 in. for the depth of the beam. If the ground slopes, any slope must be figured into the length. Adding 36 in. (3 ft.) to 7 ft. 10 in., the column length will be a minimum of 10 ft. 10 in. in length. Since most lumber comes in 2 ft. increments, a 12 ft. 4x6 column will be used and then cut down.

Place the columns in the centers of the tubes. Brace the columns using 2x4 braces nailed to stakes. Always stake two directions, usually at right angles to each other. Use a carpenters level to check plumb and level. Make sure the columns are all in alignment. Be sure to set some

sort of connector, such as a specially designed post plate, into the pier to attach the post. Local codes are often very specific about the connections allowed in post construction. Pour the concrete into the forms. Be careful not to move the columns while pouring the concrete. Use a rod or spade to work the concrete. Trowel off the top of the column and pitch the concrete slightly from the face of the column to allow the water to run off. Allow three to four days before you remove the bracing. Cure the concrete by wetting the area on a daily basis. You should now have six columns sticking out of the ground. If using 4x6s, the 6 in. faces of the columns should be parallel to the house.

Alternate. If not using Sona Tubes, pour concrete into the postholes you have dug, work the concrete, and position the connectors into the concrete. Check the connectors for alignment and plumb before the concrete begins to harden, in case adjustments are needed.

Step Five: Setting the Beams

Once the columns are in place and the concrete has hardened, you can attach the beams. You will need assistance for this part of the project. To the exterior faces of the columns, tack nail the 2x10 across the three columns, allowing 24 in. between the end of the beam and the center of the column so that you create one end of the overhang. The vertical placement of this beam on the column will be 84 in. above the foundation. Once the beam has been nailed to the first column, level it across the other two. Leave 24 in. of overhang at the other end (see p. 87). Level and tack nail to the remaining columns. Repeat this same procedure on the interior side for each column. Use the level of the beam on the exterior column face to level the interior beam. Check alignment and level again. Measure to ensure that the overhang has been provided. You can now locate the remaining 2x10s on the other rows of columns. Tack nail. Use four ½-in. galvanized carriage bolts for each connection. Drill through the beams and the column with a drill that has the same size bit as the bolts. This will give a tight fit. After connecting all the columns to beams using the bolts, you can cut off any portion of the columns extending above the beams. Our design calls for you to cut the posts flush with the tops of the beams.

Step Six: Setting the Purlins

The beams that span across the previously set up beams are purlins. To install the purlins, measure 24 in. o.c. along each row of beams. Make sure you start at the same reference point on each beam. Position a 2x6 on the marks drawn, after allowing for a 24 in. overhang on each end, measured to the centerline of the beam. Toe-nail each purlin, using four 12d galvanized nails per connection. On each end of the 2x6s, nail a 2x6 fascia board to the ends of the purlins. If your roof trellis is flush against the house, you may have to attach the end of the fascia board prior to attaching the purlins to the beams. This can also simplify the construction of the trellis. Re-measure the spacing between the purlins to make sure that the distance is 24 in. o.c., which will be necessary for construction of lattice work.

Step Seven: Installing the Lattice

The lattice work is built from 2x2 strips of wood. There are many ways to arrange the lattice: you can place it across the purlins from the edge of the trellis to the other end; you can set it diagonally across the purlins; you may inset a ledger strip of 2x2 on each face of the purlin and then position precut sections into place. These are just a few of the variations that are possible. It is easier to build the lattice in place than on the ground. Make sure that you have a safe platform from which to work. For purposes of demonstration, a double lattice work will be constructed.

Lay each 2x2 from end to end across the purlins. Make sure that any splices (joints between pieces) always fall on a purlin. Use two 12d galvanized nails per

Trellis Covered Privacy Deck 12x16

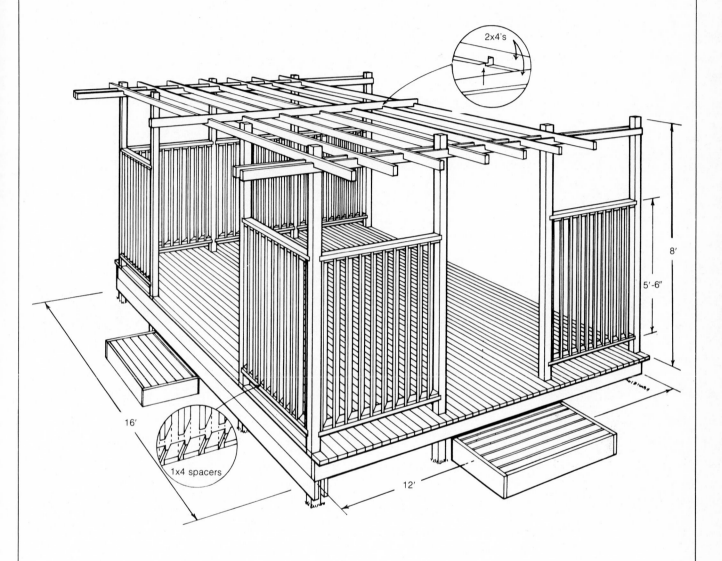

2x4's

8'

5'-6"

16'

1x4 spacers

12'

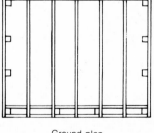

Ground plan

MATERIALS LIST

1. Main support posts: 10 pieces required. Cut to fit terrain of your deck
   (approx.) 10 pieces 4x4x10'
2. Materials for header boards: 3 pieces required 2x8x16'
3. Fascia boards:
     2 pieces required 2x8x12'
4. Joists:
     7 pieces required 2x8x12'
5. Decking:
     36 pieces required 2x4x16'
6. Trellis materials:
     Support beams: 5 pieces required 2x4x14'
     Trellis boards: 7 pieces required 2x4x18'
7. Privacy screen as per your requirements.
8. Nails and accessories as required.

This free-standing, low deck has overhead of notched 2x4s that can be left open, or filled in to provide shade.

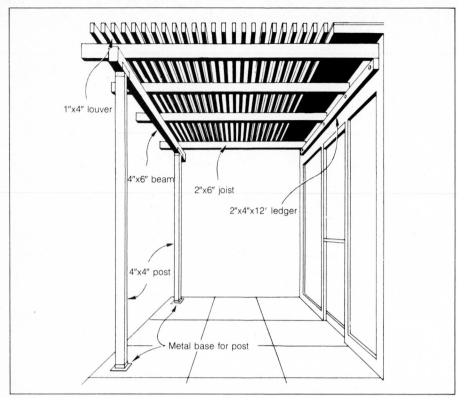

1"x4" louver

4"x6" beam

2"x6" joist

2"x4"x12' ledger

4"x4" post

Metal base for post

Allow sufficient clearance between top of the ledger and bottom of the soffit to enable later insertion of 2x6 joists. Insert joists every 4 ft.

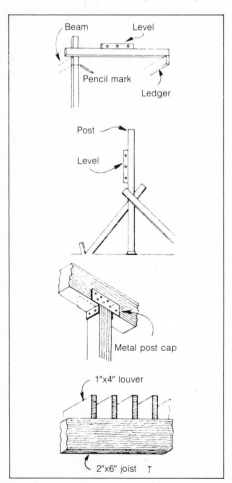

Beam   Level

Pencil mark

Ledger

Post

Level

Metal post cap

1"x4" louver

2"x6" joist

Once joists are in place, install 1x4 louvers on edge. Leave 3 in. between rafters for filtered sunlight.

connection. Space the lattice 4 in. o.c. Having positioned all the lattice on the upper part of the purlin, you are now ready to install the under layer. On the underside of the lattice — between the purlins — nail 2x2s to the bottom of the lattice at 4 in. o.c.

With the second row of lattice in place, all you have to do is add a 1x3 fascia board around the edges of the lattice, laying across the top of the purlins.

An Attached Roof Trellis
The procedures outlined above are very similar to those for an attached roof trellis. The major difference occurs in the attachment of the beams to the wall of the house. The most commonly used method is to drill through the exterior of the house and to bolt a ledger board either at the purlin or beam level. The purlins are attached to the ledger with metal hangers or angles. This can be adjusted depending upon the position of the roof relative to the eave line of your house. Do not allow the roof to rise higher than the eave level, or you will have problems with snow or with unusual movement. It is also desirable to locate the trellis below the eave line in case of movement due to wind or rain. The water runoff will be down and away rather than toward the house. The

trellis will have greater visual appeal if it is part of the house rather than if it is completely separate. An attached roof trellis resembles a lean-to. It relies on the stability of the wall for support. The purlins are attached to and supported by the ledger beam, which has been attached using 3⁄8 in. galvanized lag screws that are connected to the studs of the exterior wall. For a masonry wall, attach using 1⁄2 in. lead expansion shield and bolts. The screws should be spaced on 24 in. centers, maximum. The expansion shield and bolts can be spaced up to 36 in. centers. Joist hangers can then be used to attach the purlins to the ledger, or they can be nailed. For a roof that has much of a pitch, the purlins should be cut on an angle before attaching to the ledger. To fit the purlins smoothly to the exterior of the house, hold up one purlin to the ledger and mark the angle onto the lumber. Cut and use this as a guide for the other purlins.

Wooden screens serve as supports for overhead bolted to house fascia.

Finishing the Trellis
If you have selected redwood or cedar, the material will weather into a natural grey tone. It may cost a little more in the beginning to select a material that weathers well, but you will save in the longevity of the structure. Wood preservatives are available in most locales. Stains can be added to the materials every four or five years to guarantee a uniform appearance and a long life. You may wish to paint the wood, but this will mean more frequent touch-ups. Select your paint or stain to keep maintenance to a minimum.

OTHER INFILL MATERIALS
Here are some variations using other infill materials, based on an attached roofing design.

Lath

The laths are spaced so that sunlight (and rain) can pass through their cracks. While that may seem like a disadvantage, lath roofs do provide shade and can often save the homeowner tax dollars, since many communities in the U.S. do not consider them permanent additions to the home.

After building the framing structure (piers, posts, beams), attach the purlins to the ledger board and beams. Install fascia edge boards and nail on the best grade of lath available. Leave ½ to 1 in. spaces between lath strips, depending on the amount of light that you desire to have penetrate. Then paint the entire roof with a high-quality weather-resistant latex stain or paint. Or, let the entire structure weather naturally if using cedar or redwood.

Fabric

In certain climates, a fabric overhead cover can last a long time, and will provide shade and protection at a relatively low cost. The favorite is canvas, because it holds up best to the elements. The fabric can be attached to either a wood or pipe frame. The simplest method is to just tie the fabric to the frame after stretching it tight. Another alternative is to stretch canvas panels on cables from the house to the garage — or to supports. This offers temporary protection from the sun.

Sewing Canvas. If heavier than 10 oz. duck, or if vinyl-coated, the canvas will need to be hemmed on the special equipment found at an awning shop. If hand-sewing 10 oz. canvas, use a No. 13 Sailmaker's Needle and Dacron thread. You can have the grommets installed by the awning shop, or you can put them in yourself. A lace-on cover will require grommets about every 8 in., as well as one in each corner.

To lash canvas to the frame, use a cord or rope or ¼ in. diameter. If desired, you may also tie on the canvas, but make it look as if it is a slip-on style by cutting the canvas so it can overlap the edges around the frame.

Retractable Canvas Covering. A more complicated arrangement, but very attractive and useful, was designed by the California Redwood Association. This awning extends and retracts using a rope and pulley system.

Utilizing a heavyweight canvas cover, wood dowels of ¾ in. diameter are in-

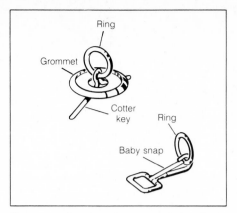

Canvas overhead can be suspended on strong cables, using cotter pins passed through grommets or baby snaps sewn to canvas. Panels are most often parallel 5 ft. strips, but wider strips may be used. To attach cable to house, use awning hinges on large screw eyes. A turnbuckle at one end of the cable will keep fabric from stretching.

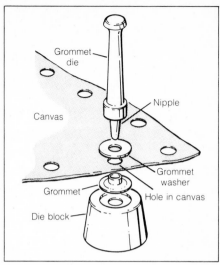

Pierce canvas for grommets. Line up each hole with block and washer; insert grommet. Align nipple; tap grommet die with hammer.

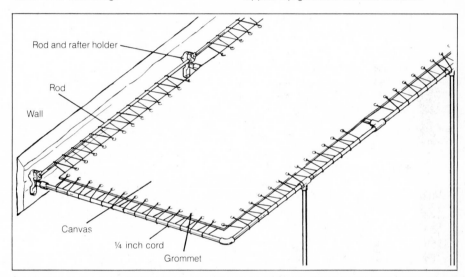

A canvas cover can be lashed to either a pipe or wood frame. When laced onto frame using a continuous cord, tension will be evenly distributed.

This redwood garden room has peaked second roof that incorporates a rain-resistant canvas covering. The canvas retracts and unfolds with a rope and pulley system.

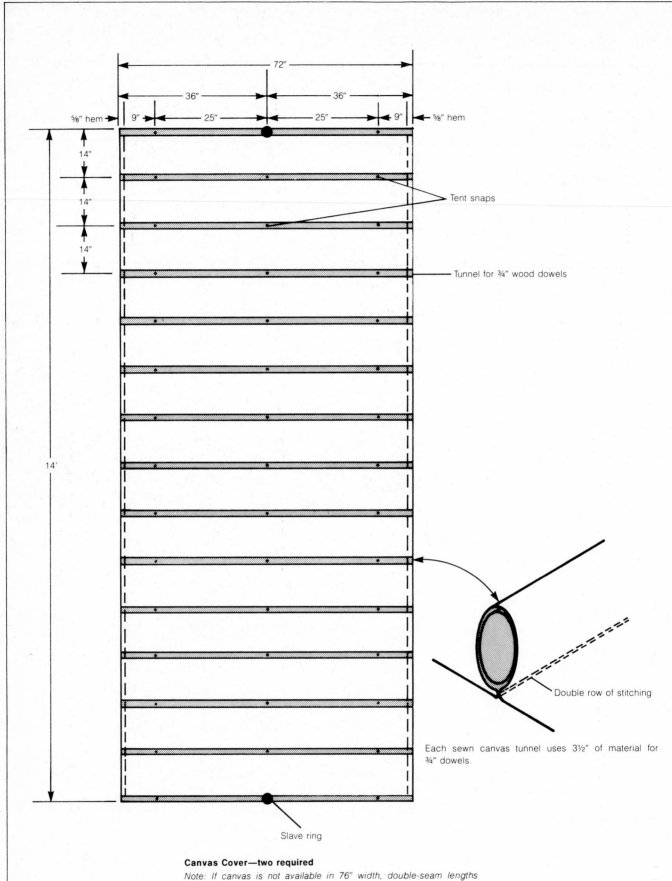

72"

36"   36"

⅝" hem   9"   25"   25"   9"   ⅝" hem

14"

14"

14"

14'

Tent snaps

Tunnel for ¾" wood dowels

Double row of stitching

Each sewn canvas tunnel uses 3½" of material for ¾" dowels.

Slave ring

Canvas Cover—two required
Note: If canvas is not available in 76" width, double-seam lengths together before sewing tunnels for dowels.

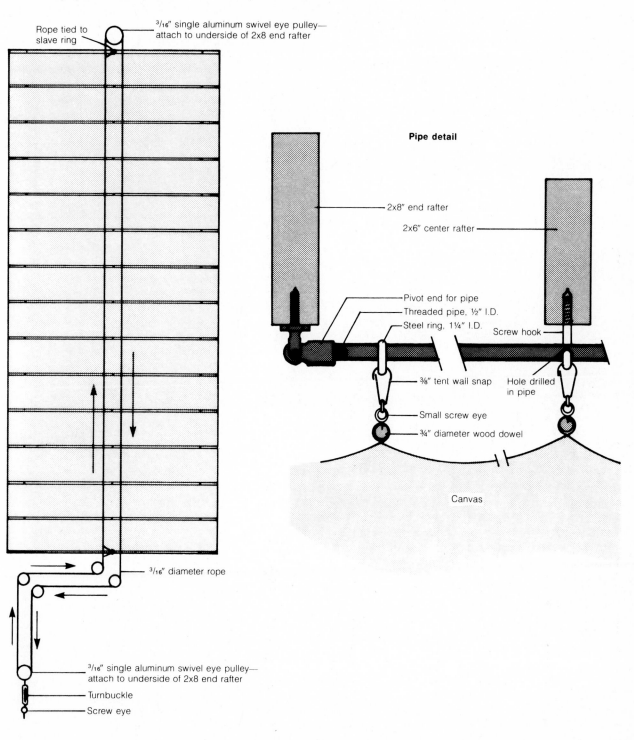

Rope plan for canvas covers

Rope tied to slave ring

$^3/_{16}$″ single aluminum swivel eye pulley—attach to underside of 2x8 end rafter

Pipe detail

2x8″ end rafter

2x6″ center rafter

Pivot end for pipe
Threaded pipe, ½″ I.D.
Steel ring, 1¼″ I.D.

Screw hook

$^3/_8$″ tent wall snap

Hole drilled in pipe

Small screw eye

¾″ diameter wood dowel

Canvas

$^3/_{16}$″ diameter rope

$^3/_{16}$″ single aluminum swivel eye pulley—attach to underside of 2x8 end rafter

Turnbuckle

Screw eye

© Meredith Corp., 1979

Removable insect proof screens fit on top of redwood 2x4 trellis and around sides of redwood garden room.

serted in folds that have been sewn every 14 in. across the fabric. The dowels will give even support across the width and create watershed "valleys" for rain runoff. Install the screw eye hooks in the dowels; there will be three screw eye hooks for each dowel. Use tent wall snaps to connect hooks to the metal rings that have been put around ½-in. galvanized pipes. You will need three pipes for each awning. At each end of the peaked rafters, the pipes are supported as well as by a center-rafter screw hook. The canvas cover parallels the slope of the rafters, but the pipes are perpendicular to the rafters. This adds to the ability to handle water runoff. The project shown has two separate awning mechanisms; each slopes from the peak on the ridge of the second roof. The rope that retracts and extends the awnings attaches to the lead or slave ring found at each end of the awning, on

The rope pulley system extends downward to turnbuckles and then out to the second pipe on each side of center post, enabling canvas to be pulled back from front of the garden room.

Rope reaches the full length of the second pipe on each side. It pulls the canvas from front to back, not from the sides toward the roof peak.

The canvas cover can be made from 76-in. wide fabric. If the larger material is not available, smaller widths can be double-stitched together.

the middle pipe. When attaching, check that the slave rings at each end connect to ropes going in the opposite direction. This allows the cover to retract along the pipes and to extend forward.

Fiberglass Panels

While adaptable fiberglass panels could easily be used over the frame previously described, it is best to set them on a good pitch—usually at least 3 in. in 12 (meaning that the roof rises 3 in. for every 12 in. of span). Set the purlins 24 in. o.c. to accommodate the 26 in. panels (standard size). They will overlap by one corrugation on each side. You can buy the panels in 8, 10, or 12-ft. lengths.

After building the framing structure (piers, posts, beams) attach purlins at the necessary angle for pitch. Then add the fascia boards to the ends of the purlins. To prevent sagging of the panels over time, we also recommend cross-bracing every 5 ft. between the rafters. Now you can at-

tach fiberglass panels to the rafters using aluminum nails and neoprene washers (available where panels were purchased). Predrill the nail holes to ease installation and aid accuracy. An optional but desirable measure is to roll out mastic along the overlaps; this will help prevent shifting of the panels once they have been connected. Add flashing — install to the side of house to cover the joint between the house and the fiberglass panel roof.

Eggcrate overhead frame takes fiberglass panels for removable shade and weather protection.

Custom flashing, designed for use with the panels, is available from building supply centers and from many catalog outlets. It is a good idea to spread mastic or caulking where the flashing meets the house wall.

Removable-Panel Installation Method. Before putting up the purlins and fascia boards, you can rout a rabbet joint into each interior edge to hold the panels. This enables you to fill in portions of the roof with the panels, or to move them around, or to remove them entirely when desired.

Permanent Roof

The permanent roof is installed in basically the same manner as the fiberglass roof panel, except that the 2x6 purlins are placed 16 in. o.c. rather than 24 in.

Build the support structure (piers, posts, beams and purlins, and fascia boards). Then nail ½ in. CDX plywood to the frame. Install a piece of metal flashing between the roof and the siding of the house, using adhesive and roofing nails.

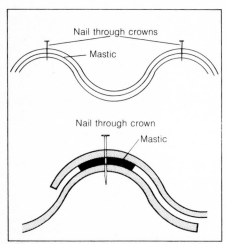
Use mastic strips along seams to prevent panel movement. Predrill all nail holes; nail through overlaps and mastic.

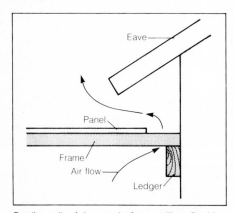
Caulk wall of house before nailing flashing through predrilled holes. Use proper nails for wood, masonry or stucco. Leave a small space between panel ends and wall for ventilation. Eave overhang will protect space from rain.

Close-set infill near the house covers walk area, leaving remainder of backyard and patio uncovered. Beams span from house to garage; using the garage avoids the need for additional support columns.

Now cover the roof, starting at the bottom, with sheathing paper, overlapping each course by two in. Nail the paper just enough to hold the paper in place. Cover with roll roofing or shingles, starting at the bottom and working up the roof.

If you use shingles, start at the bottom and lay the first row upside-down (with the tabs facing up). Nail the second row right side up and continue working, using a chalk line to keep the lines straight. Stagger the joints.

At the top of the roof, connect either roll roofing or shingles to the flashing using roof adhesive. Cover the nail holes in the side of the flashing with the same adhesive, caulking, or special roof sealer.

If desired, you can attach a gutter and downspout to the low end of the permanent patio roof, although it isn't necessary.

Since the roof of the patio will have nails showing (which many people don't find a problem), you may want to improve it cosmetically by spray painting the underside of the roof with a light-colored paint.

Materials Needed for Permanent Roof, 8x12 area. 3 sheets 4x8 ½ in. CDX plywood; 1 roll sheathing paper; 1 square roofing paper or asphalt shingles; 5 pounds 6d galvanized roofing nails.

Infill is installed in staggered pattern, both above and below beams, for shade and attractive design.

Columns, beams, and joists of varying lengths, have been painted white to emphasize the open, airy structure. Panels can be added for shade, as needed.

Attached overhead has joists set into notched beams. Corner columns serve as support for screen framing, deck, and overhead.

8 Screens, Walls and Fences

Screens, walls, and fences all perform the same functions: they give privacy and help define the outdoor living space. Your particular requirements for the deck or patio will probably dictate a combination of these three, or repetitive use of one. Of the three main privacy elements — walls, screens and fences — walls are often considered the most secure because they are built from solid masonry units and stand from 2 ft. to 8 ft. high. They are expensive to build, but the end result is worth the additional effort. Screens generally offer privacy but still let the light enter; they are usually composed of small wood pieces set at a diagonal to a frame. The fence is a vertical element providing privacy and protection. Screens are the least expensive, and the easiest to install.

MASONRY WALL

Almost every wall built of masonry units has two main parts: (1) the above ground wall, (2) the foundation or footing. The forces that act on a wall — such as wind, snow and everyday weight of the wall itself — are transferred down through the wall into the foundation. The foundation is set at an elevation below grade to reduce the chance of frost heave. The foundation transfers the forces into the soil to achieve stability. If the wall also acts as a "retaining wall," where there is a difference in ground level between both sides of the wall, an additional force must be accounted for — the overturning force. To counteract the overturning force, the footing is enlarged in the direction of the highest ground level. The size and character of the foundation is dependent on the quality of the soil you are planning to build on. For long walls, where the wall is to enclose an area completely, joints must be introduced into the wall to allow for expansion or contraction.

Above-Ground Components

Most masonry walls used for exterior gardens are a minimum of 8 in. thick for brick and concrete masonry units. The wall is composed of four ingredients that help determine its structural capability and its weathering characteristics: the masonry unit, the joint reinforcement, the mortar, and the pattern or structural bond achieved by the quality of workmanship.

Brick Masonry Units. Brick used for garden walls should meet the requirements for a grade SW (severe weather) Face Brick. Used or salvaged brick should not be chosen for exterior garden walls unless the material is graded for severe weather. There are many types of brick garden walls, with new variations appearing constantly. Perforated walls of brick resulting in brick screens are becoming more common. Perforated screen walls can be created with the types of bricks to be discussed. If you decide that a perforated wall is needed, the dimensional proportions and reinforcement should be carefully followed.

The most-used brick garden wall is the straight wall. This type of wall relies on the texture and color of the brick for its character. To determine the maximum thickness of the wall based on its height,

Unfinished redwood fence offers visual privacy without a feeling of isolation. Adjoining cement block wall has been parged with plaster for stucco finish.

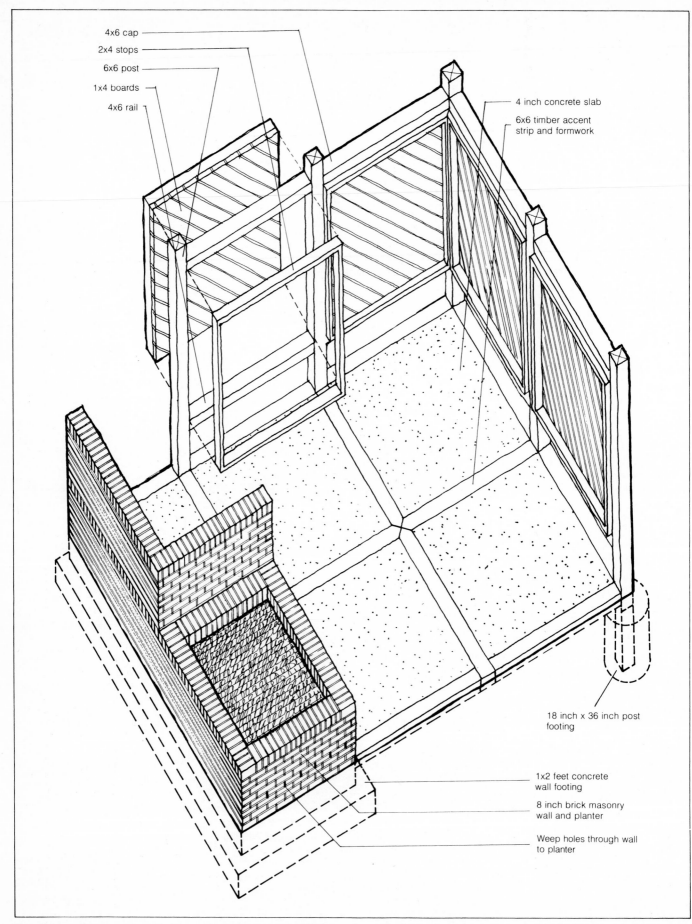

4x6 cap

2x4 stops

6x6 post

1x4 boards

4x6 rail

4 inch concrete slab

6x6 timber accent strip and formwork

18 inch x 36 inch post footing

1x2 feet concrete wall footing

8 inch brick masonry wall and planter

Weep holes through wall to planter

This diagram shows components for wood screens, fences and brick walls, and indicates how simple they are to build. The same principles that apply to building a brick wall also serve when building a planter.

the wall thickness must not be any less than the following:

Wall Height Above Grade	Thickness
2 ft.	4 in.
4 ft.	8 in.
6 ft.	10 in.
9 ft.	12 in.

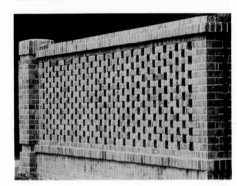

Perforated screen walls require careful placement and planning, but can result in unusual decorative effects.

The recommended thicknesses are based on a wall that will be subjected to a wind pressure of 10 lb. per sq. ft. If you live in coastal zones where this value is exceeded, the above must be increased by 1 in. for every 10 psf additional. This type of wall will be described later under "Construction of A Brick Masonry Wall." Another type of brick garden wall is the "pier" wall. A 4-in. brick wall is built between brick piers. The distance between the piers is limited by the height of the wall and the wind pressure. The piers must be reinforced. One wall that has been used for several generations is the serpentine wall. The serpentine shape provides lateral strength to the wall so that the wall can normally be built of 4 in. brick. The radius of the serpentine curve is dictated by the height of the wall. The radius of a 4-ft. wall should be twice the height of the wall above grade. This means that a serpentine wall 4 ft. above

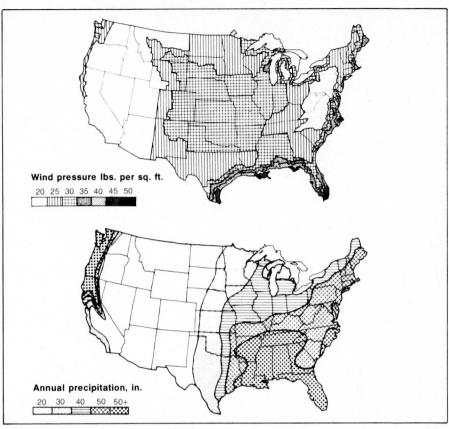

Wind pressure lbs. per sq. ft.

20 25 30 35 40 45 50

Annual precipitation, in.

20 30 40 50 50+

Exposure conditions are broken down as: severe — annual precipitation, 30 in. or over, wind pressure 30 lb. per sq. ft. or over; moderate — precipitation 30 in. or over; wind pressure 20 to 25 lb. per sq. ft.; slight — annual precipitation less than 30 in., wind pressure less than 20 in.

The outlined brick is a stretcher, laid flat with its longest dimension lengthwise along the face of the wall.

Headers are laid perpendicular to the face of the wall, short end showing. Headers connect the two wythes and create bond patterns.

Serpentine walls follow a simple mathematical relationship to assure stability, and require a wider foundation than a straight wall.

A course of headers interspersed regularly among courses of stretchers forms the common bond wall.

A course of headers every other course, with courses of stretchers in between, results in a Flemish Bond wall.

Running bond is composed entirely of stretchers. The mortar joints in alternate courses line up vertically; each vertical joint is centered over the middle of the brick below.

grade should have a radius of 8 ft. The overall dimensions of the wall should be a multiple of 4 in., to minimize cutting of the brick.

The above options for a brick masonry wall include possible decorative surface patterns. The pattern bonds are available in a variety of shapes, textures and forms. The most common is the running bond pattern. It is the easiest to use and requires the minimum of brick cutting.

Concrete Masonry Unit. Concrete masonry units or concrete block are similar to the brick masonry unit in that they are modular and form similar wall structure. Concrete block for exterior garden walls should meet the load-bearing concrete masonry unit requirement, for which your supplier will be able to provide specific, localized information. The two types of block walls are: the solid wall and the perforated wall or screen. Within those two types are a variety of patterns and textures. Generally the pattern bonds most used for solid walls are running bond and the stack bond. For screens or perforated concrete block walls, a stack bond is preferred. The perforated block is a standard shape available from the dealer. It normally is available in 4- or 8-in. widths, but availability may vary by region. For exterior application, the 4-in. block is the recommended minimum thickness for a wall up to 4 ft. From 4 ft. to 8 ft. in height, an 8-in. wall should be used. All of the walls must be reinforced. If the block is to be used in a screen configuration, all joints must be reinforced due to the delicacy of the wall.

Reinforcement. The reinforcement for the brick masonry wall and the concrete masonry wall is of two types: horizontal joint reinforcement and vertical reinforcement. The horizontal joint rein-

forcement is a very thin wire that has been formed into a miniature truss. It is laid flat in the mortar joint. Its purpose is to add stiffness to the horizontal section of the wall. It comes in different thicknesses and shapes. Durowall or Truss Wall are the trade names most often recommended. Consult your supplier for the specific type available. The #3 vertical reinforcement bar which is placed in the vertical joints of a brick wall or in the cells of a concrete block is generally a "deformed billet" bar. Once placed into the construction, the grout or mortar is then placed around it to create structural strength and stability.

Mortar. Mortar is the glue that bonds the masonry units together. The mortar type most frequently used is Type M or Type S. This type of mortar is used for exterior application only, and can be purchased in premix form.

Workmanship. The last ingredient is the most variable. It can influence the strength, quality and longevity of the wall workmanship. The art of building a wall is an experience that everyone should try. It requires experimentation and continuous trial and error. Even the most experienced mason will periodically err in the building of the wall. Workmanship is an acquired ability. This ability can be developed, and should not deter you from building a masonry wall. Once you have set the first course of bricks, it will become easier and easier.

Foundation or Footings

The second major element in a garden wall is the foundation. It is rarely seen, and yet it demands time and effort to build a suitable base. Most garden walls are continuous. They move around the garden, defining the space in a variety of forms and shapes. The foundation must be constructed to allow the wall to follow these shapes. The most-used type of foundation for a garden wall is the continuous wall footing. It is rectangular in form, built of concrete, and is reinforced. Its width is dependent on the amount of load to be transferred into the soil and the quality of the soil. The following recommendations for the size of footing must be modified for your locale:

Wall Height & Thickness	Width of Footing	Depth of Footing
4 ft. 8 in.	20 in.	10 in.
6 ft. 10 in.	22 in.	12 in.
9 ft. 12 in.	24 in.	12 in.

These are minimum sizes. If you plan to place your footing in an area where there is a high water table and the footing will be in it, or a foot above it, these sizes must be increased 50% in width and 10% in depth. There are many other types of footings, but few of them are applicable to the continuous wall requirement.

The depth of footing below ground level is determined by the local code. If you live in a northern climate, you may

Butter inside face of brick before placing on mortar bed. Cored "SCR" brick reduces weight of wall, but is not suitable for areas of heavy rainfall.

find that the bottom of the footing must be at least 36 to 48 in. below the ground level, while in a southern climate the depth of footing ranges from 12 in. to 36 in. The main purpose is to prevent frost heave, and cracking of the wall. In the event you have a wall that is "retaining" some earth at a higher level, the depth of footing measurement is taken from the lowest possible level of ground. If you have a wall that steps up or down a hill, the footing must step up or down, still maintaining its position below the surface. Always extend the foundation 12 in. beyond the finished edges of the wall, 6 in. on each side.

LAYING OUT YOUR GARDEN WALL

Whether the wall is to be built of brick or concrete, you must lay out the path of the wall. This will help you set the foundation, determine the quantities of materials, and choose the method of construction required. There are a number of considerations when laying out the wall: the position of the wall in relationship to the deck or patio area (to head off any conflicts in the construction); the overall height required (so you can decide if scaffolding is necessary); the slope of the land (to resolve the shape of the wall), and the thickness (to estimate the quantities of material required). Once you have made these decisions, transfer the information to paper as described in Chapter 4 on "Drawing your Plan."

BUILDING PERMITS

If wall construction will coincide with the building of a deck or patio, the building permit that you will apply for includes building the wall. In the event that the wall is the sole element to be built, the

This high retaining wall is the net result of regrading severely sloping terrain. The area nearest the house has been leveled to allow placement of the patio.

drawing submitted for review must show: the overall height, location of openings, distance of wall from property line, type and size of footing, material and position of the house or building relative to the wall. Once the permit has been issued, the inspector will wish to inspect the footing prior to its being filled in. Make sure you schedule an appointment at that point. This procedure varies from community to community, so it is very important that you check on the local specific requirements.

HOW TO BUILD A MASONRY GARDEN WALL

This section will provide you with the necessary construction information and

tips to be used in building brick or concrete masonry walls. For purposes of demonstration, a 4-ft. high brick wall will be constructed. There may be parts or portions of the procedure that you may wish to subcontract out. In this event, simply pick up where the subcontractor left off. The procedures outlined will apply to concrete block as well. If differences occur, they will be pointed out and explained.

Retaining walls, can double as planters; this stepped-back series of beds gives an impression of additional space and adds to the usability of the sloping ground.

Lay heavy mortar bed before filling in corner leads. Butter the ends of each brick and check the thickness of your mortar joints in each direction for a strong, even wall.

Step One: Preparing the Site

Clear the area. Any shrubs, bushes or trees should be removed to give access to both sides of the wall. Stake the approximate area in which you will work. This will give you some idea where to store your materials so that you will not have to go back and forth so much. Strip the ground surface of sod or other ground cover. Make sure that no overhead wires will enter into your work zone.

This site has been regraded for landscaping. Supporting columns for the overhead will be placed around the perimeter of the concrete.

Step Two: Staking the Foundation

To lay out the foundation prior to excavation you must stake the actual dimensions of the wall. If the wall starts at the corner of the house, use the triangulated survey method discussed in the construction of a patio or deck (Chapters 5 and 6) to determine the line. Once you have located the line of the wall, stake the interior and exterior faces of the wall, allowing a thickness of 8 in. Follow the line until you come to the end of the wall or the first corner. Stake the end of the wall or exterior corner. Connect the stakes with string so you can see the shape of the wall. Having located all openings in the wall using stakes, you can now stake out the footing line. Measure out, from either side of the wall stakes, the desired width. In this example, add 6 in. from both faces of the wall for a total width of 20 in. Drive these stakes as deep as you possibly can, since you will be excavating around them. Repeat this procedure at the other end of the wall. Connect all the stakes with line. Verify all dimensions and distances. They need not be exact to the inch, as you will be repeating this procedure again for the wall after the footing has been poured.

Step Three: Footing Excavation

Before excavating the staked-out area, place another stake along the exterior line of the footing at some distance beyond the area to be excavated. Place another stake, in line, at the other end of the wall, if possible. This will keep your line in place if the stakes are disturbed. Excavate to the required depth. Put the excavated dirt in a spot that will not interfere with pouring the footing or building the wall. Dig down to the desired level and form a trench 20 in. wide. Allow just a little on each side so that the formwork can be installed. Make sure the bottom of the trench is clear of any loose debris and is level. Use a carpenters level or a line level to check.

Step Four: Forming the Footing

The forms for the footing need not be perfect, since most of the concrete will never be seen once the grass fills in. Therefore, 2x4s and ½ in. CD plywood can be used. Cut the plywood in strips 12-in. high and 8 ft. long. Place the plywood along the lines that were staked out in Step Two. Tap the top of the plywood into the excavation. To hold it in place, drive it next to the 2x4 stake on the outside. Where the joint occurs, reinforce it with a 2x4. Stake and nail the plywood to the 2x4s. Fill in around the formwork.

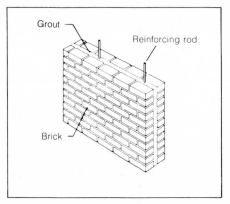

Reinforced brick walls offer higher resistance to lateral forces or loading pressures. They are often used as retaining walls.

Oil the inside face of the forms so that they can be easily removed. You should now have a formwork that outlines the footing, 20 in. wide and about 12 in. deep. If your footing will be 10 in. deep, fill in with some of the excavated soil and tamp soundly over the entire length of the form. Cut off all stakes just above the form. Place two #5 reinforcing steel bars into the form. Locate each one 3 in. from the outside edge and above the bottom of the trench. Place them and tie to a brick laid on its side. You are now ready to pour the footing.

Step Five: Pouring the Footing

Pour the concrete into the formwork. Start at one end, working the concrete by spading it or rodding it. When placing it, do not allow the concrete to fall more than three feet or the aggregate will separate from the cement. Once the form is filled along the entire length, get a small 2x4 on edge and screed the entire length using the edge of the formwork as the level. There is no finishing of the concrete required beyond the screeding. Fill in all depressions and rescreed. Once the formwork has been screeded, install #3 steel bar dowels every 32 in. on center. They should stick out of the concrete 24 in. and should be placed along the centerline of the wall. The wall will then be formed around the dowels. The hooked ends of the dowels should be carefully placed into the concrete. An alternative is to get straight dowels and simply drive them into the bottom of footing once the concrete has been poured. Make sure they are accurately placed.

Step Six: Removing the Formwork

After the concrete has been cured for three days by wetting it down on a regular basis, the formwork can be removed. Strip the formwork and fill around footing, tamping the earth down around the footing. You can now build the masonry wall.

Step Seven: Construction

Snap a chalkline on the footing to help you accurately align the block or brick. Space the brick or block over the length of the wall to determine the joint sizes. (At this point you are laying the bricks out without mortar.) Both the interior and exterior wythes should be laid out — each line of brick is called a wythe. Keep brick moist to prevent its drawing the moisture from the mortar and weakening the bond.

Starting at one corner, spread a full, thick mortar bed for the first course. Lay the exterior corner brick first, positioning it very carefully. Take another brick and "butter" the inside face. This brick is then set alongside of the first one to form the inside face of the wall. As each brick is buttered on its end, it is then brought over its final position and pushed downward into the mortar bed and against the previously laid brick. The setting motion is similar to taking a brush and scrubbing the floor. The scrubbing that takes place is what provides the bond between the bricks. After several bricks have been laid, a masons line is used as a straight-edge to assure that they are in correct alignment. To bring to proper level and plumb, tap on the brick with the trowel handle. If a brick has receded, gently tap from behind to bring face flush with line. The first course of masonry should be laid as accurately as possible, since subsequent courses will rely on the first course for alignment. Once the base course is down, build the corners by laying up the next several courses at the corner, keeping the corners always about 18 in. higher than the center of the wall. As each course is laid at the corner, it is checked for plumb, alignment and level using the masons line. At the same time, each course is checked with a level to make sure all the joints are lined up and in the same plane.

Once the corners are set, a line can be stretched between corners for each course. As you spread the mortar over the lower course, make sure it is plastic.

As each brick end is buttered and scrubbed into place, the joint between the brick — as well as the one underneath the placed brick — will ooze mortar. Simply strike off the excess with the trowel. To assure a good bond, do not spread the mortar too far ahead or it will dry out too soon. Every other course must be started with a header course. This will result in the bricks being offset by one half a brick, which is the basic running bond pattern. Always work from the corners to the middle.

Turning the Corner. First, lay down two mortar lines on the foundation, just inside the chalkline. Lay the first brick on the corner, and then butter and lay up the second brick, using your steel square to ensure that the two bricks create a right angle. Now lay up the next four bricks along the chalklines, extending out from the corner, alternating placement (see illustration), until you have a six-brick corner. Form the backup wythe in the same way, leaving enough space between this row of bricks and the first to create an exact fit for the capping course (row-locks). The bricks in this second wythe must meet at a right angle and overlap the first wythe by half a brick. In building up the second course of the first wythe, place a full brick so that it covers half of Brick 1 and half of Brick 2 (header), and the next

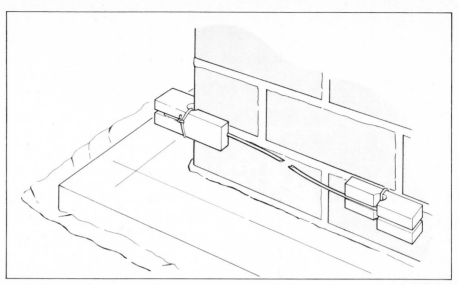

Use mason's line as guide for filling in between ends and corners of walls. Hook block around end brick of one corner, aligning with top of brick, and extend line to other end or corner of wall.

Painted stucco (plaster) coated walls offer increased brightness to patio area, provide a wind break and an attractive background for colorful or unusual plantings.

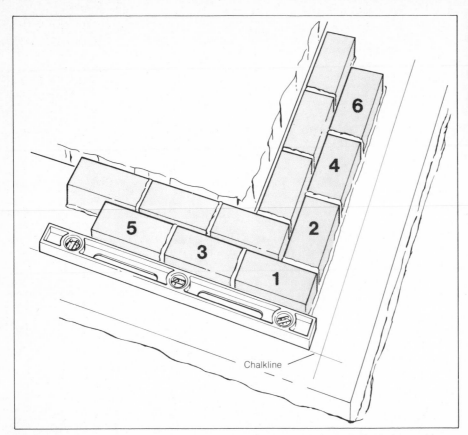

Spread two perpendicular mortar lines just inside of chalklines. Lay first brick at outside corner, and then work alternately from side to side, as shown. Build up six-brick corner lead. Then do the same for the inside wythe.

Natural boulders and cut stones in this retaining wall keep some of the natural look of the sloping terrain while protecting the patio.

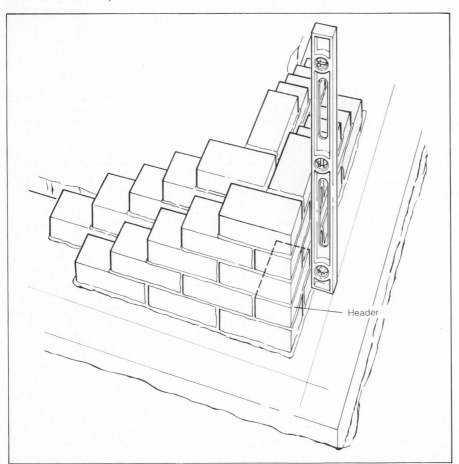

Lay header to start second course. This will offset brick and create a running bond pattern.

Capping course for a brick corner sets rowlocks to the end. Then continue rowlock bricks by placing perpendicular to previously laid row.

Brick is buttered for placement on edge as rowlock, across both wythes.

brick over half of Brick 1 and Brick 3. Continue in this manner in succeeding courses in order to create a staggered pattern (running bond).

Reinforcing. Having completed the first 6 courses (16 in. high), horizontal joint reinforcement must be set. Spread a layer of mortar about a ½ in. thick over both lines of brick (wythes). Push the reinforcing into the mortar bed until it appears fully seated. Lay the corner brick of the next course over it by buttering the bottom of the brick and placing it into position. Tap the brick until the joint is the same thickness as the others. Remove the excess mortar and repeat the operation for both the wythes. Place the ties on 24-in. centers, reaching across the two wythes to hold them together. The reinforcing will be placed every six courses vertically. After the next six courses, stagger the reinforcing horizontally so that trusses fall between the row of trusses previously set.

Tooling the Joints. When the mortar is thumb hard, but not completely set, all the joints must be tooled before the mortar sets. A joint tool with a concave or vee shape edge is the simplest to use. Draw the tool along the joint while pushing in slightly. This will cause a slight depression of the joint while at the same time smoothing it out. Do this to all the vertical joints before starting on the horizontal joints.

Flashing and Capping the Wall. As you approach the top of the wall, but

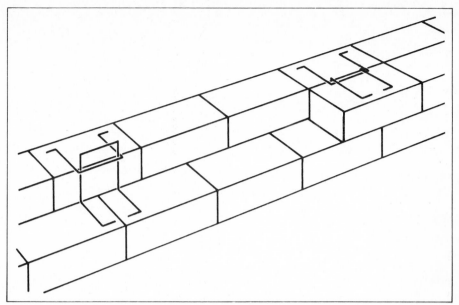

Adjustable metal mini-trusses (wall ties) handle different heights of brick wythes. Longer "U" section lies across one wythe, holding vertical arm of "L" section that lies on other wythe. For secure reinforcing, the two sections may meet at any level ranging from the base up to ½ in. from top of "L". Install ties every 2½ sq. ft. of wall area with at least ⅝ in. mortar bed.

This large, formal series of pools set with geometric forms of tile and bricks is the center of a garden which uses both natural growth and trimmed, formal plantings and planters.

Place closure brick very carefully. All edges of the opening and all four vertical edges should be buttered.

before capping the wall, the wall should be flashed. Flashing keeps the water from entering into the wall and weakening the joints. It is a very thin metal sheet or plastic cloth that is put over the length of the wall before the capping course is installed. Stop the coursing 4 in. below the top of the finished wall height. Place a layer of mortar about ½ in. thick over the wall and lay down the flashing. To cap, set the brick on its side with the weathering surface facing upwards; capping a wall is crucial to its strength. Place mortar on the sides of the brick which will be used for the capping course. Then place the brick on the flashing. Press down until the mortar oozes from the joint, and remove the excess. Repeat this procedure until the wall has been capped. Make sure that all joints have been struck and compressed lightly with the joint tool. Once the wall is finished, do not clean the surface immediately. Wait for at least a week; then scrub the wall down with a brush and a solution of hydrochloric acid in ten parts water. This will etch the brick to its natural coloring. After the scrubbing, rinse the wall.

The capping rowlock seals the flashing and unites both wythes. First lay bricks without mortar to find spacing. If partial brick is needed, place it 4 or 5 units from the end.

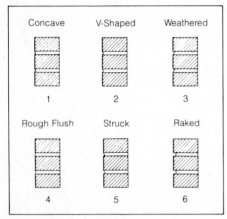

Concave	V-Shaped	Weathered
1	2	3
Rough Flush	Struck	Raked
4	5	6

Cross-sections of mortar joints: (1) and (2) small, formed with steel jointing tool, resists rain; (3) worked from below, sheds water; (4) simplest, made with trowel edge, not always watertight, also called rough cut; (5) most common, easily struck with trowel, does not shed water easily; (6) mortar removed while soft using square-edged tool, gives shadow patterns, not for areas of heavy rainfall.

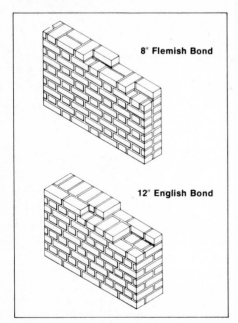

8″ Flemish Bond

12″ English Bond

Masonry bonded walls are not as resistant to rain as metal-tied walls, and should be used only in areas of slight exposure. Joints must be completely filled.

Brick, rigid in structure, can be set in easy curves as in this series of garden walls and edgings or in straight, linear patterns as in the patio surface shown.

Retaining walls of more than 3 ft. should be designed and built by a professional, since stress and pressure on an improperly engineered higher wall could cause it to give way.

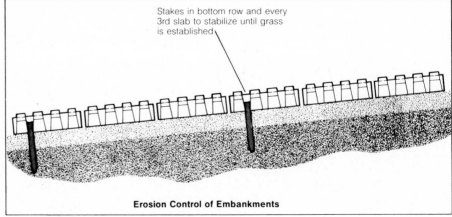

Stakes in bottom row and every 3rd slab to stabilize until grass is established

Erosion Control of Embankments

Sloping ground can be stabilized using concrete precast units. This can substitute in some cases for a retaining wall.

Step Eight: Finishing the Wall

Before filling in the area around the base of the wall, the area underneath must be treated for moisture in the ground. There are two methods that can be used. The first involves brushing on a bituminous coating that is composed of asphaltic tars. This can be purchased in most hardware stores. Cover the area that will be below ground. Make sure not to brush it onto any of the exposed area, since the black surface is not very attractive. The other method is to parge (coat) the surface with a ¼ in. layer of cement plaster to form a protective shield against the moisture. This cement plaster can be purchased at any hardware store; it is troweled on as you would apply plaster. Both methods are effective. Once you have treated the below-ground face of the brick you can infill around the wall. Tamp the earth solidly before placing next to it whatever material you had selected as a wearing surface.

Concrete block walls can be decorative as well as functional. If the wall rests on the edge of a concrete patio, a separate foundation need not be built.

Concrete Block Walls

The major difference between brick and block construction is that the block is already 8 in. wide. This means you will build only one wythe. To begin your block wall prepare a base as for a brick wall, then put a thick layer of mortar at the corner of your footing using a masonry trowel. Lay corners first, by placing the first corner block firmly into the mortar bed at the corner. Mortar all the exposed edges and set the second block in place. As you lay the block, butt it firmly against the first block already positioned. Check the square and the level frequently. Make sure all the joints are equal in size. Don't spread the mortar too far ahead, or it may harden and lose its plasticity. Place the

horizontal reinforcing in the same manner as required for brick, but every two courses rather than every six. When capping a concrete block wall, flashing is not required. Simply place solid concrete blocks on the mortar bed, making sure that the joints are well mortared.

The wall is now complete. If you had indicated any openings in the wall, they would be formed in the same way as the end of the wall. If gate hardware were required, it would normally be placed into a mortar joint or anchored into the finished material.

Concrete block with pattern in three-dimensional-relief offers dynamic design as well as traditional solidity and strength.

Spread a full mortar bed and furrow with a trowel for lots of mortar along the bottom edges of the faces of the first course.

Carefully position the first block. Lay block with thicker end of face shell up.

For vertical joints, butter only ends of face shells. Place several block on end for quick application of mortar to vertical face shells.

Bring each block over its final position and push downward into mortar bed, and against previously laid block, for well-filled vertical mortar joints. After laying three or four blocks, use mason's level to check alignment of block. Carefully check block for level, and bring to proper grade.

Make sure block is plumb; tap block with trowel handle to seat firmly in mortar. After the first course has been completed, apply mortar only to face shells of block. Build up corner leads first. Use level to check that block faces are all in same plane. Step each course back half a block. Check horizontal spacing by placing a level diagonally across the corners of the block.

Fill in between corners, using mason's line as guide. For exact placement, tip block slightly toward you until you see upper edge of course below.

If you are able to work rapidly, you can cut unset mortar extruded from newly made joints and apply it to the vertical face shells of the block just laid.

For strong joints, apply mortar to vertical faces of both block being set and block just laid.

In some areas a full mortar bed may be specified, as shown, for all concrete block construction. Check local requirements. If there is a delay that causes mortar to stiffen, remove the mortar to board and rework.

For V-shaped joints, use a tool made from a ½ in. square bar.

If supporting overhead cover, wood plates should be placed on top of wall as connecting surfaces. Place anchor bolts in cores of top 2 courses of block; fill cores with concrete or mortar.

To hold concrete or mortar in cores, place pieces of metal lath in second horizontal mortar joint from top of wall and under cores to be filled. Extend threaded end of bolt above top of wall. When filling hardens, fasten wood plate.

Carefully lower closure block into place. If any mortar falls out, leaving an open joint, remove closure block, apply fresh mortar, and reposition.

Tool horizontal joints first. Then strike the vertical joints with a small S-shaped jointer.

For continuous vertical joints, full and half-length blocks are used. This allows building paper or roofing felt to be inserted for a control joint.

Cut paper or felt wide enough to extend across joint. This keeps mortar from bonding on one side of joint and creates a control joint.

Sometimes an offset jamb block can be used at control joints, with a noncorroding metal tie bent in an open "Z" and laid across the joint.

Use L-shaped corner blocks, or lay up corner using 8x8x16 block on outside corner, and concrete brick to fill space left on inside corner.

Control joint block is available in some areas. Its tongue-and-groove shaped ends help give lateral support.

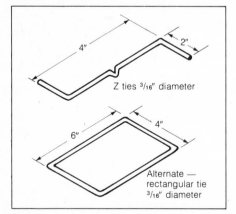

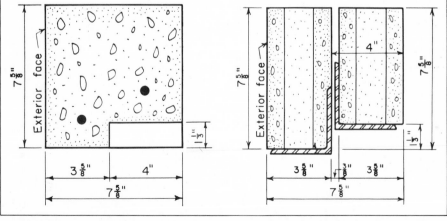

The most common wall tie for concrete block is a Z tie of $3/16$ in. diameter steel. Space at least one tie per $4\frac{1}{2}$ sq. ft. of wall area. Space vertically no more than 18 in.; space horizontally no more than 36 in. Stagger in alternate courses.

For openings in wall, precast concrete lintels are designed with an offset on the underside. Steel angles (above right) can also be used as lintels to support block over openings. To fit openings, steel lintel angles must be installed with offset on underside.

PARTS OF A FENCE AND SCREEN

For purposes of discussion, the fence and screen discussed will be of wood. While there are a number of other materials available to you, wood is the most popular material. In the same way that a wall can provide privacy, a fence or screen can also allow air movement or light to filter onto the deck or patio. There are five main parts to a fence or screen:

(1) the posts;
(2) the rails;
(3) the infill;
(4) the foundation;
(5) the gate.

The differences between a wood fence and a wood screen are mainly in the infill. The following discussion will illustrate the similarities as well as differences.

The forces that act on a fence arise primarily from wind pressure. The main problem to watch for is the overturning force, for which you need footings of sufficient depth to withstand the force. All vertical loads are transferred into the soil by the post set into the footing.

The Posts

The wood posts are usually the first structural element to be installed. They are usually 4x4 in.; for round posts, a 4 to 6 in. size may be used. The posts are usually placed on 8-ft. centers. That means there are intermediates that span from post to post; the intermediates are often called the top and bottom fence rails. Most posts are set in a posthole or concrete foundation. The bottom ends should always be treated to prevent rot. This treatment can be a bituminous substance that is brushed onto the embedded portion of the post. The height of the post depends on the height of the fence and the depth of the posthole. The following list offers height guidelines.

Five-ft. fence	2-ft. posthole	7-ft. post
Six-ft. fence	3-ft. posthole	9-ft. post
Eight-ft. fence	4-ft. posthole	12-ft. post

It is easier to work with square posts than round ones. If the fence you are using comes preassembled and uses round posts, be sure the posts are precut;

this will reduce the difficulty of construction. The wood most often used for posts includes redwood, cedar, spruce, pine or fir. Some lumber yards have pretreated material in stock, which means you will have less work in preparing the fence.

The Rails

The members that span from post to post are called the rails. The top and bottom rails are often the secondary support, and transfer the load from the infill to the posts. There are several ways to attach the rails to the posts. Top rails should be mitered at the corners. Rails are usually built from 2x4 or 2x6 material, and are the same species as the posts. Rails can also be placed diagonally across the posts to act as bracing.

The Infill

It is the infill that offers design possibilities. Some options will be illustrated in this chapter. Some of the designs are: alternate widths, basketweave, alternate panels, diagonal, lattice, to name a few.

The end of this fence is cantilevered. The support rail can be extended beyond the last post by about one-third the span between the posts.

Varying the wood infill can result in differing visual effects.

Posts and railings for wood screen or fence can become part of the pattern and design of your patio area.

The material ranges in size from 1x1 in. pieces up to 1x8 or 1x10 in. boards. The infill is attached directly to the rails and can, depending on the location of the rails, extend above and below the rails. The species are varied: redwood, spruce, hemlock, fir, bamboo, etc. Some of the infill panels are prefabricated. Your local lumber yard should have several styles available for immediate delivery.

The Foundation
The post is the support for the fence or screen. The post can be sent directly into the ground in a posthole or, if required, set into a concrete foundation. If a posthole is dug larger than is required, the post can be placed in it and concrete poured around the post. This is the least time-consuming method.

The Gate
No discussion of fences is complete without some mention of gates. Always brace a gate by attaching a diagonal from one corner to the other. This keeps the gate from warping. Gate posts should be sturdier than the fence posts, since they are subject to greater forces; 4x6 gate posts usually are used. The gate post should be set in a concrete foundation to insure stability.

The minimum width of a gate should be 36 in.; anything less might not conform to the local building code requirement.

With a prefabricated fence or screen, a matching gate is not always available. Check on the availability of parts or pieces if you select a prefabricated fence.

Laying Out your Fence or Screen
The spacing and positioning of the fence is limited by the size of the infill members. In ready-made units, an 8-ft. module is the basic size and all dimensions should be multiples of that unit. If you have a space that is somewhat less than 8 ft., select a prefabricated type that can be cut down to size easily without damaging the structural capacity. In a customized fence design, you can modify the module, as long as the maximum distance between posts does not exceed 8 ft.

Position the gate or gates in the most usable spot. If your site slopes, the fence will have to step down with the slope. This will affect the length of the posts. Try to locate the fence away from trees, since tree roots are difficult to dig through. Once you have determined the positions of all the pieces and the shape of the fence, transfer the information to paper as described in Chapter 4.

Building Permits
If you have planned your fence in conjunction with the deck or patio, the building permit will include the construction of the fence. Height is the most important factor when applying for a building permit for a fence or screen. Some local codes dictate the maximum heights permitted. When building a fence, keep in mind that the good side of the fence must always look to the outside. The inspector will make sure this is in your design. We recommend that you select a design that will look the same from either side.

CONSTRUCTION OF A WOOD FENCE OR SCREEN
The purpose of this section is to provide you with necessary construction information and tips that are used in the fabrication and assembly of both custom and prefabricated fences and screens. For purposes of demonstration, a 6-ft. screen divider will be used. If you subcontract portions out, pick up where the subcontractor leaves off. Where use of prefabricated units requires different handling than a custom screen divider, those differences in the step-by-step construction procedure will be indicated.

Step One: Preparing the Site
Clear the line that the fence will pass through. At least one foot to either side will be sufficient. Any shrubs, bushes, trees or stones that are in the line should be moved, or the fence should be designed to avoid them. The ground cover need not be stripped unless it has been called for in your landscaping. Make sure that overhead power lines or underground utilities will not interfere with any of the components. Your utility company can provide a site plan of buried lines.

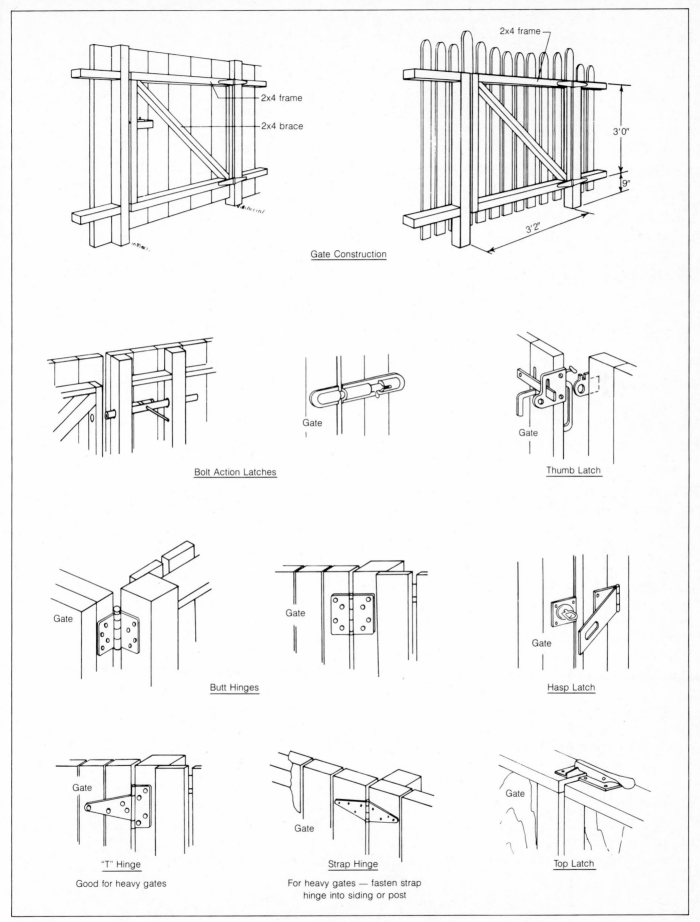

2x4 frame

2x4 frame
2x4 brace

Gate Construction

2x4 frame

3'0"

9"

3'2"

Gate

Bolt Action Latches

Gate

Gate

Thumb Latch

Gate

Butt Hinges

Gate

Gate

Hasp Latch

Gate

"T" Hinge
Good for heavy gates

Gate

Strap Hinge
For heavy gates — fasten strap
hinge into siding or post

Gate

Top Latch

Gate posts should be 4x6 or 6x6 lumber set in concrete, spaced for the gate, which must be at least 3' wide. Both glue and nail the gate for most strength. Install with ½" clearance between gate and latchpost. Use heavy-duty, galvanized metal hinges and latches for greatest durability.

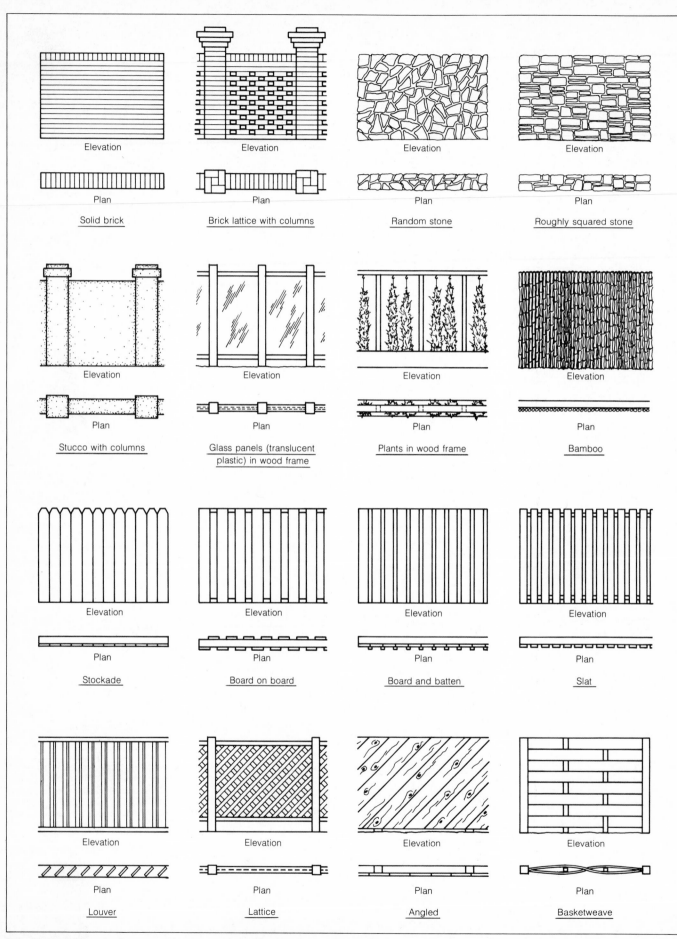

Elevation — Plan — Solid brick

Elevation — Plan — Brick lattice with columns

Elevation — Plan — Random stone

Elevation — Plan — Roughly squared stone

Elevation — Plan — Stucco with columns

Elevation — Plan — Glass panels (translucent plastic) in wood frame

Elevation — Plan — Plants in wood frame

Elevation — Plan — Bamboo

Elevation — Plan — Stockade

Elevation — Plan — Board on board

Elevation — Plan — Board and batten

Elevation — Plan — Slat

Elevation — Plan — Louver

Elevation — Plan — Lattice

Elevation — Plan — Angled

Elevation — Plan — Basketweave

The elevation gives the face-on, side view; the plan indicates the view from above.

Step Two: Staking Postholes

Once you have decided on the path of the fence, you can position the posts. In prefabricated fence, you may desire a model where center-to-center distances are 4, 6 or 8 ft. on center. Check local requirements. In our example, the posts are located on 6-ft. centers. After the spacing has been decided, measure — on a level — the distances between centers and place stakes at each point. Proceed until you have completed the path of the fence. If you require an accurate 90 degree corner, use the triangulated survey method outlined in Chapter 5. Keep in mind that the dimensions are taken from the center of each post to the center of the next post. This is especially important in prefabricated fences. Try to keep the units to even feet. This will avoid waste. Verify all dimensions again.

Step Three: The Posthole

The hardest part of the entire procedure is digging the postholes. If the soil is very hard or difficult to break into, you may want to rent a posthole digger. This cuts out a great deal of work. Auger-type diggers are good for rock-free earth. If digging through tree roots by hand, you must have a clamshell type of shovel. As you start to dig, either manually or by power, make sure the hole is vertical. This will be important in setting the posts. The depth

Eight-foot or nine-foot ties can be cut in half and used for low fences. These vertical ties should be buried about 1½ ft. in the ground. Place corner ties in a concrete footing, or dig a trench and pour concrete after the ties have been positioned and supported.

of the posthole depends upon the height of the fence (refer to the earlier section on posts for the appropriate depth). The diameter of the posthole varies from 6 to 12 in. The larger it is, the more space you have to adjust for alignment. If you plan to set the posts in concrete, dig at least a hole 12-in. in diameter.

Step Four: Setting the Posts

Be sure that the posts are correctly aligned and plumb. If the plumb is off, the fence will appear slipshod. Use a carpenters level to plumb the posts, check all posts on two perpendicular surfaces. The most effective method is to first set the end posts. Once set, connect a string between them. Level it, and then set all the other posts to that line. On a windy day, keep the string close to the ground.

If you are not planning to set the posts in concrete, simply replace the earth you dug out. Pack it evenly around the post perimeter until it is full. Tamp down as well as possible. If you will be pouring concrete around the post, fill in around the bottom of the post with some earth or gravel before pouring concrete. Always pour the concrete so it reaches to 2 to 4 in. below the ground level. This allows the ground cover to pass through the fence and around the posts undisturbed.

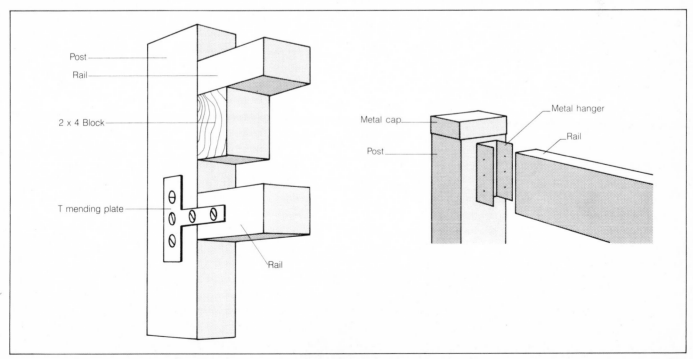

Many kinds of hangers are available to support fence rails and screening. A metal T-shaped mending plate is easy to install to stop wobbling; wooden cleats support rails. Metal post caps protect post tops from weather. Metal hangers, similar to joist hangers, can be used to strengthen joints between posts and rails.

This diagonal infill is applied to a frame that is then attached to the fence frame. To ensure that the fence looks equally good from both directions, install a matching panel with infill for each side of the frame.

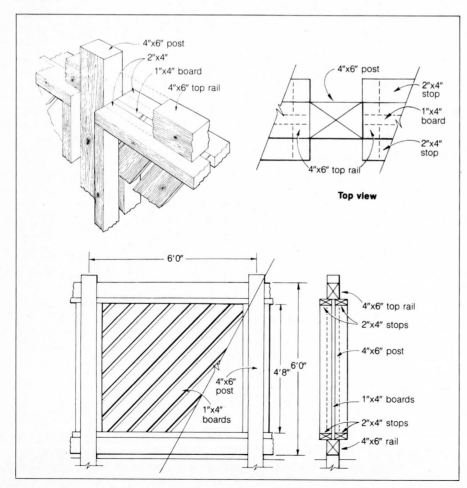

Step Five: Constructing the Screen Divider

This fence design calls for a knot-containing construction grade of wood such as construction heart redwood or a pine. The posts are 4x6 and are 8 ft. 6 in. long. Once the posts are set, check again for alignment, plumb and level.

To fit the 4x6 ft. rails on the bottom of the posts, measure 2 in. up from the ground and carry that mark to the other posts using a carpenters level. Measure the post-to-post (o.c.) distances and cut the 4x6 bottom rails to size. Attach the bottom at the 2 in. mark using 6 in. x 6 in. 12 gauge "L" straps, one to a side. Use galvanized straps and screws, purchased in a hardware store or building center. Toenail the bottom rails to the posts with 16d galvanized nails.

Next, construct two pairs of 2x4 frames that form the stops for the diagonal boards. Measure horizontally and vertically for an exact fit; there will be some variation. In cutting, leave at least 6 in. to the top of the post. After cutting the frames to size, position one of each pair of frames to the post. Allow ⅜ in. from the post centerline to the edge of the frame. Nail to posts and bottom rail with 16d galvanized nails. Sink all nail heads. Check square. Lay the other frame on a flat surface. Make sure the shape corresponds to the one already set into the posts. Position 1x4 boards diagonally across it, providing for a ¼ in. space between the boards. This may be increased to as much as ¾ in. if desired. Nail the boards to the frame using two 8d nails at each board end. Trim the boards flush with the outside of the 2 x 4 frame, or as necessary for your design. Lift the panel into the frame already nailed in place, with the 1x4 boards facing the frame already installed. Nail frame in place using 16d galvanized nails. The last step is to cut the top rails, which are 4x6 pieces cut to size, and attach with "L" straps in the same manner as the bottom rails.

Step Six: Finishing the Fence or Screen

Most materials, like redwood or cedar, do not require any additional finishing such as preservatives or sealants. In the event that the wood you have selected does require a finish, select it based on how you would like the material to weather. If you desire to paint the material, always apply a primer to the wood before the finish coat.

Construction Tips for a Fence

When you have selected a continuous fence as your space divider, the procedures described from Step One to Step Five are the same. The major difference will be in the sizes of the top and bottom rails and the method of attaching them to the posts. The use of metal hardware such as "L" brackets and the like are recommended. The rails can be attached to the outside face of the posts and cut off at the post centerlines. The infill can be 1 x 4 or 1 x 6 boards placed vertically or diagonally across the rails. The boards should be nailed with two 8 penny galvanized nails per board end. Where you desire to have the same finish on the interior as on the exterior, repeat the procedure, attaching the diagonal boards to the inside face of the top and bottom rail. The boards will overhang; trim the ends so they are at least 2 to 4 in. above ground level.

If height between elevations is slight, vertical ties can prevent portions of upper level from washing into lower level. Ties should be lined with roofing paper or shingles to prevent water and soil seepage. Bury bottoms of ties a distance equal to their height above ground, and toenail the top edges.

For drastic elevation differences, use ties vertically or stock horizontally with backsides braced. Nail furring strips to inside for support. If more than 2 ties are stacked, use heavier lumber (2x4s) as braces. Staple roofing paper over braces and against ties before grading ground level to top of wall.

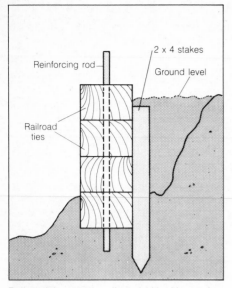

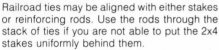

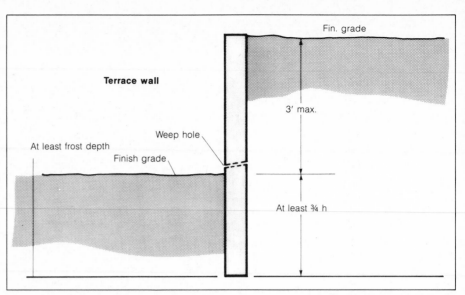

Terrace wall

Railroad ties may be aligned with either stakes or reinforcing rods. Use the rods through the stack of ties if you are not able to put the 2x4 stakes uniformly behind them.

Terrace walls can be used where the difference in grade is no more than three feet and where there is no probability of the wall having to support more than 50 lb. per sq. ft. The wall should completely fill the trench, using concrete backfill if required. Earth below lower grade should be firm, fairly dry, and not easily compressible.

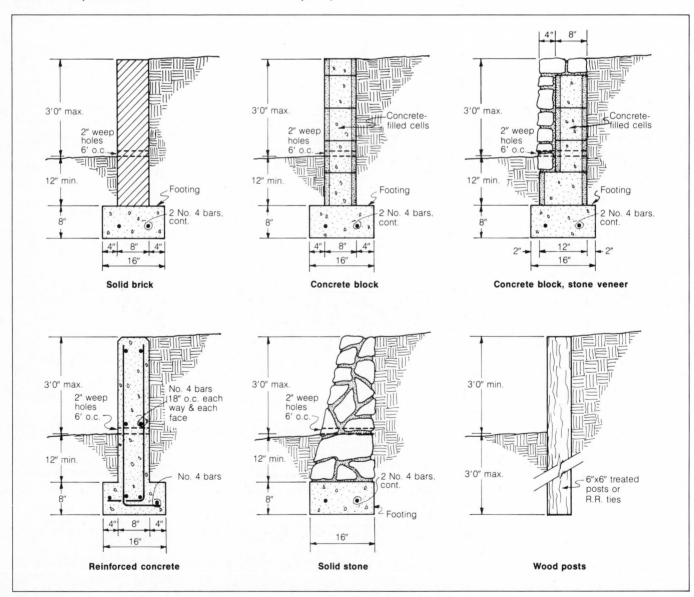

Solid brick

Concrete block

Concrete block, stone veneer

Reinforced concrete

Solid stone

Wood posts

For heights of 3 ft. or less these retaining walls will withstand most conditions. Cores in concrete block are filled for extra rain resistance.

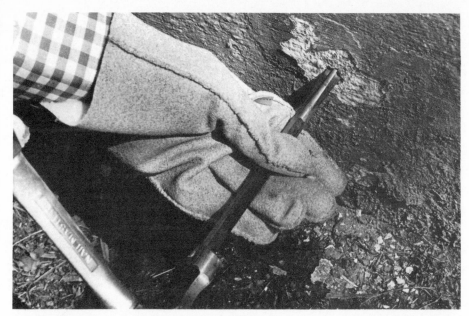

Concrete retaining walls need weep holes to keep moisture from damaging them. Drill holes about every 2 to 3 ft. and push in short pieces of hose as a lining.

Retaining walls can also serve as planters. See instructions for planters in Chapter 9.

In this chapter we will present basic plans for, and then variations on, several types of outdoor furniture and cooking areas. (See Chap. 6, "Built-in Benches.")

OPEN FIREPIT COOKING AREAS

An old-style open barbecue pit is really a firebrick-lined hole in the ground, and should be planned for an out-of-the-way area. In addition, this type of pit should have a raised rim or ledge around it, and a cover, to keep someone from accidentally stepping into it.

To build the pit, map out an area 3 ft. by 4 ft. Locate it close enough to the patio that you can build an open fire and enjoy it, but far enough to one corner so that drifting smoke won't cause discomfort. You may want to call your local National Weather Bureau office at this stage of planning to ask what the predominant wind direction is during the summer months. In addition, check your local fire codes. Open fires are prohibited in some areas. Once you have sited the firepit, dig a 2 by 3 ft. hole to a depth of 2 ft. Fill the bottom 6 in. of the hole with mixed aggregate (gravel) of the same type as is used in making concrete. You can buy a couple bushels at the local lumber, brick or garden center.

Onto this base spread two inches of coarse torpedo sand. Tamp firmly using either a 4x4 post or a hand tamper available at many local hardware stores. Once the base is level, you're ready to begin lining your firepit with firebrick. Buy firebrick at your local brickyard and, while there, ask for the name of the nearest dealer in fire clay. This substance will be mixed with standard mortar mix to make a heatproof mortar to hold the firebrick in place. Try to buy firebricks as close to the size of a common brick (7½x3⅝x2¼) as possible. That will make finishing easier. You will need 180 bricks. Face or decorative brick can be used on top of the pit.

Now, buy your grills. The easiest thing to use for a grill is one taken from an old or discarded oven. The standard size is 16 in. by 22 in. Special, heavier duty grills, made in 12-in. increments, are available at many patio centers.

Upon the sand base, begin laying your bricks in a double row around the pit. Start by laying eight bricks, in a double line of four, at one end. Then, inside that double row, lay two rows of four bricks

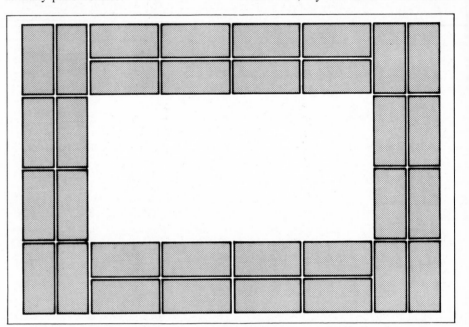

Here is an overhead view of the first brick course for a rectangular firepit. This first course pattern repeats for third and fifth courses.

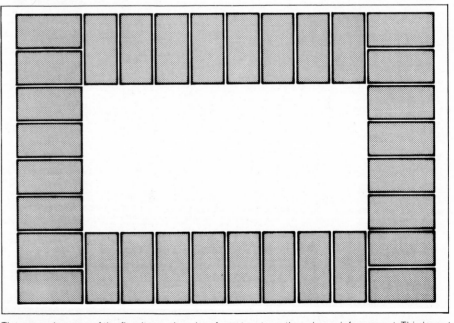

The second course of the firepit uses headers for extra strength and as reinforcement. This layout recurs for the 4th course.

each for the sides (see drawing). End this first course with another double row of four bricks.

You should be trying to keep your mortar joints at approximately ⅜ in. Keep a carpenters level at hand and check your level frequently at both top and sides. Your mortar should be a 10 to 1 mix of mortar and fire clay. For each 40 pounds of mortar mix, add four pounds of the clay.

Laying mortar beneath and to the side of each brick, start your second course by laying bricks directly across the one you have already laid. The third course should cross in the same way, following the first pattern for the first course. Alternate these two types of courses for the third, fourth, and fifth courses. Lay the sixth and final course of bricks on their sides. This will create an automatic ledge for your grills.

After the brick mortar has hardened (about one week), tuckpoint the top of the barbecue pit with wire brush and a mixture of muriatic acid and water (1 part acid to 9 parts water).

MATERIALS LIST: Open barbecue pit
2-3 bushels, mixed aggregate
2-3 bushels, torpedo sand
2 bags mortar mix
10 lbs. fire clay (or buy premixed refractory mortar, if available)
180 firebricks

Firepit Within Patio or Deck

To build a slightly more elaborate firepit in the center of your patio or deck, use cement blocks. The pit must be built before constructing the deck or patio. Connect 2x8s to the block using carriage bolts, to give a finished look and to add strength to the pit. Here are the steps as well as instructions for a table cover and a surrounding deck.

(1) Select a spot in the middle of where your patio or deck will be and lay out a 3 ft. square.

(2) Dig the square out to a depth of 4 in.

(3) Fill the hole with 4 in. of mixed aggregate. Tamp firmly.

(4) Mix mortar with fireclay and water (as in barbecue pit instructions).

(5) Lay blocks on their 3⅝ in. face, three high. Try to keep mortar joints at ⅜ in. or smaller (a minimum of ¼ in. is needed for a good bond). Use a level frequently to keep all blocks perfectly square, both horizontally and vertically.

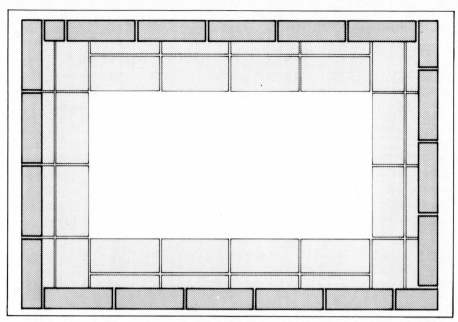

The sixth and final course uses bricks placed on edge so that the fifth course becomes a ledge for the grill. The sixth course keeps the grill in position.

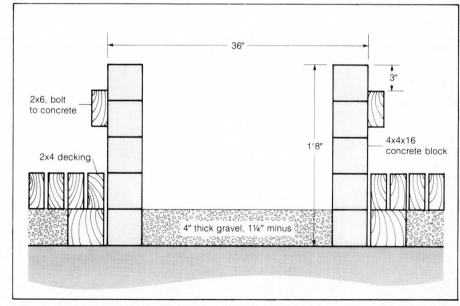

This firepit can have as many courses of 4x4x16 concrete block as desired by adjusting the excavation depth or the final height. A mitered 2x6 surround attaches with carriage bolts.

A firepit placed within a deck should utilize concrete cinder block, large gravel, and pretreated wood. The block should extend above ground level.

(6) After one week, tuckpoint; then drill eight ¼ in. holes. Each hole will be 10 in. from the corner.

(7) Cut four 4 ft. pieces of 2x6s to fit around block walls of firepit and miter corners (45 degree angles).

(8) Nail corners of lumber together around barbecue. Drill ¼ in. holes and then attach to block with carriage bolts, nuts and washers. Nuts and washers will be on the inside of the firepit. Stain and varnish the wood. To cook in the pit, support grills or oven racks on two or three bricks or cement blocks.

MATERIALS LIST: Firepit in deck
1 cu. yd. mixed aggregate
1 cu. yd. torpedo sand
32 15⅝ x 11⅝ x 7⅝ cement blocks (or 40 blocks, 4x4x16)
2 bags mortar mix, plus 10 lbs. fire clay.
4 4 ft. 2x10s
8 ⅜ in. carriage bolts.

Removable cover for the firepit is shown bottom side up. After clamping 2x4s with ¼ in. spacers, nail on 2x2 end caps. The inner 2x2 box holds the top in position so it doesn't slide.

Variation: As A Table. The firepit can also double as a table if you care to make an attractive top for it. To do so, clamp thirteen 4½ ft. 2x4s and twenty-two 2x2x¼ plywood spacers together, using long gluing clamps that are available at any hardware store. Use this photo as a guide. Check dimensions to ensure that the inside ridge (for smaller frame) will fit the outside dimensions of your pit.

BRICK BARBECUE

Built of brick (or you may use concrete block), the barbecue is lined with one wythe of firebrick backed by two wythes of SW common brick, and capped with face brick or cement block. It has tabs set in mortar at several levels to adjust the grill, and bolts on both sides for small shelves that will hold cooked dishes, sauces, and barbecue utensils.

First, cast a 4-in. slab to hold the weight of the barbecue. Set on an 8-in. bed of sand or gravel, the slab can "float" with freeze and thaw cycles, and should not crack. Here are the steps.

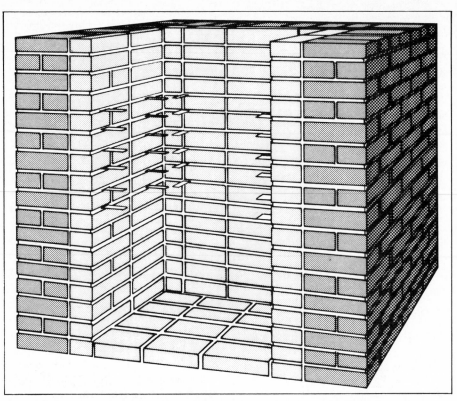

Outer wythe for this barbecue is running bond; middle and inner wythes are stack bond.

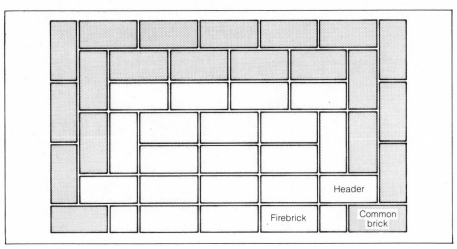

Header in base (shown) and alternate courses ties firebrick inner shell to middle wythe.

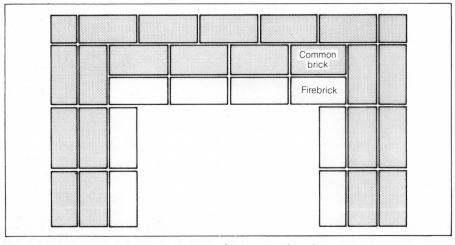

This second course layout repeats as pattern for even-numbered courses.

(1) Dig out a square, 40-in. on a side, to a depth of 8-in.

(2) Fill the hole with 4 in. of crushed aggregate; tamp firmly.

(3) Add 4 more in. of coarse sand; tamp firmly.

(4) Nail four, 42-in. 2x4s into a square form (see sketch).

(5) Oil form with motor oil. Set reinforcing mesh (welded wire) into the form, resting on 1½-2 in. stones as props.

(6) Mix two 90 lb. bags of concrete mix with water, and pour into the forms. Let concrete cure beneath wet burlap or plastic sheeting for one week.•

(7) Using fireclay mortar, build the barbecue's firebox (firebrick interior) first. Snap a chalkline onto the concrete foundation, spread a mortar bed and lay a solid base of firebrick. From the solid, one-course base, build up 16 courses of the firebox, building corner leads first and filling in. When you reach the 8th course, set 7-in. pieces of 1x⅛ in. iron plate into the mortar joints. They will extend 4 in. into the firebox. These will be the supports for the oven racks. Set brackets the same way on the next 5 courses. You can also purchase drop-in cooking units, but measure carefully to ensure that you buy one that fits the dimensions of your barbecue.

(8) Begin work on the outside two wythes of the barbecue. It is not necessary for you to use fireclay mortar for these.

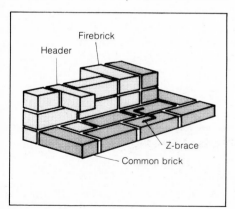

Use Z-braces to reinforce and connect outer two wythes, placing them every other course, staggered vertically. Seat Z-brace in mortar before placing buttered brick on top.

Once you have laid fourteen complete courses, set weatherproof carriage bolts into the mortar and cover with the remaining two courses. Attach brackets and side shelves to bolts after tuckpointing. Wait approximately one week before your first cook-out.

MATERIALS LIST: Barbecue.

One yd. mixed aggregate
One yd. torpedo sand
Two 90-lb. bags of concrete mix
Four sq. ft. 2x4 in. welded wire (fencing) or concrete reinforcing rods
125 firebricks, 7½x3 ⅝x2¼
340 SW common bricks
Four 90-lb. bags of mortar mix
10 lbs. fireclay
Thirty-six 7 in. strips of 1"x⅛" Iron flat plate (or reinforcing rods)
Four weatherproof carriage bolts, nuts and washers
Two A- or angle-iron brackets for shelves
Four 2-ft. 2x8s (or two standard sink cut-outs (for shelves)

BENCHES & TABLES

We will start with how to build a brick bench, for which you will need 140 bricks. The bench should be placed on a concrete slab over a prepared base, as for the barbecue. Lay out a base course 64 in. by 24 in. Set bricks seven courses high, working from corners to middle, building up a lead from corners and then filling in. Now build a wooden top out of three pieces of pretreated 2x12, connected horizontally by five pieces of 1x3 on the underside. The 1x3s will span the 2x12s and will anchor them together, and their

lengths will be the same as the interior width of the bench (24 in. minus two times 3⅝ in. — actual width of brick — equals 16¾ in.). In this case we would suggest that the 1x3s be 16½ in. long to ensure that the top fits easily into the space. The 1x3s thus held hold the top in position. Before attaching the 1x3s, place a 57 in. by 17 in. piece of roofing felt over the rectangle that corresponds to the interior area of the bench. This will help keep the inside of the bench dry, and prevent it filling up with water during a rain. You will note that the top is 9¾ in. wider than the bench. This creates a 4⅞ in. extension all the way around, leaving room for feet to dangle. If you add a cushion to the wooden top, it will be more comfortable, but will prevent your being able to leave the top out in rain or sun.

Fill the center of the bench with concrete to a level of 4 in. to 6 in. This will require two 90 lb. bags of concrete and will offer interior space for storage. Trowel the surface of the concrete so it is smooth. Let the concrete set until it has cured by keeping it under frequently moistened burlap for about a week.

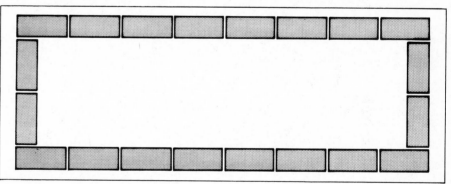

Shown is the basic plan of the first course for a brick bench. The bench may be filled with concrete or rock fill, or left open for storage, or filled with earth to create a planter. Start the next course with a header for a running bond pattern.

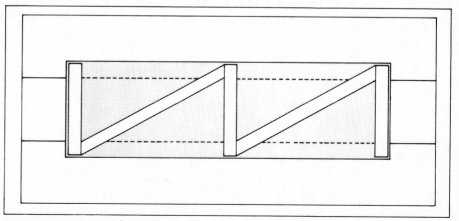

Here is a design for a wooden table top, with an overhang so that feet can dangle comfortably. Use 2x4s to brace, reinforce, and strengthen the top from underneath. As an alternative, use brick to create bench top surface, after filling in core.

Barbecues Built Using Other Materials

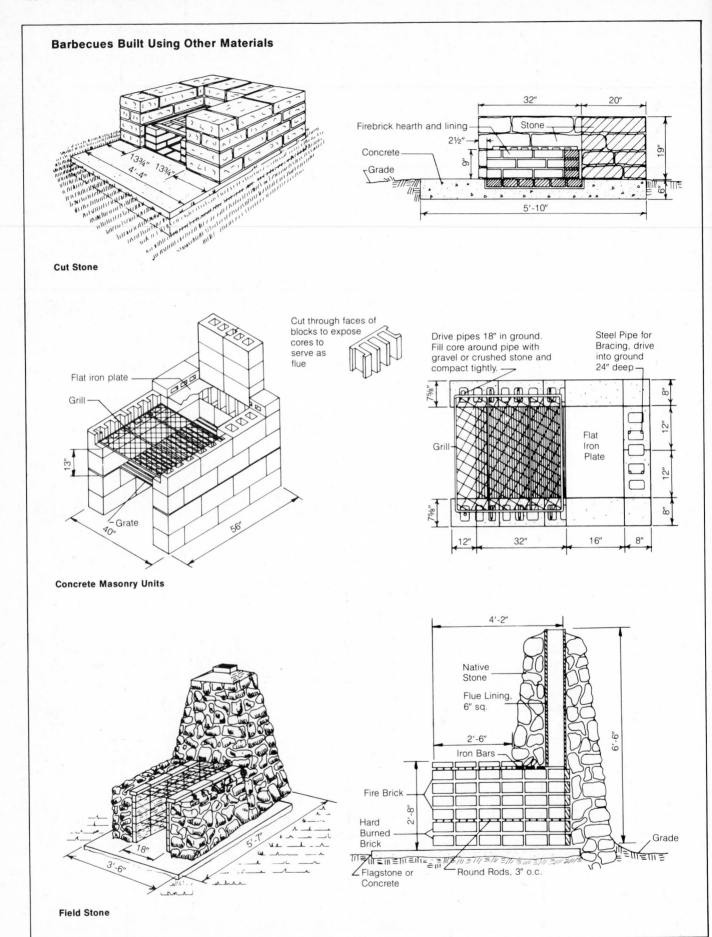

Cut Stone

Firebrick hearth and lining
2½"
Concrete
Grade
Stone
32"   20"
9"   19"   6"
5'-10"

Concrete Masonry Units

Flat iron plate
Grill
13"
Grate
40"   56"

Cut through faces of blocks to expose cores to serve as flue

Drive pipes 18" in ground. Fill core around pipe with gravel or crushed stone and compact tightly.

Steel Pipe for Bracing, drive into ground 24" deep

7⅝"   Grill   7⅝"
8"   12"   12"   8"
Flat Iron Plate
12"   32"   16"   8"

Field Stone

18"   5'-7"   3'-6"

4'-2"
Native Stone
Flue Lining, 6" sq.
2'-6"
Iron Bars
Fire Brick
Hard Burned Brick
2'-8"   6'-6"
Flagstone or Concrete
Round Rods, 3" o.c.
Grade

Barbecues built of materials other than brick follow similar procedures, and should rest always upon a concrete slab for adequate support.

Variation: Brick Table

To build a table, follow the same procedures as for a bench, but higher (and usually in a square or a wider rectangle). The table should be about 30 in. (eleven courses) high. You would need 110 bricks for a table three bricks to a side, with a wooden top. You may build the wooden top on the same principle as for the bench, or you may wish to try a dressier variation. One possibility is to fill the table with concrete once you have reached the 10th course. After curing, set the last course of bricks, covering the top with brick in whatever pattern you desire. After another week, tuckpoint with a wire brush and a mixture of 10% muriatic acid and 90% water. When dry, glue an acrylic top to the brick, using a cement recommended for the acrylic. If the company supplying the glass does not have a recommendation, use a high-quality, clear, waterproof epoxy.

Wooden Bench

The bench plan offered here is free-standing, but with a few modifications, it can become built-in seating attached to a deck rail. Build the 2x12 frame. Place the 2x12 spacers 3′ apart; these spacers determine bench width. Then put together the 2x4 frame for seating, which rests on the 2x12 frame. This is made up of 2x4 cross-members that support 2x4 fascia. Space all cross-members so that they lie on top of the 2x12 spacers. The cross-member length will depend on spacer length and on amount of overhang desired. If the bench will be attached to a fence or rail, nail the back seating frame fascia to the rails or fenceposts. If you build a corner as shown, be sure to place an additional 2x4 cross-member diagonally at the corner to ensure proper support of the staggered seating members.

Position the 2x4 decking for the seat on the top of the seating frame. Before nailing, predrill both ends of each piece to avoid splitting, then nail at each bearing. California Redwood Association recommends the use of vertical grain lumber for seat surfaces, but if flat grain material is used, lay boards with the bark side up (so that growth rings arch upwards) to avoid raising the grain.

Nails and fasteners should be stainless steel, aluminum alloy or top quality, hot-dipped galvanized to prevent stain streaks. 16d nails should be used.

This simple box bench is free-standing, but can also be constructed as a built-in. The overhang allows comfortable foot placement.

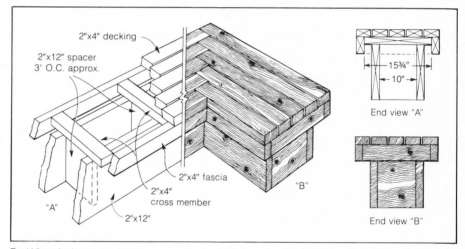

End View A shows the interior components of this bench, while End View B indicates the surface finish materials.

A laminated bench is easy to assemble, and offers design coordination possibilities since table tops, planters, and other furniture can be built in the same style.

Variation: Laminated Bench

You can make a more attractive, laminated bench by nailing good quality 2x4s together and end capping them similar to the firepit table top. The main difference is that the table top was made of 2x2s. Here are the steps.

(1) Clamp ten 6-ft. 8-in. 2x4s together

(on end) with ¼ in. spacers cut from ¼ in. plywood. Nail on end caps to outside 2x4s to create frame. Nail edges of the 2x4s to a 2x4 cap with 16d, weatherproof nails. The cap should measure 18 in., but doublecheck the dimensions and make any necessary adjustments. It could differ as much as ½ in. Remove spacers after nailing.

(2) Cut four 18½ in. 2x4 braces for the seat. Cut off the ends of the braces at a 30-degree angle. Nail and bolt braces to a 50-in., pressure-treated or naturally rot-resistant (cedar, redwood, etc.) 4x4 ft. post.

(3) Toenail the completed brace and support to the bottom of the bench, 16 in. from either end, with 16d weatherproof nails. To make a permanent bench, dig postholes and set posts alongside the patio, to a depth of 3 ft. Mix concrete and pour into the hole. Support the bench in place with boards or cement blocks (or old furniture) until the concrete cures completely — about one week.

The same bench can be built 9 ft. long (start with 8 ft. 8 in. 2x4s), but will need three supports. The first will be set exactly in the center of the bench and the other two will be 14 in. from each end, in the center of each 4x4.

The nails keep the braces in position while drilling two holes through the braces and legs to hold bolts.

Use two ⅜ x 7 in. carriage bolts to secure the braces and bolts.

Braces are nailed to 4x4 pretreated posts that serve as legs for the bench.

If building a longer bench, add another (center) leg with braces and bolts.

Toenail each brace on both sides; then toenail the ends of the braces to the outside 2x4s.

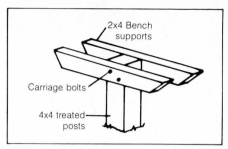

To use this bench as a built-in, attach 2x4 supports with carriage bolts to treated posts.

Butcherblock Parson Bench

This bench uses 2x4s for seatboards and for legs that extend up to become part of the bench top.

Legs. Trim four pieces 18 in. and four $14^7/_{16}$ in. (subtract the width of a 2x4 from 18 in.). Assemble short and long pieces in pairs with six 8d nails and attach to each end of a seatboard, flush on ends and edges.

Laminate. Fit a short seatboard between legs and nail every 6 in. in a zig-zag pattern. Nail-laminate eight long seatboards, alternating zig-zag nailing; then nail remaining legs and the last short and long seatboards.

Corner connections. Completed straight bench sections can be butt-joined at corners without hardware. Or they can be joined with galvanized steel straps nailed across bench edges from underneath.

Herringbone corners. Assemble a 90-degree corner working frame of two long 2x4s about 17¼ in. shorter than the outside length of one bench section. Butt-join them around the corner, nailing with two 12d nails from one board face into an adjacent board end.

Attach bench end legs as above, flush at all edges. Then trim two seatboards to fit inside legs and butt-join at the corner. Nail from each board face into adjacent board ends, and zig-zag nailing along board length, as above.

Assemble eight long 2x4s per bench section, butt-jointed at the corner and trimmed flush at bench ends. Attach outer

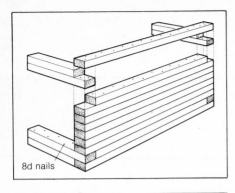

8d nails

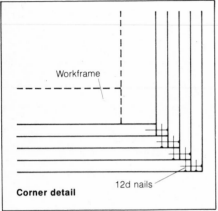

Workframe

Corner detail

12d nails

bench legs and the last short and long seatboards as above.

Center legs. Assemble four short leg pieces (14⅞ in.) in pairs. Attach the inner corner leg with one angle iron on each side. Set the outer corner leg flush with bench edges and attach with two angle irons and one metal strap.

To avoid scratching the seating surface, build the bench on edge or upside down on a flat surface. Use only noncorrosive hardware. To prevent splitting, predrill nail holes near board ends.

MATERIALS LIST:

Bench Length	Lumber used
4 ft.	2 pcs. 6'*
4 ft.	5 pcs. 8'
6 ft.	12 pcs. 6'
8 ft.	10 pcs. 8'
10 ft.	10 pcs. 10'
12 ft.	10 pcs. 12'

*Two 2x4s, 6 ft. long. Use only surface lumber. Nails, hardware: 8d nails, 12d nails, angle irons, galvanized metal strap for corner leg.

Circular Table

When building this table and benches, use either a band saw or a sabre saw capable of cutting 2 in. material.

First cut out rail pieces and notch as shown. Drill all holes in rail pieces before nailing to top pieces. Holes should be ⁷/₁₆ in. in diameter to allow clearance for ⅜ in. bolts.

Now cut pieces for the top. (1) If using a sabre saw, just cut 2x6 to length: five pieces 5 ft. 0 in., two pieces 4 ft. 0 in., and two pieces 3 ft. 0 in. Place the best side down, after marking the centers of these boards, and space them ¼ in. apart. Now line up centers and position rail pieces 8½ in. from the center line. Glue and nail with 8d galvanized box nails. Turn top over and drive a small finish nail in center of top. Using a string and pencil, mark the circular outside edge. Cut on line and then remove the finish nail in center. Finish making the top by drilling a 1⅝ in. hole in center for the umbrella shaft. (2) If using a band saw, mark and cut top pieces before attaching the rail pieces.

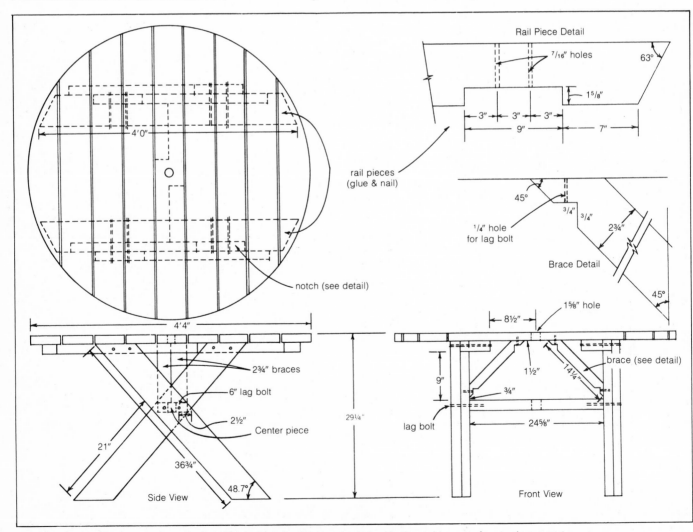

This circular table has two under-rails and diagonal interior braces, as well as horizontal braces, for sturdy support.

To make legs, cut a 42 degree angle on the end of a 2x6 and then measure 36¾ in. (long point to short point) to the other end which is the same angle. The legs can then be clamped or lightly nailed in position on rail pieces making sure that they are crossed properly and that the bottoms of the legs are parallel to the top. Mark holes and drill.

The center piece is a 2x6 that is 24⅝ in. long. Drill two ¼ in. holes in each end that are 1½ in. in from each edge and drill 1⅝ in. hole in center for umbrella shaft.

Using bolts with washers on each end, attach the legs. Fasten the center piece with four lag bolts. Next rip a 2x6 in half (2¾ in.) and cut two braces 14¼ in. long with 45 degree angle on each end. Notch and drill (¼ in. hole through brace and ³/₁₆ in. hole into leg and top).

Curved Bench

To make a curved bench, lay out two pieces of 2x6 by 4 ft. 0 in. and space ¼ in. apart. Using string and pencil swing an arc with a 4 ft. radius that reaches to 1½

in. from the outside edge of farther 2x6. Cut on this line. The piece that is cut off will be used for the other side of the bench. With the same radius point, mark pieces along string for end cuts.

Next cut rail pieces that are 10 in. long (long point to short point) with 77 degree angle on each end. Notch and drill as shown and then glue and nail to top pieces 10 in. from center.

Legs are cut from a 2x6 that has been ripped in half (2¾ in.). Cut legs 18 in. long with 56 degree angles on the ends. Position on rail pieces and mark holes. Drill ⁷/₁₆ in. hole for ⅜ in. bolt. Now bolt legs to rail pieces. Then clamp legs together at crossing and drill and bolt at 5¼ in. from the bottom side of top.

To complete the bench make braces (cut from 2 in. by 6 in. that is ripped in quarters — 1⅝ in.). The braces are 17 in. long overall. Cut 55 degree angle on end that fastens to leg and 35 degree angle on end that goes to center on bench. Attach legs with ¼ in. by 2 in. lag bolts (put in on an angle).

MATERIALS LIST:

Table

Top cut from:
1 piece 2x6, 8 ft. long
2 pieces 2x6, 10 ft. long
1 piece 2x6, 12 ft. long
Rail pieces: 1 piece 2x6, 8 ft. long
Legs: 2 pieces 2x6, 8 ft. long
Center Piece: 1 piece 2x6, 24⅝ in. long
Braces: 1 piece 2x6, 16 in. long
   (rip in half lengthwise)
Hardware: (galvanized or zinc plated)
   4 machine bolts ⅜ in. x 8 in.,
   4 machine bolts ⅜ in. x 6 in.,
   32 washers ⅜ in.,
   4 lag bolts ¼ in. x 2 in.,
   4 lag bolts ⁵/₁₆ in. x 6 in.

Benches (three)

Tops cut from: 3 pieces 2x6, 8 ft. long
Rail Pieces: 1 piece 2x6, 6 ft. long
Legs: 1 piece 2x6, 10 ft. long (rip in half)
Braces: 1 piece 2x6, 3 ft. long
   (rip in quarters)
Hardware: (galvanized or zinc plated)
   6 machine bolts ⅜ in. x 8 in.
   6 machine bolts ⅜ in. x 6 in.
   6 machine bolts ⅜ in. x 4 in.
   36 washers ⅜ in.
   12 lag bolts ¼ in. x 2 in.
Nails (galvanized) 3 lbs. 8d box
Glue

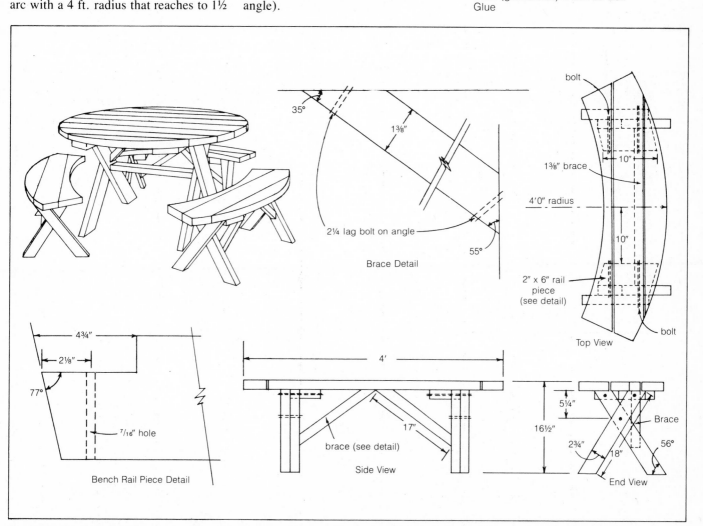

35°
1⅜"
2¼ lag bolt on angle
55°
Brace Detail

bolt
1⅜" brace
10"
4'0" radius
10"
2" x 6" rail piece (see detail)
bolt
Top View

4¾"
2⅛"
77°
⁷/₁₆" hole
Bench Rail Piece Detail

4'
17"
brace (see detail)
Side View

5¼"
16½"
2¾"
18"
Brace
56°
End View

The pieces for the curved bench are all cut from one piece of wood, moving the inside portion to the outside to complete the curve.

Staggered heights of cut-off, vertically placed railroad ties can edge both a patio and a planter at the same time.

PLANTERS

Brick or concrete block planters can be built in the same manner as brick walls, tables, and benches. Railroad tie planters are also popular, and instructions on how to build them follow. In addition, three wooden planters are offered.

Horizontal Panel Planter

A horizontal panelized planter calls for stacking square frames together on edge to form planter sides, then attaching outer rails and base. This planter measures 24x18x24 in.

Frames. Trim twenty 1x4 pieces 22½ in. Nail together five square frames with two 6d nails per board end; stack frames to form planter sides.

Rails. Cut Rails "B" and "C" to fit. Nail "B" rails from inside the planter with two 4d nails per frame. Nail "C" rails from inside with five nails as shown.

Base. Trim two 2x2's, 21 in., and two 19¼ in. to fit inside planter. Assemble with one 10-penny nail per corner. Cut six 1x4's, 21 in. and nail them to 2x2's, ⅛ in. apart. Use two 6-penny nails at each board end.

Insert the base into the bottom of the box. Extend 2x2's about ⅜ in. below paneling and nail from inside with five 10-penny nails per side.

MATERIALS LIST:
1 pc. 8' 1x4
2 pcs. 6' 1x4
1 pc. 8' 2x2

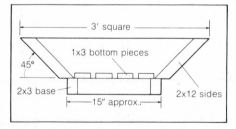

Mitered Planter Box

This mitered planter measures 3 ft. square at the top. Trim four 2x12s to 3 ft. Miter cut 45 degrees straight across board ends, then across board edges. Assemble with 16d nails.

Assemble 15-in. square base with mitered or butt-joined 2x3's. Glue and nail top and base as shown, and fit in four 1x3 bottom pieces about 13½ in. long.

MATERIALS LIST:
1 pc. 12' 2x12
1 pc. 6' 2x3
1 pc. 6' 1x3

Concrete masonry planters can be built several courses high, following the same procedures as for brick masonry walls and planters.

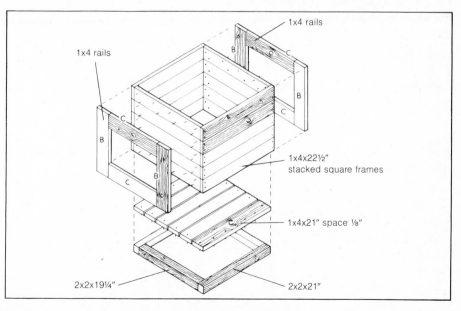

Laminated Planter

The design given earlier for a laminated bench can be used to produce a large, attractive planter that matches the style of your bench. The same principles, although not covered here, can also be applied to many other types of indoor and outdoor furniture. We recommend any of the following types of wood: Douglas Fir, Hem-Fir, Engelman Spruce, Idaho White Pine, Lodgepole Pine, Sugar Pine, Western Larch, Western Cedar, and Ponderosa Pine.

The floor of the planter, which is 3 ft. sq. is made up of 2x6 tongue & groove wood that is blind-nailed to 2x2 cleats. Cut the floor pieces 33 in. so they will meet the side sections of the planter. The floor fits within the planter frame.

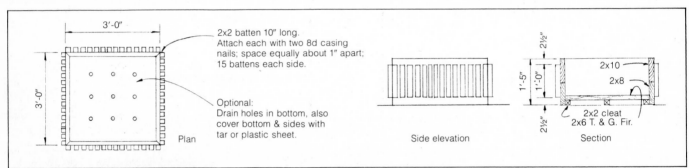

3'-0"

3'-0"

2x2 batten 10" long. Attach each with two 8d casing nails; space equally about 1" apart; 15 battens each side.

Optional: Drain holes in bottom, also cover bottom & sides with tar or plastic sheet.

Plan

Side elevation

2½"

1'-5"   1'-0"

2½"

2x10

2x8

2x2 cleat
2x6 T. & G. Fir.

Section

Each side of the planter will be built using one 2x8 plus one 2x10. The four pieces of 2x8 and 2x10 can be precut from the 12 ft. length indicated in the Materials List. The 2x2s are battens that join the 2x10 and 2x8, giving strength and style. To ensure even spacing between the 2x2s, use a predrawn spacer board on which the spaces have been marked.

Miter the corners and then join them using 8d nails. The side sections will fit around, and are nailed to, the floor piece. Cleats on the underside of the floor will hold the planter off the ground; this is an especially good idea if you have added the optional weep holes shown in the diagram.

Once the sides have been joined, add two 2x2s at each corner for a well-finished look.

MATERIALS LIST
2x10 1 pc 12'
2x8 1 pc 12'
2x6 1 pc 12' t&g
2x6 1 pc 8' t&g
2x2 1 pc 9'
2x2 6 pcs 10'
8d & 16d galvanized nails

Side sections of this simple planter are of overlapping 2x2s held together with long spikes or bolts.

Railroad Tie Planters

Railroad ties should be placed in trenches for stability, but check first that service lines are not in the area where you will be digging your placement trenches. Electric cables have been found as little as 6 in. below the surface. While some types of railroad tie installations only require 3 in. trenches, others necessitate 2 ft. holes. This depends on whether the ties are used horizontally, one course high, horizontally in two courses, or in vertical lengths.

If your plans include an irrigation system, lay the pipe before installing the ties. If there is even a slight possibility that sprinkler heads might be desired, bury a length of pipe that extends from the outside of the intended planter area to the inside of the planter. Extend the pipe far enough into the planter area for ample working room. It should be buried just a little deeper than the depth of subsequent ties. The pipe should be capped to keep dirt out of the line. Mark the spot, or at least make a mental note of its location, so you won't have to dig up plants and sections of the lawn to find it later. Even if you never use the pipe, you have wasted very little money, especially if you have used plastic pipe.

Horizontal, one course high. For better stability and uniformity, particularly if several ties will be laid consecutively, place the widest dimension face down. A trench depth of 3 in. leaves an exposed height that will accent the planter. Since the side placed face down could be damaged or irregular, prepare the trench accordingly. Mound soil beneath missing chunks or indentations in the bottom side of the tie so it will be level. Use a spirit level to achieve alignment. To encourage tie ends to butt up against each other, try a series of sharp, quick blows on one end. Toenail the ends together with 16d nails to insure they will stay flush. If possible, drive nails into the connecting ties at their bottoms, so they can be hidden with fill dirt. Use galvanized nails; they resist moisture and tend not to rust.

Fill the inside of the planter with topsoil and level off just above ground level. In order to keep water and expensive soil conditioners from draining out from between natural gaps where the ties meet, staple a narrow strip of tar paper to the inside of the planter, overlapping at the corners. A double layer will ensure a long-lasting seal. If you cannot find a

Machines that ride on top of rails have shears mounted on each side to sever both ends of the ties just inside the rails. The ends can be either squeezed off, or cut.

small amount of tar paper and do not want to spend the money for a whole roll, asphalt roofing shingles will do. The gaps where ties adjoin are the result of erosion, and sometimes give tie ends a rounded-off look. Even when butted together and toenailed, the tie ends do not form an exact fit.

Staple or nail the tar paper with 1 in. roofing nails if a staple gun is not available. The staples or nails should be placed at the tie joints on the inside of the planter, and can be hidden with fill dirt. If any of the tar paper still shows after filling with dirt, you can trim it off with a utility knife. Tar paper will resist moisture and last longer than most other plastics that might be used.

The fill dirt will not only hide the tar paper, it will reinforce one side of the ties. The other side can be reinforced with braces, although if everything else has been done properly, additional support of a one-tier planter is not necessary.

Once ties have been aligned, leveled, toenailed and sealed, fill outside edge of the trench even with the ground level. Use the head of the sledge hammer to pack the earth tightly alongside the ties. Sprinkle both sides of the ties with water. The water washes off the dirt that will invariably spill as the planter is being filled, and hardens the fresh earth so it forms a bond with the ties.

Although the nature of railroad ties forbids geometric perfection, they should be placed in as uniform a manner as possible. Flush outside edges look best, and most of the uneven interior of a planter

will be hidden once it has been filled.

Plant Root Systems. Ties can be installed in close proximity to root systems of existing plants. However, be careful not to disturb entire root systems, particularly of small bedding plants such as flowers.

Horizontal, Two Courses. Ties can be placed two courses high to elevate the planter. A single planting area can be subdivided with ties to provide a unique fortification for each plant and an interesting division in ground levels. The height of each subdivision can be varied by alternately positioning ties that are one course high and then ties that are two courses high. These arrangements do not have to be restricted to square or boxlike shapes. The ties of each planter can be positioned diagonally for a triangular effect. Eight-foot ties used in this way create a very big planter. Smaller planters built with 4 ft. lengths may seem a little small; 9 ft. ties can be cut in half to provide two 4½ ft. sections. Your choice will depend on the size of the area to be landscaped.

There are several ways to arrange ties horizontally for planters. Overlapped corners can be toenailed or bolted for stability.

To keep a planter watertight, staple tar paper or roofing shingles to the inside of the planter, overlapping at corners. A double application will guarantee a good seal.

Hide sprinkler heads inside planters; clamp the ties to backs of ties for support.

Horizontal ties can be accented with vertical ties placed at corners; however, you must increase the depth of the trench at corners.

Ties placed two high must be nailed together for stability. However, the toe-nailing process mentioned previously will not be sufficient. If you nail on the inside of the planter the top tie will be pulled inward, so that it will not rest evenly on the lower tie. Theoretically, nails pounded on the other side will force the tie back into the correct position. However, if the outside edge becomes splintered as a result, the damage will show. Even if the outside edge does not splinter, the top tie will still be top-heavy.

The best way to brace the top tie is to attach short sections of furring strips or other 1x2s to the inside of the planter. If you happen to have 2x4s they can be used instead. Smaller sized wood, however, will provide sufficient bracing strength

and is less expensive. Each strip should be about one foot long in order to span the gaps between ties. Each end of the strip should be nailed to a separate tie using 8d nails, positioning braces diagonally for better reinforcement. Be sure the end attached to the top tie is still positioned low enough on the inside of the planter to be hidden by the fill dirt. The number of braces used depends on the length of the ties. Eight-foot ties should have four supportive braces; four-foot lengths need only two.

The wooden braces should be treated with creosote or some other wood preservative, since replacing braces that have deteriorated prematurely due to dampness in the planter would be a time-consuming project. Creosote can be distasteful to

work with; a few notes on its use are given below. Install the braces before applying tar paper to the inside of the planter.

Creosote. You can apply creosote to exterior ties using an old paintbrush that you know you will never use for anything again. Avoid getting any creosote on your skin, or breathing any vapors. Wear a painter's mask so you will not inhale the fumes. Don a long-sleeved shirt and gloves to protect your skin. If any of the creosote does get on your skin, immediately rinse with rubbing alcohol and wash with soap and water. If any ends up on plants or grass, wash off at once. Use a small piece of plywood as a protective edging when applying creosote to ties that are already in place. The plywood will catch drips from the paintbrush, and keep the preservative from bleeding through the grass. Store creosote in warm places during cold weather.

Ties Used Vertically. Vertical ties should extend at least 8 in. above ground. This means the minimum length, cut specifically for this purpose, should be about 12 in. A piece with 8 in. showing will be slightly higher than connecting horizontal ties. Vertical pieces must at least be high enough to establish a subtle difference in height, and in some cases a height contrast is even better.

Long borders of horizontally placed ties in a straight row can be enhanced by an occasional shorter length placed in the upright position. This interrupts the pattern and prevents monotony. The outside edge of the vertical piece should be flush with the rest of the border. As always, ties should be nailed together for support. The frequency of these pieces can vary, but they look good when positioned every 8 ft. or so. This is based on convenience, since tie lengths are normally 8 or 9 ft. More frequent intervals would require extra work to cut up the long sections. For an unusual and attractive planter, install every other tie at alternating heights, or stepped in threes.

Trench depth for ties placed in the upright position depends on tie length. Two-foot sections are a usable size when building vertical planters, and will look good in most areas. Trenches for 2 ft. lengths should be about 8 in. deep., leaving 16 in. above ground. If longer lengths of ties are used, trench depths should vary accordingly; usually the trench depth should be one-quarter to one-third the en-

Creosote should be brushed onto railroad ties before their installation to prevent insect infestation and ensure longevity.

The flexibility of vertical tie placement enables circular planters, varying heights, and contrasting rough or smooth textures.

Place the ties in a trench around the patio before installing brick. This requires precise measurement and placement for correct fit.

Vertical ties can butt to concrete masonry planters for a visual break from low beds and uniform lines.

Gravel or bark chips layered inside railroad tie planters can add the final touch to a Western or desert landscaping theme.

tire length of the tie.

If a staggered effect is desired, varying amounts of earth can be placed under each tie to establish heights from 19 to 22 in. Dirt should be packed at the base of each tie as it is positioned. Then plumb and toe-nail the tie to its predecessor with 16d nails. Wherever possible, nails should be driven on an angle from the corners of a shorter tie into the side of its taller neighbor. Since tie placement sometimes restricts hammer freedom, nailsets can be used to finish the job. For the best appearance, the nail head should be pounded flush with the top of the tie. Additional nails should be used along the inside edges wherever possible.

The dirt at the base of the ties should be tamped, moistened, allowed to settle, and then repacked. An effort to fill cracks between the ties should be attempted. Sand is an excellent filler. It is much finer than dirt and it easily penetrates the narrow gaps between ties and fills any voids in the trenches. The cost and effort re-quired to place ties in concrete can be avoided by securing them in this manner.

Cutting the Ties. Two-man lumber saws can be used, but cutting will still be a lot of work. If a significant number of cuts are to be made by hand, pine or other softwoods should be selected. The blades must be sharp, and various household oils should be applied to both sides of them periodically. It requires much less effort to cut with properly lubricated blades.

Extreme caution must be used when cutting ties, particularly if you use a chain saw or other power saw. Do not try to support the end being cut with your free hand. If the tie has any cracks, it could have small stones in its interior. When the blade of a power saw strikes a stone, the saw sometimes bucks erratically, and you do not want a hand anywhere near the blade. Wayward nails, stubborn knots and other imperfections in the wood can also disrupt the blade. The operator should always stand well behind and off to one side of the cutting tool.

When cutting with a chain saw, place a stable 6 in. block under the tie, a few inches from each side of the groove. This raised cutting surface keeps the blade from striking the ground, and leaves both hands free for operating the saw. Chain saws are by far the most commonly used equipment for cutting ties. They will sputter and cough, but can cut easily through a tie. However, renting one might be difficult, especially if you admit what you are planning. If you do rent one, keep the blade well oiled and at the proper tension.

Circular saws with carbide-tipped blades can be used to cut all but the center of a tie by making cuts on all four sides. The tie should be placed on level ground, and the extension cord should be kept free from the cutting surface and out from under the feet. As the tie is rotated, special care must be taken to insure the blade stays in the same groove, so the cut surface will be smooth. A handsaw can then be used to finish the cut. Wear glasses to prevent chips from flying into an eye.

Railroad ties (and also telephone poles) can be cut using a two-person saw, but it is hard work and requires caution.

Exterior lighting, when placed wisely around a deck or patio, can enhance and extend the usefulness of the exterior space. Accent or task exterior lighting can increase the mood or add to the apparent size of your outdoor room. Whether you are planning to light the walkways or paths for safety, spotlight an important site feature or area, or provide overall illumination for night-time entertainment, there are basic rules that should be followed.

(1) Try to provide enough light for the task at hand, but do not overlight. Too much light can ruin the atmosphere of an exterior space. Too much light can also cause surface glare. Always use several small lights, strategically placed, instead of one or two powerful ones. This will give flexibility, and help avoid a "whitewashed" look.

(2) Try to arrange the lighting so that the light is seen, but the source is not. A bare spotlight is unsightly. Where possible, allow for indirect lighting. It will cast a uniform light level on the area without accentuating its location. There can be a magical quality to night lighting; if the source is visible, that quality is lost.

(3) Backlighting at night provides a visual effect that is seldom available to any area in the daylight. It can transform a commonplace plant dramatically, creating shadow or decorative effect.

(4) Try to locate your lighting with efficiency in mind. A well-placed series of lights in some cases can extend the interior lights you already have. The exterior lighting should complement your interior lighting.

(5) Try to keep the distance between lights to a minimum. Remember that all the lights must be connected to a power source. The more spread out the lighting is, the more costly the installation will be.

The night lighting around this pool is subtle and well hidden. A 75 watt flood highlights the leaves of the foreground tree. Small yellow lamps shine out from under the lanterns, and three PAR floods behind the screen are aimed obliquely to create leaf shadow patterns.

A pair of shielded bullet housings direct the light from 75 watt R30 blue-white lamps. Indirect lighting under trees forms canopy of light.

Uplighting at the foot of the wall and behind the stair balustrade adds footing safety without destroying the romantic quality of night lighting. The incandescent lamps have dimmers; downlights are hidden in the trees (Garden designer: Robert J. Lamont).

It can be seen that exterior or outdoor lighting falls into two general categories: functional and decorative. While decorative lighting can add a new dimension to the exterior space, functional lighting is required to light up high-use areas such as steps, stairs, gates, walkways and outdoor grills. The functional lighting should be considered first in laying out your lighting design. Once you have decided on your functional requirements, decorative aspects of lighting can then be introduced. In some cases you will find that, with slight modification, your functional lighting may be used decoratively.

EXTERIOR ELECTRICAL POWER
Indoor and outdoor electrical circuits are identical. The circuit used for interior power is the same for the exterior space. The major difference is in the materials used for the exterior electrical power distribution. All exterior receptacles must be waterproof. They are available in a variety of designs, with snap-closing covers or screw-on covers. In considering the location of exterior power receptacles, try to place them in an area where you will be using the greatest number of appliances for outdoor entertaining, or where the outdoor lighting source will be. It is possible to purchase exterior lighting fixtures with a power outlet or receptacle already installed. If at all possible, all exterior electrical power circuits should be controlled from the interior of the house. In addition, most electrical codes require that you install a GFCI receptacle for all exterior uses. This ground fault circuit interruptor is a safety device that prevents short circuits; the National Electrical Code (NEC) requires it for exterior application. They are expensive, and therefore their placement should be carefully considered. If you have a master control unit or an automatic time switch to power the lighting, you must have an override feature from a remote location. Most devices have this provision already incorporated into the design. It is recommended that all lighting circuits be separate from other exterior power circuits. This allows flexibility in the control of power and lighting.

Exterior Electrical Lighting
There are primarily two types of exterior electrical lighting available to you: the standard voltage (120 volts) or the low-voltage (12 volts). Before you install either system, verify which system is acceptable through the building inspector's office. The National Electrical Code is applicable to most areas; however, there may be local restrictions or amendments. While the low-voltage system may be more suitable for a very small garden space from a control point of view, a standard 120-volt system with interior control is recommended for a normal-sized garden area and patio or deck.

There are many different lighting fixtures. Some are used only for in-ground application, while others are only wall-mounted. In choosing lighting fixtures, select a type specifically for exterior usage. If any interior-fixture model is used in an exterior application a breakdown can occur.

Planning the Circuits
Using the plan for your exterior space, locate the position of your electrical service panel. This will give you a good idea of the path that power will follow in moving from the interior to the exterior of the house. Locate the lighting fixtures and the receptacles according to your design. If you plan on exterior switches, indicate their positions. Again, consider using three-way switches that will give you control from inside the house. If you have electrical circuits to the front of the house as well as the back, you might want two separate circuits for the purpose. Locate all fixtures and receptacles so that they are easily accessible for both installation and for future maintenance. Try to keep the

A 5 ft. mushroom lamp unit highlights chrysanthemums in the flower box. The fixture is spiked into the lawn, directly behind the box. Spotlights focus on other areas of the yard.

total distance between fixtures to a minimum. By laying out a plan of circuits and the fixtures, you will be able to estimate quantities of materials, and the tools, required to accomplish each task.

Electrical Underground Materials. Before bringing the wire from inside the house to outside, you must decide not only on the type of wire to be used but also how the circuits will be built. Most building codes dictate that all outdoor wiring must be placed in rigid conduit from the point at which it leaves the house to the point it disappears underground. It is very important that you check with your local code to determine your specific requirements. Most underground wiring can be UF cable, which is a plastic-sheathed cable designed to be buried directly in the ground. It is available in a three-wire configuration with ground. Where the wiring will emerge from the ground on a regular basis, rigid conduit is recommended in combination with type TW wires that have moisture-resistant coverings. When using rigid conduit, there are several types available to you: thin-wall plastic, rigid thin-wall metallic type (EMT), or thick-wall metal type. Plastic is the easiest to work with, although the method of assembly is similar for all three types. They all require a trench of at least a foot deep, in which the conduit is placed.

INSTALLATION PROCEDURES
While the procedures to be discussed apply to exterior wiring requirements, they are general descriptions for a method of installation. If you are not very familiar with electrical wiring standards or circuitry, it is strongly recommended that you have a licensed electrician actually connect the wiring. You will find that you can arrange to complete a significant part of the installation prior to the electrician's work (digging the trench, putting up the junctions boxes) but do not take any chance with live wires. In many areas, building codes require that this stage be carried out by a licensed electrician.

Exterior Wiring Setup
This part of the procedure involves connection of the interior wiring to an exterior conduit. You can connect through the foundation wall or through the frame wall. If you plan to connect through the foundation wall, junction boxes to which the conduit will be attached must be positioned over the opening on the inside of the foundation wall, so that the conduit LB fitting and nipple extend through the wall into the junction box. Always drill the hole at a point that you know will not interfere with other underground utilities and where you will have easy access from the outside.

Position the LB fitting where you plan to drill and check that the fitting will not overlap with a siding joint (if you have wooden siding; for cinder block, see below). Drill a ¼ in. test probe to doublecheck your measurements. Then use a ⅞ in. spade bit to bore through the joist.

Mount the junction box on the interior, over the hole, then find a nipple that reaches through the wall to the box, and screw the nipple to an LB fitting. Place the nipple in the hole to test its position. Adjust the conduit so that it will run from the fitting into the trench. Remove the nipple and LB, connect them to the conduit, and then insert the nipple back into the wall. Now strap the conduit to the outside foundation. Caulk all around the nipple. Inside the house at the junction box, attach the nipple using a star nut and then screw a plastic bushing onto the nut.

For Cinderblock Foundation. Use a ⅞ in. star drill to make the hole. Choose a block which is in the second course down from the siding; the blocks should be hollow here. Pound the hole through. For a

Outline box area with tape. Drill holes through block with ½ in. masonry bit on ⅜ in. drill. Tap out any material left between the holes.

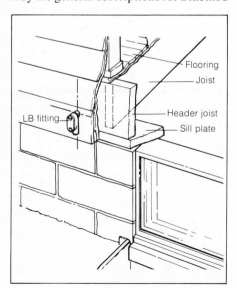

Find hole location by using a reference point accessible from both sides of the wall. The hole must be at least 3 in. from joists, sill plate, and flooring.

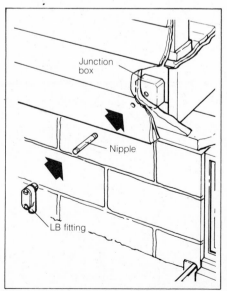

Mount box on inside wall over the hole. Choose a nipple that will reach through wall and into junction box; screw nipple to LB fitting.

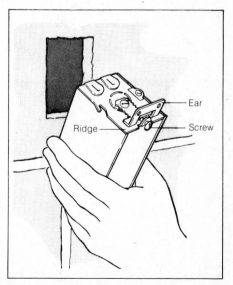

Loosely insert screws into fixture-mounting tabs of the box so mortar will not get into screw holes. Edge of the box should be about 1/16 in. out from wall.

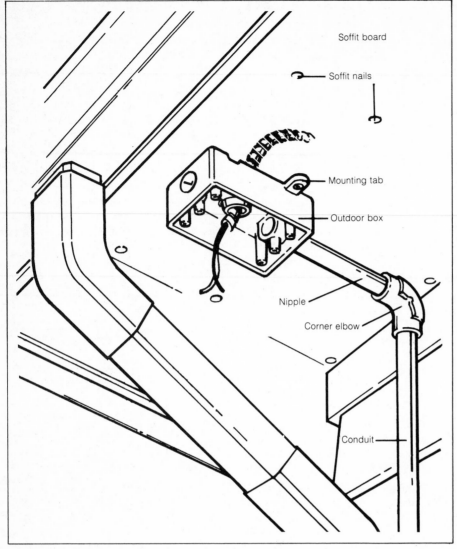

Hold assembled outdoor box, corner elbow, section of conduit, and nipple against soffit board; keep conduit against house siding. Position box between rows of soffit nails.

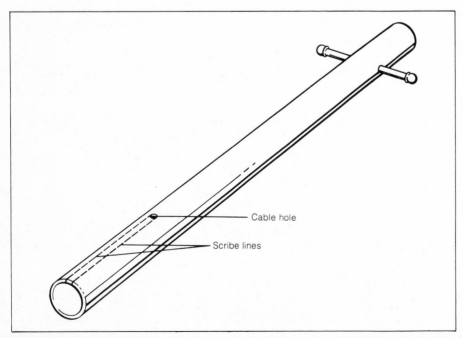

To slot a post for conduit, first mark 18 in.-long lines, ⅞ in. apart, onto post. Lines will extend beyond UF cable hole in post. Use a special hacksaw to cut along lines.

clear, round hole, rotate the drill one-eighth turn following each hammer tap.

How to Install a Box into Cinder Block. Place the box next to the cinder block and outline its shape with tape. Drill 6 to 8 holes into the central, hollow portion of the block, using a ½ in. masonry bit on a ⅜ in. drill. With the holes completed, use a ball-peen hammer and a cold chisel to knock away any material left between the holes. Then chip out the edges of the box opening until it will hold the box.

If the cinder block has been stuccoed over so that you cannot find the seams, make a test hole using a star drill. When your test probe finds the hollow center — an area where the drill does not meet any resistance — insert a stick into the hole. Tap around to find each side of the hollow. Now you can follow the steps above to create a box midway between the sides.

To install, loosely insert screws into the fixture mounting taps (so mortar won't get into the holes screw). Adjust the ears of box so that its edge is about ¹/₁₆ in. from the wall. (You will later add the cover-plate gasket to form a tight seal all around the ridge.) Slide the box into place and mortar it in. Use a putty knife and be sure that the gap between the box and the edge of the hole has been completely filled. This protects the unit from wet weather conditions. Once the mortar has dried, you can take the screws out of the mounting tabs.

Thread the wires through the junction box, from the interior to the exterior, through the conduit. The procedure is similar for wire exiting through an eave or through a frame wall.

Exiting Wire Through an Eave. It is a good idea to have a helper to hold the various components. The job will go faster. Position the assembled outdoor box, corner elbow, section of conduit, and nipple, against the soffit board. Keep the conduit next to the house siding and place the box between 2 rows of nails in the soffit. Using the box as a template, mark the soffit a cable hole and then indicate the holes required for mounting screws. Use a ³/₃₂nd in. bit to drill holes for ¾ in. No. 8 screws; use a 1¹/₈ in. spade bit to drill a hole for the cable.

After fishing the cable from an indoor circuit and out through the cable hole, fasten on a two-part connector. Screw the box to the connector. If shape of the connector makes it necessary, you may need to enlarge the cable hole with a rasp before you are able to line up the mounting tabs on the box with the screw holes. Mount the box on the soffit. Now fasten the conduit to the wall and the nipple to the soffit board. Bend the conduit as necessary to run it into the trench. If feasible, run the conduit alongside a downspout; it will be less visible.

Lamp Post Setup. Mark your guidelines, 18 in. long and ⅞ in. apart, onto the post. Cut out strip using a special hacksaw which will grip the blade both at one end and at the center. Bend out the ⅞ in. strip and saw it all the way off. Smooth edges sharp corners, or burrs using a file. If the lamp post will be in the middle of a conduit run, cut another slot that faces the first.

Dig a hole that is 2 ft. deep and about 8 in. wide. If you are using UF cable you do not need conduit. If using anything else, curve the conduit until it rises from the ground and is positioned over the center

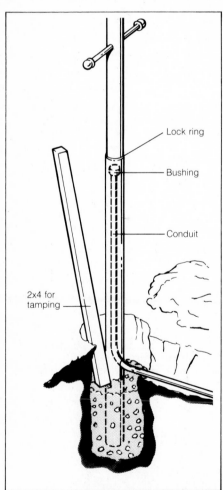

Lock ring

Bushing

Conduit

2x4 for tamping

To anchor a post, dig the hole 2 ft. deep, 8 in. wide. Bend conduit (unless using UF) so it comes up in the middle of the hole — almost to the lock ring on an adjustable post, or nearly to full height of a·fixed-length post.

of the hole. The conduit should be nearly as high as the lock ring on an adjustable post, or to nearly the top of a post of fixed length. This will make the conduit easier to fish through later on. Use a plastic bushing to cap the conduit, and slip the post over the conduit. Place alternating layers of dirt and large gravel around the post, using a 2x4 to tamp and compact. Use a level to check the post's vertical position. Fill the hole in only to the bottom of the trench. When you backfill the rest of the trench later, fill in the rest of the hole.

Digging A Trench

Once the wire has exited from the house, you must dig the trench. Always stake out the trench, keeping it as straight as possible. If it has many turns or angles, your assembly will be more difficult. If you use plastic conduit, the trench should be 8 in. wide and a minimum of 12 in. deep. If the conduit will go under a sidewalk, dig out both sides to a sufficient depth. Pass a length of conduit under the walk, pushing or tapping it through the space you have dug. You can then connect up the other pieces of conduit. When the conduit surfaces to be connected to a light fixture, bring the conduit up inside the cell of a concrete block. This will act as a brace, and as a solid base for the lighting fixture. Always try to make the wiring connection at least 12 in. above ground level. If the circuit continues, put the conduit back down through the block and continue underground. Fill in the block cells with excavated dirt. Always follow any recommendations that come with the lighting fixture you have purchased. If possible, buy a unit that has a built-in ground fault interrupter.

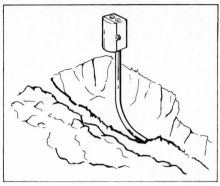

For end-of-run box, dig trench for cinder block 4 in. high. Extend conduit 8 in. above ground; fasten box with threadless connector.

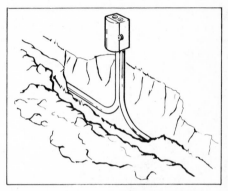

For middle-of-run box, install as for end of run but use box with 2 conduit openings. Fasten second conduit same as first.

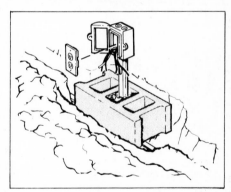

Lower cinder block over the box. Fill in core with gravel. Fish wiring through the conduit and then install receptacle.

Ground fault interrupters ensure that any potentially lethal current is cut off before a serious shock can be received. A test/reset button is particularly important for exterior wiring.

Index

Glossary

Absorption The weight of water a brick or tile unit absorbs, when immersed in either cold or boiling water for a stated length of time.

Absorption rate The weight of water absorbed when a brick is partially immersed for one minute, usually expressed in either grams or ounces per minute.

Admixtures Materials added to mortar as water-repellent or coloring agents or to retard or hasten setting.

Aggregates Crushed stone, gravel or other material used with cement and water to form concrete.

Air-entrained (concrete) Concrete which has been mixed with an admixture which causes tiny bubbles of air to be held in the mixture as the concrete sets. Air-entrained concrete is more workable and less vulnerable to frost.

Ammoniacal copper arsenate A water-borne wood preservative which can be applied to lumber.

Ashlar Masonry composed of rectangular units of burned clay or shale, or stone, generally larger in size than brick and requiring proper bonding; having sawed, dressed or squared beds, and joints laid in mortar. The units may vary in size and produce a random pattern. Stone is cut square and is usable for walls or patio wearing surfaces.

Auger A screw-threaded tool used for boring holes.

Backfilling A process whereby earth is removed from an area to permit construction and is then used as support for the construction to return earth to an area from whence it was removed.

Backlighting A technique of casting light behind objects or locations in order to provide background illumination or to silhouette an object or location.

Beam Lumber or steel supports for joists used in either the deck flooring or in the overhead cover.

Blocking Addition of cross braces between joists in the form of short sections of lumber nailed perpendicular to the joist. The addition of blocking increases stability of the joists (see illustration p. 68).

Bond(s) In brick, refers to: (1) the methods of interlocking or tying together individual units so that the whole construction is stable, or (2) the pattern made by a series of bricks and mortar joints, or (3) structural adhesion of the mortar, brick and reinforcing material.

Brace(s) Any of several structural ties that distribute or resist weight or pressure. A brace gives extra stability to a structure. Types for a deck include: K-brace, X-brace, Y-brace (designation based on obvious appearance) and a temporary brace which may be used during construction and removed when permanent supports are complete.

Broom finishing Texturing of a concrete surface by stroking with a stiff broom while the concrete surface is still fresh.

Butter The process of applying mortar to brick or to other masonry units.

Capping The process of finishing the top of a masonry wall. The capping gives a visual finish as well as structural solidity. Usually placed over flashing to keep rainfall from entering the lower wall, the capping unites the two sides of a wall. The capping pattern is usually different from the pattern of the wall.

Chalkline A string coated in chalkdust which when pulled taut against a surface and released will leave a straight line mark on a surface. This chalkline is used to mark a guideline for masonry construction.

Chromated copper arsenate A waterborne wood preservative which can be applied to lumber.

Cleats Blocks of wood, usually cut from 2x3 or 2x4, which are nailed to the inside of the stringers for support, as for treads in a flight of stairs. The cleats support the treads which are also attached to the stringers.

Collar joint The large vertical and longitudinal joint which lies between the wythes of a two (or more) wythe wall.

Common In brick the term refers to ordinary building brick as opposed to a specialty brick or other masonry unit such as firebrick or glazed brick.

Concrete A basic building material used for footings, poured foundations, walks, drives and streets, as well as for patio wearing surfaces. Concrete consists of a mixture of cement, sand aggregate and water. Concrete continues to harden over a long period of time and becomes harder and stronger with age, although it is subject to cracking under the pressure of heat, cold, and water.

Conduit A protective covering for electrical wiring usually in the form of a flexible or solid-wall metal tube. It is required for any exterior or exposed wire circuits.

Control joints The lines cut into a concrete surface to ensure that when the slab cracks under normal water, frost, or heat pressures, it will crack only along these control joint lines. These are cut to a depth of ¼ to $1/5$ the thickness of the slab, and placed every 4 to 10 ft. in each direction. Failure to use control joints will cause uneven fracturing of the slab surface.

Course In masonry work a course represents one layer (horizontal row) of brick or block in a wall.

Coverplate gasket A flexible material placed between a junction box and the coverplate to ensure an air- and weather-tight seal.

Crazing A series of very fine cracks which may appear on the surface of a concrete slab either because the surface was allowed to dry too quickly under certain weather conditions or due to improper surface finishing (floating).

Creosote A derivative of coal tars, this oily liquid can be used, with special precautions against inhaling the noxious vapors, as a brush-applied wood preservative, especially where the wood will be on contact with the soil. Because it stains the wood, it should not be used where wood is to be painted.

Cross bracing Reinforcing structural supports which extend, on a diagonal, from one support column to another to increase the load-bearing capacity of the columns. At times cross bracing is used between joists to increase stability.

Darbying A smoothing of the surface of a concrete slab after initial leveling. Darbying is done with a darby tool or a long, smooth piece of lumber or steel.

Deformed billet A reinforcing rod used to increase stability and unity of a vertical masonry construction. Deformed indicates that the rod has a twisted shank which allows the mortar to grip the rod securely for maximum stability to the wall.

Dog's Tooth A brick pattern in which a brick is set so that one end or one face projects from the plane of the wall.

Dusting A powdery coating which appears on the surface of a newly set concrete slab. This usually occurs when: silt has been used in the concrete mixture; the second floating was done while there was still a coating of water on the wet concrete; or, the curing time was too brief.

Efflorescence A powder or stain sometimes found on the surface of masonry which results from a deposit of water-soluble salts.

Elevation A drawing done to scale that shows the details of any vertical surface, plane or face of a planned construction.

EMT wire A type of rigid but thin wall conduit suitable for exterior use in decks or patios. It should be used in combination with TW wires which have their own moisture-resistant covering.

Expansion joint A planned break in the continuous surface of a patio or wall into which a compressible material has been placed to absorb pressure when the surface expands when heated. This joint prevents buckling or crumbling of the surface or structure. Commonly used materials for expansion joints are wood, oakum or asphalt. Expansion joints are required wherever dissimilar materials adjoin since they will expand and contract at different rates.

Exposed aggregate A decorative surface treatment of concrete created when the smooth wearing surface of the concrete slab is washed away before the concrete has fully hardened to reveal a layer of coarse stone aggregate which has been embedded just below the surface.

Face In masonry, a layer of brick or block which covers interior construction. It also refers to the wearing or exposed surface of a masonry unit.

Fascia In construction, a horizontal board finishing the edges of a deck or roof by covering the ends of the decking boards. Fascia gives a finished appearance to exposed joints.

Firebox The inner wythe of a firepit or barbecue, in which the fire is laid.

Fireclay A compound which is used in mortar for fireboxes. Fireclay increases the capacity of the mortar to withstand extreme heat.

Fishing electrical wire A procedure in which a length of stiff wire is used to pull new electrical wiring through a space in a wall or through a length of conduit. The "fishing" wire is inserted from the location of the desired electrical connection back to the new wiring. The new line is then attached to the "fishing" wire and both are pulled through to the location of the new connection.

Flashing A thin, impervious material placed in mortar joints to prevent water penetration, or in some cases to provide water drainage. Also referring to an impervious material used for the same purpose where deck ledger boards are attached to house walls.

Flemish Bond A brick-laying pattern in which each course of brick is laid so that stretchers alternate with headers both horizontally and vertically.

Floating A finishing process in laying a concrete slab. After the surface has been leveled, a smooth piece of wood or steel is drawn across the surface of the wet concrete. Once the concrete has set to the point where there is no moisture apparent on the surface, a second floating is done to ensure that the final surface is level, smooth, and unmarred.

Footing The portion of a foundation which directly transmits the structural load to the ground. For decks, footings are usually placed only where the posts will be located. Footings also are required for support columns for overhead cover and for some fence posts.

Galvanized A technique in which one metal is coated with another through electrical ionization. Nails, screws and other fasteners, as well as hardware used in exposed exterior construction, should be galvanized because metal treated this way will not rust and stain adjacent areas.

GFCI Ground Fault Circuit Interrupter, also known as Ground Fault Interrupter, is a device which will shut off current to an electrical outlet whenever there is a failure in the grounding system of the electrical wiring. The purpose is to eliminate shock hazard. GFCI protected outlets are mandatory on all exterior wiring and in all newly wired bathrooms. Most units have test buttons to make sure they are working properly. The GFCI may be reset to allow operation of the outlet after the ground failure has been repaired.

Headers In brick masonry, headers are brick set in a course so that the small face or end of the brick is visible on the wall surface. In a two-wythe wall, the header lies across both wythes to tie them together in a structural bond.

Infill In overhead cover, any material which is used between or above supporting members; in fences, railings and screens, any material used between supporting members.

Isolation joint The same type of joint as an expansion joint.

Joints In masonry, the mortar-filled spaces between masonry units.

Joists Structural members that are laid parallel to one another from beam to beam in order to support a floor or ceiling. Sizes depend upon spacing and amount of load.

Lag screw or bolt A large screw, up to 6 in. in length, which has a square head that is turned with a wrench rather than with a screwdriver.

Lath Thin, narrow strips of wood which are often used as partial infill for overhead cover, lightweight trellises, or decorative screens.

Lattice A structure made up of wood or metal strips. Often made with lath infill.

LB fitting A connector for conduit, an L-shape fitting which allows wiring to make a right angle turn. It is usually used at the point the wiring emerges from the house wall and is used to direct the wiring (in the conduit) to the ground. The LB fitting has an access plate which allows for opening the fitting to guide the wiring through the conduit.

Lead The section of a wall built up and stepped back on successive courses. A line is attached to the leads as a guide for

constructing a wall between them.

Ledger A horizontal board attached to the side of a house or other wall to support the deck on overhead cover. It is secured with lag screws and expansion shields to masonry walls and with carriage bolts or spikes to wooden walls.

Lintel A beam, used to support masonry, placed over an opening in a wall.

Masonry Brick, tile, stone, block, or other material, usually small enough to be handled by one man, that bonds together with mortar to form a permanent structure.

Mason's line A length of twine which is held at each end by an L-shaped block. The line can be stretched tight when the blocks are hooked to the corners of a wall. The line is used as a straightedge guide and it permits the mason to check the evenness of the course being laid.

Moderate weather (MW) A type of brick which can only be used in areas where there is not much variety or severity of weather conditions.

Mortar An elastic mixture of cement, sand and water which is used to bond units of masonry together.

Nominal dimension A dimension which is greater than the actual dimension of a piece of lumber or of a masonry unit. In lumber, supposedly the wood size before it has been milled. A brick nominal size usually allows for a ½ in. mortar joint to give the full nominal dimension.

Parge (or parget) A coat of cement mortar on the face of a masonry wall, similar to a smooth stucco; also the process of applying such a coat.

Patterns In masonry there are many regularly used methods of laying units which create recognizable patterns which have been named; i.e., English Bond, Flemish Bond, basketweave.

Pavers Man-made units, frequently identified as "paving bricks" which are either brick or molded concrete. There are many types, styles and sizes. Some interlock in patterns and when properly set in a

base of sand or concrete will withstand a great deal of weight or pressure.

Perforated walls A one-wythe masonry wall in which the pattern of the units is staggered and hole spaces have been left.

Pier An isolated column of masonry, usually a support for a section of wall or other separate structural unit. When such a unit is integrated into a wall of the same type of material, it is a pilaster.

Pitch (grade) The angle or slope of a basically horizontal surface. In construction, usually built into a roof or exterior floor or slab for purposes of drainage.

Plumb On a straight vertical line. A wall which is plumb is straight up and down with no lean. When constructing a wall or deck or roof, plumb must be checked regularly to ensure vertical stability.

Portland cement A type of cement (not a brand name), this combination of many elements is largely lime and silica and is basic to the making of concrete and mortar.

Posthole A deep hole into which a post is set and concrete poured. This is an alternative method of setting posts rather than building footing forms. Postholes may be dug with a hand posthole digger or with a mechanical, auger type digger.

Purlin A horizontal structural roof member which supports rafters.

Railroad ties Thick, square lengths of timber which are set into the bed of a railroad track and to which the tracks are attached. Railroad ties are durable and are frequently used in landscaping to secure low, stepped back changes of grade.

Reinforcing In masonry structures, rods, mini-trusses or metal ties which reach from one wythe or course to another through the mortar for greater stability and permanence.

Retaining walls A wall built with the specific intent of holding back or securing a slope of ground, especially where the slope has been cut back to give a larger, even area at a lower level. The retaining wall must be designed to withstand enormous pressure and requires a substantial footing to redistribute the pressure to the ground. Most retaining walls require the drilling of weep holes to relieve the build-up of ground water pressure.

Risers   In stairs, the board which supports the front edge of a tread. A cleat-supported tread can exist without a riser in a flight of open stairs.

Rowlock   A brick laid on its face edge so that the normal bedding area is visible in the wall face (sometimes spelled *rolok*). This placement of brick is often used as a capping course on top of a wall.

Scaling   Fracturing of the wearing surface of a concrete slab into chips or "scales" of approximately $3/16$ in. thickness. It is usually caused by a freeze/thaw cycle occurring before the concrete is fully set, by the use of salt or other deicing chemicals, or by performing the surface finishing on the concrete too early in the setting process.

SCR   Trademark of the Brick Institute of America (Structural Clay Research) for brick with perforations in core. Screeding. The first surface finishing process in making a concrete slab. After the concrete has been poured, a screed (usually a heavy, straightedged piece of lumber) is used to level the surface to remove any high or low spots.

Severe weather   A type of brick, designed to withstand the most extreme weather conditions; best choice for exterior work in the northern climates.

Slump   A test for the consistency of concrete conducted by filling a conical tube with concrete and measuring the subsequent difference in height after the concrete has settled and the tube has been removed.

Slushed joints   A method of filling vertical joints in masonry after the units are in place by throwing the mortar into the spaces using a trowel. This technique is not suggested for any exterior construction work.

Soffit   The underside of a beam, lintel, arch or eave overhang.

Soldier   A brick which is placed in an upright position with the long, narrow face outwards. (A brick placed vertically with the broad face outward is a sailor.)

Spacers   Uniformly sized pieces of plywood, or nails or other material, set between construction components to maintain a set, even distance between units during placement or nailing.

Spall   A small fragment removed from the face of a masonry unit by a blow or by severe weather conditions.

Story pole   A marked pole for measuring masonry courses during construction.

Stretcher   A brick which has been laid in a course with the long, narrow face outward; the most common placement of a brick.

Stringers   Wood or metal supports for a flight of stairs, running at an angle from the lower to the upper level. Stringers may be cut out and the treads attached to the cuts, or cleats may be attached to the inside of the stringers so the tread attaches to the cleats.

Struck joint   A mortar joint which has been finished off, smoothed and evened after the brick, block or stone has been put into place.

Template   A pattern which shows the size and shape of an area to be cut out or away.

Tooling   Compressing and shaping the face of a mortar joint with a specially shaped tool, not a trowel, to create a struck joint.

Torpedo sand   A very good sand base for construction of patios, firepits and barbecues. It is of medium texture and creates a better base than fine mason's sand.

Tread   On a flight of stairs, the level surface on which one steps.

Trellis   A latticework used as a light screen or as a support for climbing plants.

Troweling   A final finishing of the surface of a concrete slab, for an extremely smooth face on the slab. In bricklaying, the application of the mortar, also "buttering".

Truss   A prefabricated metal reinforcement. In masonry a small metal tie used to increase the stability of a wall.

Tuckpoint   The filling in of cut-out or defective mortar masonry joints using fresh mortar.

TW wires   Electrical wires which have moisture-resistant insulation covering. Used in combination with solid, weatherproof conduit, these wires will provide the safest type of exterior wiring.

Type M   A type of exterior mortar which can be purchased premixed in bag form.

Type S   A type of exterior mortar which is also available premixed.

UF cable   A plastic-sheathed cable, specifically designed for exterior use, which is completely water and weather proof. If it meets local codes, it can be used directly in an exterior trench without conduit.

Wall tie   Any of a variety of prefabricated metal reinforcing pieces designed to conform to the requirements of different types of masonry construction.

Water retentivity   That property of a mortar which prevents the rapid loss of water to masonry units of high suction. It prevents bleeding or water gain when mortar is in contact with relatively impervious units.

Weep hole   A hole drilled in a retaining wall to allow water to seep through and thus relieve pressure against the wall. The holes should be lined with pipe or hose so that the wall will not be weakened.

Wythe   In brick masonry, each continuous vertical section of masonry one unit wide. A masonry facing is usually one wythe deep. A free-standing wall may be two or more wythes deep.

Z-brace   A z-shaped metal wall tie or reinforcing unit, used for masonry.

Associations
Contributors
Manufacturers

AA Wire Products Company
6100 South New England Avenue
Chicago, Illinois 60638

American Plywood Association
Box 1119A
Tacoma, Washington 98401

Michael Bliss
Landscape Architect
222 Sunset Drive
Encinita, California 92024

Bowmanite Corporation
81 Encina Avenue
Palo Alto, California 94301

Brick Institute of America
1759 Old Meadow Road
McLean, Virginia 22101

Eric Brubaker
2306 Grovecrest Avenue
Palm Harbor, Florida 33563

Samuel Cabot, Inc.
1 Union
Boston, Massachusetts 02108

California Redwood Association
One Lombard Street
San Francisco, California 94111

Rick Clark
Photographer
10843 North 45th Lane
Glendale, Arizona 85304

Ego Productions, Photography
James M. Auer, Charles·Auer
1849 North 72nd Street
Wauwatosa, Wisconsin 53213

Erecto-Pat
Oakwood Manufacturing, Inc.
P. O. Box 519
Oxford, Michigan 48051

Filon/Vistron Corporation
1540-T Midland Building
Cleveland, Ohio 44115

General Electric Company
Lamp Division
Nela Park
Cleveland, Ohio 44112

Georgia-Pacific Corporation
900 SW 5th Street
Portland, Oregon 97204

Dennis Getto
Milwaukee, Wisconsin

Glidden Coatings & Resin Co.
˙Glidden Durkee Div.
900 Union Commerce Building
Cleveland, Ohio 44115

Philip Graham, Jr.
Landscape Architect
St. Petersburg, Florida

Hillwood Manufacturing Co.
21800 St. Clair Avenue
Cleveland, Ohio 44117

Herb Hughes
3033 Willow Lane
Montgomery, Alabama 36109

Johnson's Nursery, Inc.
W180 N6275 Marcy Road
Menomonee Falls, Wisconsin 53051

Kent Keegan
Department of Architecture
University of Wisconsin-Milwaukee
Milwaukee, Wisconsin 53201

Koppers Co., Inc.
Koppers Building
Pittsburgh, Pennsylvania 15219

Lasco Industries
3255 East Miraloma
Anaheim, California 92806

Leviton Manufacturing Co., Inc.
59-25 Little Neck Parkway
Little Neck, New York 11352

Lied's Green Valley Gardens
N63 W22039 Highway 74
Sussex, Wisconsin 53089

Marshalltown Trowel Company
P. O. Box 738
Marshalltown, Iowa 50158

Midwest Plan Service
Permission to reproduce from:
MWPS-21, *Home and Yard
Improvements Handbook* — 1978
Ames, Iowa 50011

**National Concrete Masonry
Association**
P. O. Box 781
Herndon, Virginia 22070

National Swimming Pool Institute
2000 K Street, Northwest
Washington, D. C. 20006

Richard V. Nunn
Media Mark Productions
Falls Church Inn
6633 Arlington Boulevard
Falls Church, Virginia 22045

Portland Cement Association
5420 Old Orchard Road
Skokie, Illinois 60077

Rain Jet Corp.
501 South Flower
Burbank, California 91503

**Reichhold Chemical/Reinforced
Plastics Division**
18747 Sheldon Road
Middleburg Heights, Ohio 44130

Sakrete, Inc.
P. O. Box 17087
Cincinnati, Ohio 45217

Tru-Test
Cotter & Co.
2740 Clybourn Avenue
Chicago, Illinois 60614

Warp Brothers
4647 West Augusta Boulevard
Chicago, Illinois 60651

Wausau Tile
P. O. Box 1520
Wausau, Wisconsin 54401

Western Wood Products Assoc.
Yeon Building
Portland, Oregon 97204

Wonderbrix
Brick Master/SK Sales
P. O. Box 2849
Livonia, Michigan 48151

Metric Conversion Charts

LUMBER

Sizes: Metric cross-sections are so close to their nearest Imperial sizes, as noted below, that for most purposes they may be considered equivalents.

Lengths: Metric lengths are based on a 300mm module which is slightly shorter in length than an Imperial foot. It will therefore be important to check your requirements accurately to the nearest inch and consult the table below to find the metric length required.

Areas: The metric area is a square metre. Use the following conversion factors when converting from Imperial data: 100 sq. feet = 9.290 sq. metres.

METRIC SIZES SHOWN BESIDE NEAREST IMPERIAL EQUIVALENT

mm	Inches	mm	Inches
16 x 75	⅝ x 3	44 x 150	1¾ x 6
16 x 100	⅝ x 4	44 x 175	1¾ x 7
16 x 125	⅝ x 5	44 x 200	1¾ x 8
16 x 150	⅝ x 6	44 x 225	1¾ x 9
19 x 75	¾ x 3	44 x 250	1¾ x 10
19 x 100	¾ x 4	44 x 300	1¾ x 12
19 x 125	¾ x 5	50 x 75	2 x 3
19 x 150	¾ x 6	50 x 100	2 x 4
22 x 75	⅞ x 3	50 x 125	2 x 5
22 x 100	⅞ x 4	50 x 150	2 x 6
22 x 125	⅞ x 5	50 x 175	2 x 7
22 x 150	⅞ x 6	50 x 200	2 x 8
25 x 75	1 x 3	50 x 225	2 x 9
25 x 100	1 x 4	50 x 250	2 x 10
25 x 125	1 x 5	50 x 300	2 x 12
25 x 150	1 x 6	63 x 100	2½ x 4
25 x 175	1 x 7	63 x 125	2½ x 5
25 x 200	1 x 8	63 x 150	2½ x 6
25 x 225	1 x 9	63 x 175	2½ x 7
25 x 250	1 x 10	63 x 200	2½ x 8
25 x 300	1 x 12	63 x 225	2½ x 9
32 x 75	1¼ x 3	75 x 100	3 x 4
32 x 100	1¼ x 4	75 x 125	3 x 5
32 x 125	1¼ x 5	75 x 150	3 x 6
32 x 150	1¼ x 6	75 x 175	3 x 7
32 x 175	1¼ x 7	75 x 200	3 x 8
32 x 200	1¼ x 8	75 x 225	3 x 9
32 x 225	1¼ x 9	75 x 250	3 x 10
32 x 250	1¼ x 10	75 x 300	3 x 12
32 x 300	1¼ x 12	100 x 100	4 x 4
38 x 75	1½ x 3	100 x 150	4 x 6
38 x 100	1½ x 4	100 x 200	4 x 8
38 x 125	1½ x 5	100 x 250	4 x 10
38 x 150	1½ x 6	100 x 300	4 x 12
38 x 175	1½ x 7	150 x 150	6 x 6
38 x 200	1½ x 8	150 x 200	6 x 8
38 x 225	1½ x 9	150 x 300	6 x 12
44 x 75	1¾ x 3	200 x 200	8 x 8
44 x 100	1¾ x 4	250 x 250	10 x 10
44 x 125	1¾ x 5	300 x 300	12 x 12

METRIC LENGTHS

Lengths Metres	Equiv. Ft. & Inches
1.8m	5' 10⅞"
2.1m	6' 10⅝"
2.4m	7' 10½"
2.7m	8' 10¼"
3.0m	9' 10⅛"
3.3m	10' 9⅞"
3.6m	11' 9¾"
3.9m	12' 9½"
4.2m	13' 9⅜"
4.5m	14' 9⅓"
4.8m	15' 9"
5.1m	16' 8¾"
5.4m	17' 8⅝"
5.7m	18' 8⅜"
6.0m	19' 8¼"
6.3m	20' 8"
6.6m	21' 7⅞"
6.9m	22' 7⅝"
7.2m	23' 7½"
7.5m	24' 7¼"
7.8m	25' 7⅛"

All the dimensions are based on 1 inch = 25 mm.

NOMINAL SIZE (This is what you order.)	ACTUAL SIZE (This is what you get.)
Inches	Inches
1 x 1	¾ x ¾
1 x 2	¾ x 1½
1 x 3	¾ x 2½
1 x 4	¾ x 3½
1 x 6	¾ x 5½
1 x 8	¾ x 7¼
1 x 10	¾ x 9¼
1 x 12	¾ x 11¼
2 x 2	1¾ x 1¾
2 x 3	1½ x 2½
2 x 4	1½ x 3½
2 x 6	1½ x 5½
2 x 8	1½ x 7¼
2 x 10	1½ x 9¼
2 x 12	1½ x 11¼

WOOD SCREWS

SCREW GAUGE NO.	NOMINAL DIAMETER Inch	NOMINAL DIAMETER mm	LENGTH Inch	LENGTH mm
0	0.060	1.52	³/₁₆	4.8
1	0.070	1.78	¹/₄	6.4
2	0.082	2.08	⁵/₁₆	7.9
3	0.094	2.39	³/₈	9.5
4	0.0108	2.74	⁷/₁₆	11.1
5	0.122	3.10	¹/₂	12.7
6	0.136	3.45	⁵/₈	15.9
7	0.150	3.81	³/₄	19.1
8	0.164	4.17	⁷/₈	22.2
9	0.178	4.52	1	25.4
10	0.192	4.88	1¼	31.8
12	0.220	5.59	1½	38.1
14	0.248	6.30	1¾	44.5
16	0.276	7.01	2	50.8
18	0.304	7.72	2¼	57.2
20	0.332	8.43	2½	63.5
24	0.388	9.86	2¾	69.9
28	0.444	11.28	3	76.2
32	0.5	12.7	3¼	82.6
			3½	88.9
			4	101.6
			4½	114.3
			5	127.0
			6	152.4

Dimensions taken from BS1210; metric conversions are approximate.

BRICKS AND BLOCKS

Bricks

Standard metric brick measures 215 mm x 65 mm x 112.5. Metric brick can be used with older, standard brick by increasing the mortaring in the joints. The sizes are substantially the same, the metric brick being slightly smaller (3.6 mm less in length, 1.8 mm in width, and 1.2 mm in depth).

Concrete Block

Standard sizes

390 x 90 mm
390 x 190 mm
440 x 190 mm
440 x 215 mm
440 x 290 mm

Repair block for replacement of block in old installations is available in these sizes:
448 x 219 (including mortar joints)
397 x 194 (including mortar joints)

NAILS

NUMBER PER POUND OR KILO

Size	Weight Unit	Common	Casing	Box	Finishing
2d	Pound	876	1010	1010	1351
	Kilo	1927	2222	2222	2972
3d	Pound	586	635	635	807
	Kilo	1289	1397	1397	1775
4d	Pound	316	473	473	548
	Kilo	695	1041	1041	1206
5d	Pound	271	406	406	500
	Kilo	596	893	893	1100
6d	Pound	181	236	236	309
	Kilo	398	591	519	680
7d	Pound	161	210	210	238
	Kilo	354	462	462	524
8d	Pound	106	145	145	189
	Kilo	233	319	319	416
9d	Pound	96	132	132	172
	Kilo	211	290	290	398
10d	Pound	69	94	94	121
	Kilo	152	207	207	266
12d	Pound	64	88	88	113
	Kilo	141	194	194	249
16d	Pound	49	71	71	90
	Kilo	108	156	156	198
20d	Pound	31	52	52	62
	Kilo	68	114	114	136
30d	Pound	24	46	46	
	Kilo	53	101	101	
40d	Pound	18	35	35	
	Kilo	37	77	77	
50d	Pound	14			
	Kilo	31			
60d	Pound	11			
	Kilo	24			

LENGTH AND DIAMETER IN INCHES AND CENTIMETERS

Size	Inches	Length Centimeters	Inches	Diameter Centimeters*
2d	1	2.5	.068	.17
3d	1/2	3.2	.102	.26
4d	1/4	3.8	.102	.26
5d	1/6	4.4	.102	.26
6d	2	5.1	.115	.29
7d	2/2	5.7	.115	.29
8d	2/4	6.4	.131	.33
9d	2/6	7.0	.131	.33
10d	3	7.6	.148	.38
12d	3/2	8.3	.148	.38
16d	3/4	8.9	.148	.38
20d	4	10.2	.203	.51
30d	4/4	11.4	.220	.58
40d	5	12.7	.238	.60
50d	5/4	14.0	.257	.66
60d	6	15.2	.277	.70

*Exact conversion

PIPE FITTINGS

Only fittings for use with copper pipe are affected by metrication: metric compression fittings are interchangeable with Imperial in some sizes, but require adaptors in others.

INTERCHANGEABLE SIZES		SIZES REQUIRING ADAPTORS	
mm	Inches	mm	Inches
12	⅜	22	¾
15	½	35	1¼
28	1	42	1½
54	2		

Metric capillary (soldered) fittings are not directly interchangeable with imperial sizes but adaptors are available. Pipe fittings which use screwed threads to make the joint remain unchanged. The British Standard Pipe (BSP) thread form has now been accepted internationally and its dimensions will not physically change. These screwed fittings are commonly used for joining iron or steel pipes, for connections on taps, basin and bath waste outlets and on boilers, radiators, pumps etc. Fittings for use with lead pipe are joined by soldering and for this purpose the metric and inch sizes are interchangeable.

(Information courtesy Metrication Board, Millbank Tower, Millbank, London SW1P 4QU)